Discrimination, Jobs, and Politics

D1553742

Discrimination, Jobs, and Politics

The Struggle for Equal
Employment Opportunity
in the United States
since the New Deal

Paul Burstein

The University of Chicago Press
Chicago and London

PAUL BURSTEIN is associate professor of sociology at the University of Washington.

The University of Chicago Press, Chicago 60637
The University of Chicago Press, Ltd., London

94 93 92 91 90 89 88 87 86 85   54321

Library of Congress Cataloging in Publication Data

Burstein, Paul.
  Discrimination, jobs, and politics.

  Bibliography; p.
  Includes index.
  1. Discrimination in employment—Law and legislation—
United States—History. I. Title.
KF3464.B83   1985
ISBN 0-226-08134-6   344.73'01133'0262   85-4802
ISBN 0-226-08135-4 (pbk.)   347.3041133'0262

For my father and the memory of my mother

Contents

Preface

When my father graduated from one of the nation's best state universities in 1937, as class valedictorian with a degree in the eminently practical field of accounting, he could not find a job. Part of his problem no doubt lay in the fact that the United States was still suffering from the Great Depression and jobs were difficult to find for most people. But my father also faced another problem, as the dean of his college explained in a letter my father kept for many, many years: most accounting firms and many other kinds of businesses would not hire Jews. It was years before my father found satisfactory employment.

By the time I finished school in the early 1970s, the labor market had changed a great deal. Most employers did not discriminate against Jews, and Jews had learned ways to prosper in the face of the anti-Semitism that remained. The trend, if not the result so far, has been similar for other groups. Although many employers still discriminate against blacks, women, and members of other groups, the changes that have taken place in the past forty to fifty years have been substantial indeed. It is difficult to imagine, for example, having to call out the army to see that blacks are allowed to work as bus drivers; but that is what happened in Philadelphia, Pennsylvania (not Philadelphia, Mississippi) in 1944.

This book is about the struggle for equal employment opportunity (EEO) in the United States since the New Deal, and about the consequences of that struggle. It shows how the employment opportunities available to women and members of minority groups have been affected by general social trends and by the organized activities of groups seeking fair treatment through lobbying, demonstrations, legal action, and election campaigns. It considers how American political institutions respond to pressures placed upon them in the name of justice and equality. And it examines a crucial turning point in American history; as the historian J. R. Pole has written about this period, "For the first time in American history, equality became a major object of government policy; and also for the first time, with perhaps the exception of the Freedmen's Bureau of the Reconstruction period, governments not only made laws but constituted themselves instruments of egalitarian policy'' (1978, 326). The battle for EEO legislation has, of course, been won; but, as this book shows, the passage of legislation is only part of the struggle. The opportunities available to women and members of minority groups are affected by public opinion and the activities of many private organizations concerned about EEO, as well as by election outcomes and their implications for the enforcement of EEO laws. The outcome of a particular election may seem to foretell a setback or an opportunity for proponents of EEO; but whether either is realized depends upon public opinion and continuing political and legal struggle at least as much as upon who is elected.

This book was a long time in the writing, for a variety of intellectual and professional reasons. Parts of the analysis of the consequences of EEO legislation therefore include data running only through the end of the 1970s, rather than into the 1980s as one might like. I am sure my conclusions are not affected by this bit of datedness, but there was nothing I could do about it in any case.

I have accumulated many debts while working on this book, and I am glad to have the opportunity to acknowledge, if not repay, them now. David Mayhew's assistance and encouragement were invaluable; from the point of view of a young sociologist venturing into the terra incognita of congressional politics, he could not have been more helpful. For reading and commenting on the entire manuscript, I am grateful to Claude Fischer, Bill Gamson, Jack Gibbs, Peter Harris, Dave Knoke, Seymour Martin Lipset, William J. Wilson, and Mayer Zald. For advice, assistance, encouragement, crucial conversations, and other forms of help too varied to describe, I thank Robert Belton, Richard Berk, Dan Cornfield, Joe Feagin, Owen Fiss, Jan Grigsby, Margo MacLeod, Stanley Masters, Robert Robinson, Rachel Rosenfeld, Ronnie Steinberg, Jack Walker, Marlie Wasserman, and Herbert Weisberg. Peter Harris, Jan Grigsby, Carol Boyer, Brad Bullock, and Karen Swalin were outstanding research assistants. Jo Anne Bradford did a fine job of word processing. And grants from the National Science Foundation (SOC-7825037) and the Vanderbilt University Research Council were indispensable.

Finally, I thank my wife, Florence Katz, for good discussions, great editing, and other things: ''For thy sweet love remember'd such wealth brings / That then I scorn to change my state with kings.''

1 Democratic Politics and Equality of Opportunity

Much of the appeal of democratic government, both in the United States and around the world, has rested on the belief that people are more likely to achieve basic civil rights and economic opportunities under a government that rules by the consent of the governed than under any other system. Yet is has long been known that tyranny is possible even under a democratic government, and that the poor and powerless will always be at a disadvantage in the marketplace and in politics. Much of the effort of the framers of the American Constitution was devoted to reducing the likelihood of tyranny, including the tyranny of the majority over minorities, and many of their dreams about the future of the country rested upon the hope that most Americans would remain economically independent (Dahl 1956, chap. 1; 1967, chap. 3).

Ever since the United States was established, one of its central problems has been the contrast between its democratic and egalitarian promise and its actual performance. The American political system has long been one of the most democratic in the world, and it is so today. It has seemed to promise, to its citizens and the millions who have migrated here or hope to, that this could be a country in which people would be treated as equals and would have equal economic opportunities. Yet the promise has never been fulfilled. Blacks have suffered most obviously and acutely from discrimination in every aspect of life; their treatment has been a blatant, long-term challenge to American ideals. But women and members of many other racial, religious, and nationality groups have suffered from discrimination as well. As recently as the 1960s, it was common for employers seeking white-collar workers to specify that they were interested only in Protestant or "Nordic" applicants, and of course blacks and women were almost totally excluded from many types of jobs.[1]

The conflict between American ideals of "liberty, equality, justice, and fair opportunity for everybody'' and the everyday American expression of prejudice and discrimination has been identified by Gunnar Myrdal as the American dilemma (1962, lxix–lxx). The purpose of this book is to discover whether democratic politics can help resolve the dilemma. Can the possibilities democratic politics seems to afford actually be used to gain more equal rights and better economic opportunities for groups that have been the victims of discrimination?

The book focuses on the struggle for equal employment opportunity in the United States since the New Deal. There are two reasons for focusing on equal employment opportunity (EEO). First, economic rights and opportunities are an essential aspect of modern community life and political conflict. As T. H. Marshall has written, to be fully a member of a modern community, a person must have the civil rights necessary for individual freedom, including "liberty of the person . . . the right to justice . . . and . . . the right to work, that is to say, the right to follow the occupation of one's choice in the place of one's choice, subject only to legitimate demands for preliminary technical training" (1964, 71, 75). And once fully a member of a community, a person will discover that politics revolves around economic issues more than anything else (Lipset and Rokkan 1967; Tufte 1978). Second, the book considers EEO because those involved in the twentieth-century struggle for equality in the United States have so often emphasized its importance. As soon as the modern civil rights movement began, black leaders and the black public placed EEO at or near the top of their lists of goals. At the 1949 hearings on EEO in the United States House of Representatives, both Clarence Mitchell, testifying on behalf of the National Association for the Advancement of Colored People (NAACP), and Representative Adam Clayton Powell, one of the chief congressional proponents of civil rights legislation, emphasized that passage of an EEO bill had first priority in their legislative program, taking precedence over bills dealing with voting, lynching, and segregation in public accommodations. Paul Norgren and Samuel Hill, longtime observers of the civil rights movement, concluded that "Discrimination in employment . . . has been the predominant target from the outset. It has been a major motivating factor, even when the declared objective of the demonstrations has been the removal of racial barriers in other areas" (1964, 4). Employment discrimination has been a central concern to those fighting discrimination against women, Jews, and other groups as well.[2]

The book attempts to answer two questions about the struggle for EEO. First, why did Congress decide to prohibit employment discrimination when it did and in the way it did, by adopting EEO legislation in 1964 and strengthening it in 1972? Second, to what extent has the struggle for EEO, including the demand for EEO legislation, improved the opportunities available to groups that suffered from employment discrimination?

Why Congress acted is an important question at two levels. First, and more concretely, the movement for equal treatment in all aspects of life, most conspicuously by blacks but by other groups as well, has been one of the most important public issues of our time, probably exceeded in importance in most people's minds since the 1940s only by threats of war and economic depression (Smith 1980). Demands for equal treatment by blacks, women, Hispanics, and other groups are an important political issue today and are likely to remain so for some time.[3] If we are to understand American society and politics, it seems essential to learn how and why Congress responded as it did on an issue of such intense concern.

Second, and more generally, discovering why Congress acted as it did on an important issue will help resolve a debate central to the study of democratic politics. According to many mainstream political theorists, the actions of a democratically elected legislature like the United States Congress are ultimately caused by the preferences of the public, as expressed through elections, letter writing, lobbying by voluntary organizations, and so on, perhaps modified a bit by institutional constraints (such as constitutional limitations on what Congress may do by simple majority). These theorists would hypothesize that congressional action on EEO was affected most strongly by public opinion.[4] Others argue, however, that Congress does not generally respond to public opinion but reacts to the demands of business and other elites, threats of violence, well-financed pressure groups, or the needs of its own members for power or influence. C. Wright Mills argued, for example, that "In the standard image of power and decision, no force is held to be as important as The Great American Public. . . . The opinion that results from public discussion is understood to be a resolution that is then carried out by public action. . . . But we must recognize this description as a set of images out of a fairy tale . . . an assertion of a legitimation masquerading . . . as fact. . . . The issues that now shape man's fate are neither raised nor decided by the public at large" (1956, 298, 300;

see also Pilisuk and Hayden 1965; Domhoff 1967; Katznelson and Kesselman 1975, chap. 9; Piven and Cloward 1971). Analyzing why Congress acted as it did on EEO will add to our knowledge of the determinants of congressional action; the weight of the evidence may tip the scales one way or another in debates about what democratic legislatures respond to.

The book is concerned not only with the causes of democratic political action, but with its consequences as well. The proponents of EEO legislation (as well as civil rights legislation in general) clearly believed that the democratic political process may be used to change the formal and informal rules by which jobs and incomes are allocated in a society—to change how employers decide whom to hire and promote, how unions decide whom to admit to membership, and how, in general, people are treated in the labor market. Many social scientists and political activists believe that democratic politics can affect economic outcomes. Even Karl Marx believed the working class could change the distribution of power in capitalist society through voting and peaceful political organization.[5]

Again, however, there are those who disagree, who are convinced that the political system of the contemporary United States cannot be used effectively to redistribute job opportunities and income to members of minority groups and women. They claim that potentially effective policies for redistributing opportunities and income are not likely to be allowed on the public political agenda; that if they manage to get on the agenda, they will not be adopted; that if adopted, they will not be administered effectively; and that if administered effectively, the rich and powerful will discover ways to evade their consequences, rendering any apparent gains illusory.[6] In this view, laws purporting to equalize opportunity are only symbolic, and attempts to produce economic or social change by direct action will be suppressed. Determining the extent to which the movement for EEO has succeeded will help us gauge the limits and possibilities of democratic politics in the continuing struggle over equality.[7]

What We Already Know

Despite the importance of the struggle for EEO, we actually know very little about it. Anyone who wants to know why the legislative debate on federal EEO legislation took thirty years—from the introduction of the first EEO bill in 1942 until the passage of the Equal Employment Opportunity Act of 1972—or why the present law says what it says will discover that no studies of the entire fight for EEO have been published. There have been a number of studies of the passage of the Civil Rights Act of 1964, which included the basis for today's EEO law as Title 7. They fail to deal with EEO specifically and to follow the legislative battle through to its conclusion in 1972, however, and they have two additional significant weaknesses.

First, they are vague about why Congress acted when and as it did. Collectively, previous studies provide a long list of factors that supposedly affected Congress, including public opinion, civil rights demonstrations, violent attacks on demonstrators, media coverage, lobbying by civil rights groups and religious organizations, competition for black votes in the North, parliamentary maneuvering in Congress, the personalities of political leaders, and so on.[8] Exactly how these factors were related to congressional action and to each other, however, and how important each was, is often unclear even in the best analyses. Robert Dahl has written, for instance, that the brutal suppression of civil rights demonstrators in Birmingham, Alabama, in 1963 "helped generate the public pressure and support necessary to the passage of legislation" (1967, 419); Anthony Oberschall agreed that only such confrontations "would outrage public opinion and pressure the federal government to enact such legislation" (1979, 62). Now what exactly does it mean to "generate" public pressure or "outrage" public opinion? Does this mean that violent attacks on demonstrators caused many people to *change their minds* about civil rights for blacks, or does it mean that people were simply moved to act upon beliefs they *already had?* These two interpretations have radically different implications—the former suggests that the civil rights movement had the power to alter public opinion, the latter implies no such thing—but I find it impossible to discern in the texts what is meant.

Second, even if Dahl and Oberschall (and others) were clear, we would still have little idea precisely how important each factor was or how the factors were related to each other, because the data required for the necessary analysis have not been available. No one can say how strongly Congress was affected by public opinion, for example, or by demonstrations, violence, media coverage, or other factors, because no one has examined in detail how public opinion changed between 1942 and 1972, how many civil rights demonstrations there were annually, how much violence was directed at blacks and when, or how any of these related to congressional action on EEO over the thirty-year period. Nor do we know as much as one might think about the effect of the struggle for EEO on the economic status of the groups that suffered from discrimination. A number of econometric studies of the effect of EEO legislation have been published, but almost all of them treat the EEO law detached from its social and political context, as if the movement that led to the passage of legislation had never occurred, and as if the enforcement of EEO legislation proceeded automatically, entirely unaffected by public attitudes about EEO, the civil rights and women's movements, or the continuing political debate. As a result, no one knows whether improvements in the opportunities and incomes available to women and members of minority groups are due to the enforcement of federal EEO laws or merely to social and political changes in the society that would be occurring anyway (see Berger 1967, 3).

This book began as an attempt to answer some important questions about democratic politics and the struggle for EEO. It turned into an effort to improve how we *study* democratic politics as well. Why don't we already know why Congress responded as it did to the movement for EEO, or what the consequences of the movement have been? I think there are two reasons. First, until recently neither the theories nor the research methods needed to answer the questions have been available. No one knew, for example, how to systematically describe the development of social movements over time or how to gauge their consequences. Now we do know to a substantial extent. Our ability to analyze congressional action, public opinion, social movements, and other relevant social, political, and economic phenomena has increased tremendously.[9] This study rests upon the advances made by others.

No one has previously used these advances to study the movement of EEO, however. I think this is because of the traditional academic division of labor, which constitutes the second reason so little is known about the movement for EEO. Much has been learned about Congress, public opinion, social movements, and so forth, but the new knowledge is scattered among academic disciplines. Most of the work on social movements has been done by sociologists, who have almost no interest in formal political institutions and who have therefore not tried to show how such movements affect Congress.[10] Political scientists are interested in Congress, of course, but have little place for social movements in their theories or empirical analysis.[11] Sociologists and economists are both concerned about discrimination in the labor market, but sociologists almost never study how the law may affect discrimination, while economists, who do consider EEO enforcement, virtually ignore the social and political context in which discrimination and law enforcement take place.[12] A few people do try to cut across disciplinary boundaries to deal with all aspects of the struggle for equality, but they are typically historians, lawyers, or journalists who fail to draw on social science theory or methods; their arguments therefore remain vague and their conclusions imprecise.[13]

This book is an attempt to use the advances made by sociologists, political scientists, economists, and others, but to use them to answer broad questions about EEO and democratic politics rather than about variables that are the focus of one discipline or another. To the extent that the attempt succeeds, it can contribute to our ability to analyze issues of broad public concern as well as phenomena of interest to social scientists in particular fields. As it turns out, crossing disciplinary boundaries proves to be important, because the explanations of congressional action and changes in economic outcomes described below do not fit within conventional disciplinary niches.

EEO Legislation: The Beginnings

The tension between the American promise of fairness and the experience of discrimination led to organized struggle for equal opportunity in employment. By the 1930s and early 1940s, blacks and Jews were especially active, organized, and public in their protests, and members of other groups expressed their resentment as well. The leaders of groups that were discriminated against tried a variety of approaches to gain equal treatment: promoting education and training, attempting to persuade employers and union officials to change their practices, running educational campaigns to reduce prejudice, and the like. But many came to believe that educating group members and cultivating goodwill would not end discrimination. They concluded that only the government could do so.[14]

The earliest post-Reconstruction efforts to end employment discrimination through statutes focused on state governments. The first law requiring that men and women be paid the same amount for doing the same work was adopted by the Michigan legislature in 1919, and the hearings that eventually led to the passage of the first fair employment practices law protecting minority groups were held in New York in the late 1930s. Attention soon shifted to the federal level, however. Blacks in particular realized that a federal law would be necessary, because most of them lived in the South where no state government would pass an antidiscrimination law. In addition, residents of the more liberal states worried that the passage of EEO laws in their states would simply encourage businesses to move elsewhere; a federal law would remove the incentive to do this.[15]

As the depression ended and employment levels rose, blacks came to see federal action as especially urgent and appropriate because many of the new jobs were created by the government itself, in defense industries. Not wanting blacks to be kept out of the new jobs, and believing that President Roosevelt could influence the hiring patterns of defense contractors, A. Philip Randolph and other black leaders urged the president to sign an executive order banning discrimination in defense industries. Unless such an order was signed, they threatened, ten thousand people would march on Washington to protest employment discrimination. President Roosevelt responded in June 1941 by signing Executive Order 8802, which declared that "there shall be no discrimination in the employment of workers in defense industries or government because of race, creed, color, or national origin" and required that all defense contracts have a nondiscrimination clause.

The likely power of the executive order was modest. Only defense contractors and the federal government were covered. Enforcement was to be in the hands of a five-man Committee on Fair Employment Practice, whose members were to receive reimbursement for expenses, but no pay. No sanctions against those who disobeyed were specified. And the legal status and power of such orders was somewhat uncertain.[16] Nevertheless, the order was the first federal executive or legislative action since Reconstruction explicitly intended to reduce discrimination in the private labor market. It was important because it ended what Myrdal called "the tradition of federal unconcernedness" about employment discrimination (1962, 416).

The first bill proposing to prohibit employment discrimination in most of the private labor market was introduced in Congress the next year, and the campaign for EEO legislation soon became a central part of the struggle for federal action on civil rights. We all know the eventual result of the legislative debate. It is now an "unlawful employment practice" for an employer "to fail or refuse to hire or to discharge any individual, or discriminate against any individual with respect to his compensation, terms, conditions, or privileges of employment, because of such individual's race, color, religion, sex, or national origin," or to "limit, segregate, or classify his employees or applicants for employment in any way which would deprive or tend to deprive any individual of employment opportunities or otherwise adversely affect his status as an employee, because of such individual's race, color, religion, sex, or national origin" (42 U.S.C. 2000e et seq.). Employment agencies and labor unions are similarly constrained. Individuals who feel they have been discriminated against may complain to federal agencies empowered to sue alleged discriminators on their behalf, and individuals may sue alleged discriminators on their own. If their claims are upheld, they may be given the jobs, promotions, and pay they were deprived of and have their attorneys' fees paid. The federal government expected to spend more than $350 million during the 1983 fiscal year to enforce the laws against employment discrimination (U.S. Office of Management and Budget 1982, 27), and major corporations have had to pay tens of millions of dollars and to make major changes in their personnel practices as the result of suits against them (see Wallace 1976; Peres 1978).

Thus the campaign to enlist the power of the federal government in the fight against employment discrimination succeeded. But the struggle was a protracted one. By the time Congress passed its first EEO law as Title 7 of the Civil Rights Act of 1964 and amended it in 1972, EEO bills had been the focus of intense scrutiny—in more than twenty-one congressional hearings, argument covering thousands of pages of the *Congressional Record,* and countless public and scholarly debates. The intensity of minorities' concern with EEO had had to confront resistance so strong that President Kennedy's 1963 civil rights bill failed to include a section prohibiting employment discrimination because the president believed it would be rejected. Title 7 was added to the bill by congressional committees, but the bill itself was passed only after two hundred thousand people gathered in Washington for the largest civil rights demonstration in American history.

A Preview

The first part of this book—chapters 2 through 5—examines what Congress did during the thirty-year debate on EEO, and why. The focus of much study of democratic politics is the debate between those who believe legislatures respond primarily to the public's preferences and those who believe they respond to something else. The analysis that follows shows that congressional action was the product of a complex interplay among ideas about how to deal with employment discrimination, public opinion, social protest, and political leadership.

Chapter 2 sets the stage. It asks why people started to think that the federal government should do anything at all about employment discrimination, what sorts of ideas people had about what the government should do, and how support for the ideas that became today's EEO law grew over the years. Most people tend to assume that today's civil rights legislation is the product of the dramatic events of the early and mid-1960s—the sit-ins, the March on Washington, the violent attacks on peaceful civil rights demonstrators in the South, the Democratic landslide in the 1964 election, and so forth. Chapter 2 considers the possibility that most people are wrong, that EEO legislation had its genesis in the later part of the New Deal, and that its passage was the result of a slow but steady growth of support that began long before the 1960s.

Chapters 3 through 5 focus on why Congress passed EEO legislation when it did. Chapter 3 analyzes the influence of public opinion, considering, in essence, the very simple possibility that Congress adopted EEO legislation simply because most Americans wanted it to. Chapter 4 examines the effect of the civil rights movement on congressional action. Most accounts of the passage of civil rights legislation attribute great importance to the civil rights movement, particularly its highly publicized demonstrations. The chapter attempts to ascertain the extent to which the standard conclusion is correct and to show how strongly whatever effect the movement had depended upon the changes in public opinion described in chapter 3 and upon other aspects of the social and political context.

Chapter 5 considers how congressional action on EEO was affected by three factors of immediate, day-to-day concern to politicians: elections, lobbying, and presidential and congressional leadership. It examines how the formal and informal institutions of American government influence the way Congress responds to public opinion, social movement activity, and other manifestations of the public's preferences discussed in chapters 3 and 4. Do American political institutions enhance the government's capacity to respond to the public, or do they weaken it? As it turns out, today's EEO laws may be described as the product of a meeting between old ideas about laws with new opinions about equality, a meeting organized by social protest and brought to fruition by political leadership.

The second part of the book—chapters 6 and 7—analyzes the consequences of the struggle for EEO. The analysis speaks to contemporary debates among those who believe that EEO laws have had little or no impact, those who see some modest positive effect on the incomes of those who have been discriminated against, and those who believe that EEO laws are having vast, disruptive consequences for American society. Chapter 6 shows that the laws appear to have had some of the effect intended by their supporters—a reduction in discrimination and subsequent increase in the incomes of women and members of minority groups. Some of the changes in incomes since the 1960s seems to have been brought about, however, by the same forces that led to the passage of the EEO laws. Both the laws themselves and the forces that brought them about are of continuing importance. Chapter 7 considers the future of equal employment opportunity and the possible consequences of forces that may speed up or slow down the rate at which the incomes of women and members of minority groups approach those of white men; it also assesses the likely future of reverse discrimination.

Some Caveats

Every book has its real and apparent limitations. Here are four that readers knowledgeable about Congress or civil rights are likely to notice immediately.

First, EEO is treated as a public and congressional issue in its own right. This means it is not treated as just part of an overall ''package'' of civil rights issues. I think chapter 2 shows that there is justification for this treatment, even though it runs contrary to what is customary in studies of congressional action. Although EEO legislation was first adopted as one part of the Civil Rights Act of 1964, partly as a result of the same forces leading to the adoption of legislation on other issues, EEO legislation had a history of its own, and its consequences can and should be analyzed separately from the consequences of civil rights legislation in other areas, such as public accommodations or voting. Analyzing EEO legislation on its own, independent of other, non–civil rights issues, also means ignoring, for the most part, the interrelations among issues that members of Congress consider and the logrolling that sometimes occurs. Unfortunately, no one has yet developed a satisfactory way to take logrolling into account in quantitative analyses of legislative behavior. I do not think that the inability to do so affects the analysis in any serious way, but it would have been better to deal with it directly were this possible.

Second, the first part of the book focuses almost entirely on EEO legislation, paying little attention to legislation mandating that women doing the same jobs be paid equally, or to executive orders on EEO. That is because Title 7 is the keystone of federal EEO policy. Equal pay laws mean little in the absence of more general EEO laws, for example, because employers can always avoid paying men and women equally by simply excluding women from jobs, a type of action that equal pay laws permit but EEO laws do not. The history of the federal equal pay law is in fact quite similar to that of the EEO law, so the conclusions reported below would not be altered by a detailed analysis of equal pay legislation.

Third, state EEO laws have generally been ignored (except in chap. 3), even though many were adopted before Title 7. This is because they were never enforced in any meaningful sense, for reasons that will become clear, and because they have not contributed to the public debate on EEO (see Blumrosen 1971).

Finally, the analysis of the consequences of the struggle for EEO focuses almost entirely on its implications for nonwhites and women, despite the historical importance of discrimination against other groups, the rising concern about discrimination against Hispanics (a national-origin category, not a racial one), and the fact that "nonwhite" includes Asians, American Indians, and other groups as well as blacks. This analysis, like so many others, has simply been influenced by the United States Bureau of the Census, which has traditionally presented its data in terms of male/female and nonwhite/white categorizations, and not in other ways. Other sources of information are available on other groups, but none provides the time-series data needed for the analyses presented in the second part of the book. This should not bias the results presented, but it is important to remember that other groups have suffered from discrimination, that they have dealt with it in many ways, including political ones, and that many consequences of their struggle and adaptation may be seen in the American labor market today (Lieberson 1980; Jencks 1983a,b).

The analysis begins as chapter 2 describes how Congress dealt with demands for EEO legislation.

2 Ideas and Politics in the Congressional Debate on Equal Employment Opportunity

What should the federal government do about discrimination in employment? For most of American history the answer was simple: nothing. Until the end of the nineteenth century, the labor market was virtually unregulated by federal, state, or local governments; the government would no more protect people from discrimination than it would protect them from working twelve hours a day or in unsafe conditions (Steinberg 1982, chaps. 1, 3).

Change began as the depression ended. President Franklin D. Roosevelt initiated the first post-Reconstruction federal action against employment discrimination in 1941 when he issued an executive order banning discrimination by the federal government and defense contractors. The first bill proposing to prohibit employment discrimination in most of the labor market was introduced in Congress the next year.

But sustained, active involvement by the federal government in the struggle against discrimination was a long time coming. As World War II ended, Congress blocked attempts to enforce Roosevelt's executive order. It took twenty-two years to pass the first comprehensive EEO law, as Title 7 of the 1964 Civil Rights Act, and another eight to provide the federal government with broad enforcement powers.

This chapter begins the explanation of why today's EEO law passed when it did and says what it says. My approach is somewhat unconventional. As Nelson Polsby has written (1984, chap. 1), most studies of the development of public policy focus on the period just before legislative enactment, when the debate is the most dramatic, the pressures brought to bear on Congress the most conspicuous, and the role of the president most prominent. This is certainly what most studies of the passage of

Margo W. MacLeod coauthored an earlier version of this chapter, which appeared in the *American Journal of Sociology,* November, 1980 (© 1980 by The University of Chicago).

civil rights legislation do (see, for example, Dye 1971, chap. 5; Sundquist 1968, chap. 6; Wirmark 1974; Lytle 1966; Orfield 1975, chap. 5). Yet it is very unlikely that most public policies are rapidly devised in the period just before enactment, and most sophisticated politicians and political scientists realize they are not. Little attention has been paid, nevertheless, to the process of policy development, to what Polsby calls "the politics of inventing, winnowing, and finding and gaining adherents for policy alternatives . . . before moving alternatives from unlikely to possible to probable candidates for inclusion on an agenda for enactment" (1984, 3). This chapter steps back from the enactment stage. It considers how today's EEO law was "invented" and the nature of the process through which it gained adherents; and it shows that to understand legislative change, one must examine not only the usual array of pressures brought to bear on Congress, but the development of ideas and their acceptance as well.

The chapter focuses on four questions. First, why did Congress wait until the 1940s to consider EEO legislation? Employment discrimination was hardly a new problem.

Second, why does today's EEO legislation say what it says? The civil rights movement that preceded the passage of EEO legislation was widely seen as a movement for the rights of blacks, yet the law prohibits discrimination against Jews, Hispanics, women, and other groups as well. For members of these groups, this is no small matter. How did it come about? Why does the law prohibit discrimination by state and local governments and labor unions as well as private employers? Why does it establish enforcement procedures that many people have described as cumbersome and inefficient? Answering these questions will show that we cannot understand today's EEO law as merely the product of pressures placed on Congress in the period immediately before enactment; historical forces and ideas that are often ignored or forgotten were important as well.

Third, how did support for EEO legislation grow? A systematic description of the growth of support makes some hypotheses about passage more plausible than others. If congressional support increased gradually from the 1940s on, for example, the search for explanations might focus on factors that displayed a similar pattern, such as public opinion, which was slowly and steadily becoming more liberal. If support had long been low but increased dramatically in the months before passage, however, it would make more sense to hypothesize that dramatic events, such as the 1963 March on Washington or the attacks on demonstrators in Birmingham, were crucial. We cannot hope to explain the passage of legislation if we cannot even describe the process leading to it.

Fourth, why did congressional interest in new EEO legislation drop virtually to zero after Title 7 was amended in 1972? Few people would say that the present laws have eliminated employment discrimination from American life, so why have there been no attempts to significantly improve the law?

To answer the four questions, this chapter examines the congressional proposals made since 1942 for prohibiting discrimination in employment. It makes four points: that congressional debate on EEO began soon after implementation of an EEO law seemed feasible to interested members of Congress; that congressional debate on EEO revolved around a small number of generally similar proposals introduced in the 1940s and was little affected by subsequent events and ideas; that the growth of support for EEO legislation was generally slow and incremental; and that congressional action on EEO ceased in the early 1970s because the agenda established in the 1940s had been completed.

The Beginnings of Congressional Action: Why the 1940s?

Employment discrimination was not new in the early 1940s. Why were the first federal EEO bills introduced then, rather than sooner or later?

People's political actions are predicated upon their sense of possibility. As Stinchcombe has argued (1978, 40), people do not seek political change simply because they are oppressed—it is really the "conviction of the possibility of reform . . . the gradual spreading of the conviction that perhaps a better alternative is really possible" that is the basic psychological precondition of political action. Before many people could be expected to work for government action against discrimination in employment, the passage and implementation of appropriate legislation would have to be seen as real possibilities.

Before the late 1930s and early 1940s, however, there was every reason to believe that the passage of federal EEO legislation was not only unlikely, but virtually impossible. The federal government could, it was acknowledged, treat its own employees without discrimination (though in fact discrimination was the norm), and could reduce discrimination by private employers to some extent by granting contracts only to those that did not discriminate (Bonfield 1967). But the federal work force was very small and the government's involvement in the private economy slight, except in wartime. With regard to the labor market as a whole, the federal government appeared powerless to act—the Supreme Court had long since placed very narrow limits on what the government could do against discrimination and on its power to regulate the labor market.

The federal government had acted against discrimination shortly after the Civil War; the Civil Rights Acts of 1866 and 1871 initially appeared to prohibit a broad range of private as well as public acts of discrimination, possibly including employment discrimination. These statutes were so narrowly construed by the Supreme Court in the *Civil Rights Cases* of 1883 (109 U.S. 3), however, that they were essentially nullified. These cases made it appear impossible for the federal government to do much about discrimination in the private labor market on the basis of the Thirteenth and Fourteenth Amendments to the Constitution (Gunther 1975, chap. 11).

The Court also restricted the federal government's power to regulate the economy generally, including the labor market. The Court generally struck down federal laws regulating labor relations and limited the power of the states in this area as well. By the mid-1930s, the Court had struck down federal laws attempting to regulate child labor, retirement and pensions, minimum wages and maximum hours, and other aspects of labor relations (Gunther 1975, chap. 3; see also chap. 9). Such precedents made it exceedingly unlikely that any meaningful federal EEO law would withstand judicial scrutiny. In making its decisions, the Court not only interpreted particular statutes and constitutional amendments, it also helped define and limit congressional debate—it made proposals for action appear pointless. Thus, at least until the late 1930s, even widespread latent support for an EEO law could probably not have been translated into political action. There was no point in urging Congress to pass a law, and no reason for members of Congress to vote for one, if it would surely be struck down by the Supreme Court.[1]

By the late 1930s and early 1940s, however, three crucial changes had taken place that made effective federal action much easier to imagine. First, the size of the federal government increased dramatically in response to the depression: the number of civilian federal employees rose from 580,000 in 1929 to 1,042,000 in 1940, and the federal budget increased from 3.0 percent of the gross national product to 9.1 percent. World War II accelerated these trends. Thus the number of jobs over which the federal government exercised some power increased tremendously.

Second, and more important in the long run, the Supreme Court responded to the turmoil of the 1930s, the controversies over its striking down important items of New Deal legislation, and other factors by starting to reverse its stand on federal intervention in the economy. In a series of landmark cases, the Court upheld the power of the federal government to regulate employment relations on the basis of its power to regulate interstate commerce. By the mid-1940s, the Court decided cases that appeared to legitimate this extension of federal power to employment discrimination (Gunther 1975, chap. 3). These cases greatly changed the legal and symbolic environment and made it possible to argue convincingly that the Supreme Court would uphold federal EEO legislation (see, for example, House Report 1165 accompanying the major 1949 House EEO bill, H.R. 4453).

Third, by the late 1930s the Court was rather clearly becoming more sympathetic to members of groups suffering from discrimination. Between 1880 and 1935, the Supreme Court had been willing to hear only sixteen cases dealing with discrimination on the basis of race, religion, national origin, or sex, and those plaintiffs who managed to gain a hearing were almost as likely to lose as to win—the record was nine victories for those claiming they had suffered from discrimination and seven defeats.[2] Between 1936 and 1945, however, the Court heard seventeen cases—more in ten years than in the previous fifty-five—and the balance shifted decisively in favor of those claiming they had suffered from discrimination, as they won twelve cases and lost five. Partly as a result of a sophisticated, well-coordinated, and farsighted legal campaign by the NAACP (Myrdal 1962, 830–31; Berger 1967, chap. 3), it became increasingly clear through the 1940s and 1950s and into the early 1960s that the Court was going to be sympathetic to legal attacks on discrimination. By 1964, when the Civil Rights Act was passed, the Supreme Court had heard 106 discrimination cases since 1936, and had ruled ninety times in favor of those allegedly suffering from discrimination.

Shortly after these changes in the legal environment, members of Congress began to introduce EEO bills—in 1941 to give Roosevelt's Executive Order 8802 the force of law, and in 1942 to prohibit discrimination not only by the federal government and defense contractors, but by private employers and labor unions as well. It would be a long time before such a bill would become law, but such an outcome had entered the realm of the possible. Why the Supreme Court changed its policies is an important question, but with regard to congressional action on EEO, the crucial point is this: shortly after the Court's decisions began to indicate that an EEO law *could* be passed, members of Congress began to propose that one *should* be passed. What, then, did they propose?

Legislating Equality: What Members of Congress Proposed

For those familiar with state and federal EEO legislation, certain phrases form a litany seemingly sanctified by history, repeated through the years. Perhaps the most familiar phrase is "race, creed, color, or national origin"—the bases on which discrimination is prohibited. The phrase was in Roosevelt's executive order, in most of the hundreds of EEO bills introduced in Congress, and in many state laws; the word "sex" was added to the litany in 1964 and is now taken for granted. But other important phrases recur too. In most bills and state laws, the commission established to enforce the law against employment discrimination "shall endeavor to eliminate any unlawful employment practice by informal methods of conference, conciliation, and persuasion." Those who are found to have engaged in an unlawful employment practice are required to stop the practice and take "such affirmative action, including reinstatement or hiring of employees, with or without back pay," as may be appropriate.[3] In addition, the overall structure of state and federal laws is always the same: individuals or members of an EEO commission may complain to the commission that an employer, a labor union, or an employment agency has discriminated; the complaint is investigated; if it has merit, the commission may issue an order, enforceable in the courts, that the discrimination be stopped, or the commission or aggrieved individual may sue to have discrimination stopped, and if discrimination is found to have taken place, specific penalties may be imposed.

The bills *could have* been written very differently, however. For example, they could have been modeled on the Civil Rights Act of 1866 (now 42 U.S.C. 1981), which has been used in certain employment discrimination cases in recent years. The 1866 act reads: "All persons within the jurisdiction of the United States shall have the same right . . . to make and enforce contracts, to sue, be parties, give evidence, and to the full and equal benefit of all laws and proceedings for the security of persons and property as is enjoyed by white citizens, and shall be subject to like punishments, pains, penalties, taxes, licenses, and actions of every kind, and to no other."

This law is not similar to Title 7 or to any bill proposed in Congress since the 1940s. It was the product of an age that did not lump together race-religion-national origin-sex, had not invented the term "affirmative action," did not recognize labor unions and employment agencies in federal law, and had not invented powerful administration agencies. An American EEO statute need not be like Title 7.[4]

Prohibiting employment discrimination through legislation was, from the legislators' point of view, a new and untried idea in the early 1940s. Those who introduced and debated EEO bills were proposing major legislative innovations. How did they come to write the law as it exists today?

Analyzing EEO Bills

Beginning in 1942, hundreds of EEO bills were introduced in Congress; most had little chance of becoming law, but each represented someone's idea about what EEO legislation should be like and had some chance to influence the content of the law ultimately enacted. My first step in describing the complete range of proposals was to compile a list of all bills dealing primarily with EEO in a major part of the private labor market, drawing on the indexes of the *Congressional Record* and the *Congressional Index* (Commerce Clearing House 1949–78), congressional hearings on EEO, and histories of congressional action (e.g., Ruchames 1953; Kesselman 1948; Sovern 1966).

My next problem was to summarize the bills in a way that would convey their essence but avoid excessive detail. Because the number of bills to be described was so great, the coding scheme had to describe as simply as possible the elements of bills seen as basic by most legislators, groups potentially affected, and legal observers. A careful reading of previous work on analyzing legislation, many bills, much testimony and debate, and prior work on EEO laws led to the development of a coding scheme in which bills were analyzed and coded along five dimensions:[5]

1. which groups the bill proposed to protect (racial minorities, religious groups, etc.);

2. which organizations and individuals were prohibited from discriminating (employers, labor unions, etc.);

3. which employment practices were declared unlawful (discrimination in hiring, in terms and conditions of employment, in training, etc.);

4. how the law was to be enforced (what rights and powers were given to aggrieved individuals, government agencies, etc.);

5. what penalties discriminators were subject to.[6]

In order to show how a congressional consensus gradually formed around the bill that became Title 7, as amended (referred to hereafter simply as Title 7), the analysis considers the popularity of different proposals, as well as their content. The unit of analysis, therefore, is the *sponsorship*—one member of Congress sponsoring one bill.[7]

Who Is to Be Protected against Discrimination

When Title 7 was brought to the floor of the House, it prohibited discrimination on the basis of race, religion, and national origin. This seemed natural to most people at the time, but it was hardly inevitable. The earliest federal "antidiscrimination law" prohibited only religious discrimination (with regard to qualifications for "any office or public trust under the United States," in Article 6 of the Constitution), while the post–Civil War amendments and the laws passed to effectuate them dealt only with race. The earliest attempts to prohibit employment discrimination (mostly in the 1920s and 1930s), covering narrow segments of state or local labor markets, varied in their definitions of the social groups to be protected (see Bonfield 1967; Bardolph 1970). And since the mid-1960s, various jurisdictions have prohibited discrimination on the basis of age, marital status, physical handicap, sexual orientation, and other factors.[8]

Figure 2.1 shows that, however many proposals might have been made, few were made. Considering only four characteristics—race, religion, national origin, and sex—sixteen combinations of prohibition were possible (sex only, race only, race and sex, race and national origin, etc.). But nearly all the proposals were of just two types—race, religion, and national origin (before 1964), and race, religion, national origin, and sex (after 1964). The notion of prohibiting discrimination on the basis of race and religion, but not national origin, gained some early popularity, particularly in the Senate (the argument being essentially that "we are all Americans"), but it never gained much support. Two early bills proposed prohibiting discrimination on the basis of age, sex, race,

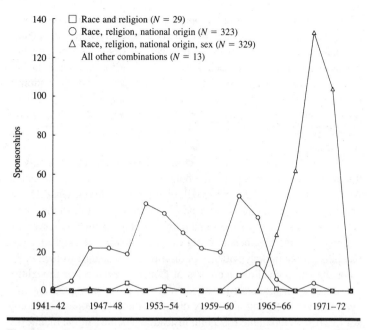

Fig. 2.1. **Groups protected from discrimination: sponsorships in the House and Senate**

and color, and one or two later ones included age, but there were virtually no other combinations.

In addition, most proposals made at any given time are the same, and the House and Senate are so similar that their bills can be combined in one figure. These facts suggest that the process of writing and introducing bills probably involved a great deal of coordinated social action and little independent, imaginative legislative drafting.

Why these proposals and no others? We cannot know for sure, but three factors seem especially important. The first modern EEO law, the 1945 New York State Law against Discrimination, prohibited discrimination on the basis of race, religion, and national origin. The New York law was much discussed in congressional hearings during the late 1940s and served as a model for congressional bills; one of its chief sponsors, Irving Ives, was elected to the United States Senate in 1946 and became an active proponent of EEO legislation.[9]

A second influence on the proposals was the power of three groups that were strongly represented in the early congressional hearings, either by their own organizations or by members of Congress who conspicuously represented them. Each was able to fight for its own inclusion: one racial group, blacks; one religious group, Jews; and one national-origin group, Hispanics (a major congressional proponent of prohibiting discrimination on the basis of national origin was Senator Chavez of New Mexico, who was especially concerned about Mexican-Americans).[10]

The third influence could be described as pure conventionality in thinking. The best example is the failure to prohibit sex discrimination. As noted, two early bills proposed doing so. In addition, while House and Senate subcommittees were holding hearings on EEO bills, other subcommittees, often of the same committees and sometimes even involving the same members of Congress, were holding hearings on equal pay bills and compiling evidence of discrimination against women in the labor market; sometimes members of Congress even asked thoughtful questions about sex discrimination. Yet this never prompted anyone, even women testifying about sex discrimination, to propose including sex discrimination in the EEO bill; instead, the politics of the manifestly inadequate equal pay bills developed separately.[11]

Thus, sponsors proposed few alternatives. What about relevant amendments offered by others in committee or on the floor? EEO bills were passed by the House in 1950 (a bill with no enforcement powers), by the House and Senate in 1964, by the House in 1966 and the Senate in 1970, and by both House and Senate again in 1972 (essentially completing the present law). For the most part, those who were not sponsors either supported the sponsors' bills or opposed EEO legislation; they had few new ideas to contribute. The House and Senate voted on 134 amendments during debates on EEO legislation.[12] Of these, only 16 dealt with who was to be protected by the legislation, and most of these were minor or were intended to prolong the debate (such as specifying that a bill did not protect communists or proposing to ban discrimination against white, Protestant Americans).

Just two proposed changes were significant. The bill that became Title 7 originally prohibited age discrimination. This prohibition was eliminated when the bill was amended in committee, and a motion in the House to put it back into the bill was defeated.[13]

The change of real consequence began as a joke of sorts. During the

House debate, Representative Howard Smith of Virginia, who opposed all civil rights legislation, moved that a prohibition against sex discrimination be included in Title 7. His aim was to complicate the debate and confuse the liberals, who were divided on the wisdom of banning sex discrimination. The initial response to the motion was, in fact, laughter (U.S. Congress, *Congressional Record,* 1964, 2576–77).

The eventual response to Smith's motion was real innovation, however (though he was probably not pleased by the result). Congress had long been considering equal pay legislation (to give women equal pay for work equal to that of men) and EEO legislation but had dealt with them separately. Smith's "joke" brought them together. Once the proposal had been made, members of Congress found it difficult to argue that discrimination against women was not serious (since many hearings on equal pay bills had shown that it was) or that sex discrimination was not a proper subject for legislation (since the Equal Pay Act had been adopted the year before). And a small but hardworking group of women took advantage of the opportunity to lobby strenuously for the proposal and to make voting against it difficult (see Robinson 1979). Smith's motion therefore passed, 168 to 133, and stayed in the final bill. The adoption of the ban on sex discrimination has been described as an "accidental breakthrough" (Orfield 1975, 299), but it was one for which the groundwork had been thoroughly, if inadvertently, laid in the many previous hearings and debates about sex discrimination.

Coverage: Who Is Prohibited from Discriminating

Roosevelt's executive order and pre-1945 state antidiscrimination laws prohibited discrimination only by government agencies and private firms with government contracts. The earliest proposals to prohibit discrimination by a wider range of organizations were therefore significant innovations.

The first EEO bills dealt only with private employers. As figure 2.2 shows, however, sponsors quickly agreed among themselves that labor organizations should be prohibited from discriminating in membership and the treatment of members. Although most early bills prohibited employers from hiring through employment agencies that discriminated, members of Congress eventually realized that not covering employment agencies themselves provided a loophole in the bills. From 1955–56 on, therefore, virtually all bills covered private employers, labor organizations, and employment agencies.[14]

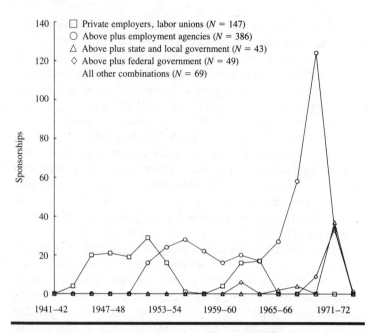

Fig. 2.2   Groups prohibited from discriminating: sponsorships in the House and Senate.

Prohibiting discrimination by these three types of organizations remained the most popular proposal right up through their inclusion in Title 7 as passed in 1964, but the approach of passage saw an upsurge of innovative proposals that presaged future developments. Beginning in 1961–62, some bills added prohibitions of discrimination by local and state governments and by the federal government itself to the usual list of organizations covered. The diversity of proposals increased at this point as well.[15]

Support for prohibiting discrimination by governments gradually increased. By the time Title 7 was amended in 1972, sponsors were quite evenly divided into three groups: those who favored the existing coverage of private employers, unions, and employment agencies; those who advocated covering state and local governments as well; and those who wanted to cover the federal government in addition to all the other types of organizations.

Nevertheless, the most striking thing about the proposals is how standardized they are. Nearly all of them belong to one of the four distinct types described in figure 2.2. Among all the sponsors, 77 percent favored just two combinations: prohibiting discrimination by private employers and labor organizations (21 percent) and by those plus employment agencies (56 percent). Only the sixty-nine sponsors listed last in the figure—fewer than 10 percent of the total—favored a combination other than the four specified.

The degree of agreement among sponsors at any given time was usually even greater than these figures indicate. Sponsors generally disagreed among themselves in only two circumstances: during transition periods when a new proposal displaced an old one (as when employment agencies were added), and just before bills passed, when involvement tended to peak. At any other time, agreement was likely to be extremely great.

Coverage was the focus of more attention in committee and on the floor than was the question of which groups to protect; the House and Senate voted twenty-four times on amendments affecting coverage. There were two central issues: how small a union or employer had to be to be exempted, and whether state and local governments would be covered (see Congressional Quarterly 1964, 352, 374; Congressional Quarterly 1972, 251, 254–56). In the 1950 House-passed bill, employers with fewer than fifty employees and unions with fewer than fifty members were exempt; in the present law the number is fifteen. And state and local governments are covered. Some of the other proposals narrowed coverage a bit (Indian tribes are exempt—see Congressional Quarterly 1964, 364), some broadened it (an exemption for the employers of certain kinds of educational personnel was ended), and some merely tightened the language of the bills. But the essential provisions defining coverage were not challenged by novel proposals.

Unlawful Employment Practices

Because the purpose of EEO bills is to prohibit discrimination, one might expect considerable disagreement about precisely what activities were to be declared unlawful. This was not the case. A standard list of proscribed practices was developed in the mid-1940s; although there were changes over the years—mostly closing loopholes—on the whole little attention was paid to this dimension. The pattern was a recurring one: a wide range of possible proposals, the early settling on a particular proposal, and little subsequent change.

This point is probably best made by quoting comparable sections from an early bill, the one introduced onto the floor of the House in 1950, and the present law. The key sections of the 1950 bill as it affects employers, for example, are brief:

It shall be an unlawful employment practice for an employer—
(1) to refuse to hire, to discharge, or otherwise to discriminate against any individual with respect to his terms, conditions, or privileges of employment, because of such individual's race, color, religion, or national origin; and
(2) to utilize in the hiring or recruitment of individuals for employment any employment agency . . . which discriminates. . . .
It shall be an unlawful employment practice for any employer or labor organization to discharge, expel, or otherwise discriminate against any person, because he has opposed any unlawful practice or has filed a charge, testified, participated, or assisted in any proceeding under this act. (U.S. Congress, House Special Subcommittee of the Committee on Education and Labor 1949)

Parts of the 1972 law are almost identical with the 1950 bill (and with most of the bills introduced in the interim); changes often involve spelling out the same idea in more detail:

It shall be an unlawful practice for any employer—
(1) to fail or refuse to hire or to discharge any individual, or otherwise to discriminate against any individual with respect to his compensation, terms, conditions, or privileges of employment. . . . to discriminate against any individual . . . because he has opposed any practice made an unlawful employment practice by this title, or because he had made a charge, testified, assisted, or participated in any manner in an investigation, proceeding, or hearing under this title. (Title 7)

The 1972 law adds that it is an unlawful employment practice for an employer "to limit, segregate, or classify his employees or applicants for employment in any way which would deprive or tend to deprive any individual of employment opportunities or otherwise adversely affect his status as an employee." This clause is present, virtually word for word, in the 1950 bill, but there it is applied only to labor unions; in the 1972 bill it applies to employers as well.[16]

Little attention was paid to defining unlawful employment practices during floor debate. The House and Senate voted on this issue just eleven times, seven of them in the 1964 Senate. Only one of the seven motions was adopted—one permitting employers to give professionally developed tests to employees and applicants for employment, provided the tests are not used to discriminate.

In sum, sponsors did no more than clarify definitions within a given context, and other members of Congress had little to add. Reliance on the early draft bills was nearly total.

Enforcement

Enforcement is a crucial element of all laws, and EEO laws are no exception. If enforcement provisions are very weak or cumbersome, questions about whom the law "protects" or what practices are declared unlawful become moot. In fact, probably more than half the text of most bills, and more than two-thirds of the text of many (including Title 7) has been devoted to enforcement. Four issues have been considered especially important. First, could aggrieved individuals initiate potentially binding legal proceedings on their own, or must they work exclusively through an administrative agency? Second, must complaints of discrimination be dealt with only case by case, or would class actions or similar group actions against alleged discriminators be possible? Third, would a special federal agency be created to administer the law? If so, would it have enforcement powers or be limited to educational programs and conciliation efforts? Finally, would enforcement be primarily administrative (with an administrative agency issuing cease-and-desist orders to discriminators) or judicial (with aggrieved parties suing alleged discriminators in federal court)?

The number of enforcement mechanisms that could be devised from the combinations of these possibilities is large. In addition, other standard enforcement procedures—making discrimination a criminal offense prosecuted by district attorneys, merely giving individuals the right to sue—could have been considered.

As with other dimensions of EEO bills, however, the number of proposals made was very small; about 90 percent of all proposals were of just four types. Before 1963–64, the only proposal made by a significant number of sponsors was for an enforcement mechanism modeled on the National Labor Relations Board—aggrieved individuals would have to complain to an administrative agency, which would deal with complaints primarily case by case and have the power to issue judicially enforceable cease-and-desist orders against those found to discriminate.

The legislative outcome in 1964 did not reflect what sponsors proposed, because in the 1964 Congress, as in every Congress in which EEO bills reached the floor, most attempts to amend the bills in committee and on the floor focused on enforcement procedures—of the 134 amendments voted on between 1950 and 1972, 81 concerned enforcement.

The change began in the House committees that wrote the basic version of the Civil Rights Act of 1964 (see U.S. Congress, House Committee on Education and Labor 1963; U.S. Congress, House Committee on the Judiciary 1963). The enforcement provisions of what was to become Title 7, which began by calling for administrative enforcement, were amended so that the Equal Employment Opportunity Commission (EEOC) created by the title was to sue alleged discriminators in federal court; if it did not sue, aggrieved individuals could sue on their own. This change was widely seen as the most significant one made in committee and was seen by proponents as weakening the bill (Blumrosen 1971, chap. 1).

The amended enforcement procedures were the object of intense debate. The House voted on fifteen amendments to the enforcement procedures, the Senate on sixteen, and the closest votes in both houses concerned enforcement. The amendments that made their way into the bill finally adopted were written by the Senate leaders, who proposed a substitute for the original bill. The major changes concerned enforcement (see the testimony of Senator Humphrey, U.S. Congress, *Congressional Record,* 1964, 12295–99).

The most important change, and focus of the greatest amount of future debate, was removing from the EEOC the power to bring suit. Instead, individuals unable to resolve their complaints of discrimination through state agencies or the conciliation procedures of the EEOC had to bring suit on their own. Proponents of EEO legislation saw this change as weakening the bill, particularly because many of those discriminated against would be poor and legally unsophisticated. So as not to impose the entire burden of enforcement on individuals, the federal courts were empowered to appoint attorneys for complainants, to permit cases to go forward without payment of the usual costs or fees, and to award attorneys' fees to prevailing parties. The attorney general was permitted to intervene on behalf of aggrieved individuals and to initiate suits where it appeared that discrimination was systematic or institutional. The leadership substitute passed by a vote of seventy-six to eighteen, and, after some additional amendments (most notably, one that limited the attorney general's intervention to cases he certified were of general public importance), the Senate adopted the bill, which was then passed unchanged by the House and signed by the president.

Liberals were dissatisfied with this outcome, believing that the enforcement scheme adopted would be ineffective, but their bills after 1964 did not suggest a return to the original proposal. Instead, two new disputes arose. The first was between those who wanted to keep the system adopted in 1964 and those who wanted to give the EEOC the power to initiate binding legal action; this disagreement shows up in figure 2.3 with regard to the third and fourth kinds of sponsorship listed. The second was within the group that favored amending the law, between those who wanted to give the EEOC the power to issue cease-and-desist orders and those who favored giving it the power to go to court.

The other notable development after 1964 was the introduction of bills that proposed weakening the existing law (something that happened

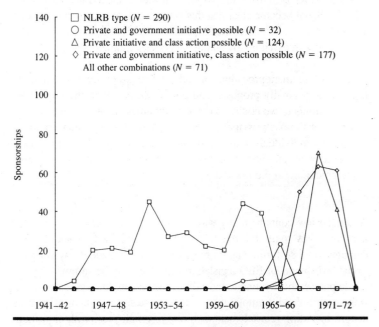

Fig. 2.3   Enforcement: sponsorships in the House and Senate.

very rarely with regard to other dimensions). For example, twenty-three sponsors after 1964 favored a proposal that would have eliminated the possibility of suits by aggrieved groups (rather than individuals acting separately), and there was also an upsurge in the number proposing legislation that was unenforceable. Faced with the prospect that a law would be passed, some opponents of a meaningful law apparently tried to affect the legislation outcome by sponsoring bills that would have symbolic significance only.

The House passed a bill giving the EEOC cease-and-desist powers in 1966, but the Senate did not vote on EEO that year; in 1970 the Senate passed a similar bill, but not the House. Finally, in 1972, both the House and the Senate voted on amendments to Title 7. The bill introduced onto the floor of both houses would have given the EEOC administrative enforcement powers. The House voted first, on a substitute taking away the EEOC's power to issue its own orders but allowing it to sue alleged discriminators; the amendment was accepted, 202–197. Voting in the Senate was just as close; it rejected the court enforcement alternative twice by votes of 41–43 and 46–48 and then accepted it by a vote of 45–39 when it became clear that this was the only way to secure enough votes for passage (Congressional Quarterly 1972, 248). Today's EEOC therefore enforces Title 7 by taking alleged discriminators to court when lesser means fail.

The enforcement procedures in today's law are vastly more complex than those originally proposed and give more power to the courts and less to administrative bodies. Yet the continuities are significant as well. Liberals as far back as the 1940s wanted proceedings that could be initiated by individuals, class action suits, administration of the law by a special agency, and administrative enforcement. All but administrative enforcement are in the law today.[17]

Penalties

American law contains many ways of dealing with persons who break the law: they may be fined, imprisoned, enjoined, made to pay damages, and so forth. The proposals seriously considered by congressional proponents of EEO legislation, however, can be summed up in a single phrase: those found to have discriminated are to "cease and desist from such unlawful employment practice and to take such affirmative action, including reinstatement or hiring of employees, with or without back pay, as will effectuate the policies of the Act." This is the wording of the bill passed by the House in 1950, and substantially identical language is found in the large majority of EEO bills introduced. Although some pre-1945 state laws and two 1942 congressional bills proposed criminal penalties for discriminators, such penalties were never proposed in Congress again (see the discussion in Bonfield 1967).

Figure 2.4 shows the possibilities most often considered. There were three: no penalty; restoring the complainant to his "rightful place" by giving him the job, promotion, or whatever, of which he had been unlawfully deprived; and awarding damages in the amount of pay lost, expenses incurred, and so on, as well as restoration of rightful place.

To some extent, sponsors restricted the range of their proposals because they had learned by the mid-1940s that certain approaches, particularly those involving criminal penalties, would not work if only because judges and juries would not impose such sanctions on discriminators (Bonfield 1967). It is nevertheless striking that sponsors' notions of what would work were so limited. Over 80 percent of the sponsors favored the "rightful place plus" penalty; after the passage of Title 7 in

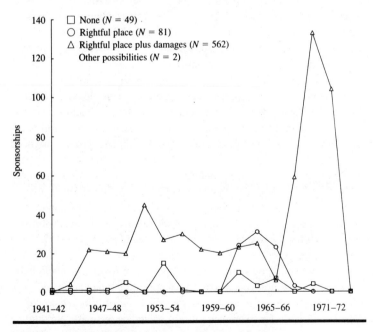

Fig. 2.4   **Penalties: sponsorships in the House and Senate.**

1964, this was virtually the only proposal made. Support for the "rightful place only" option peaked in the mid-1960s, presumably as a compromise favored by those who wanted only a weak bill to pass. Bills that proposed no penalty (and that were stated to have the virtue of focusing on "education" and "voluntary" action against discrimination) were continually proposed but never became very popular among sponsors.

Here more definitely than with regard to other dimensions, sponsors limited themselves to a very narrow range of possibilities and disagreed little among themselves. And only two motions dealing with penalties were ever voted on by the House or Senate. The proposals made in the 1940s emerged virtually unaltered in the 1960s and 1970s as the law of the land.

Growth of Support for EEO Legislation

In 1942 congressional support for federal EEO legislation was minimal—the first EEO bill had just one sponsor. In 1944 the first congressional hearings on EEO bills were held—a sign of increasing attention and some support. In 1964, 290 representatives and 73 senators voted for a bill containing a meaningful, though compromised, EEO title. And in 1972, 303 representatives and 73 senators were willing to vote for a significantly stronger bill.

This description, which is consistent with the notion that congressional support for EEO increased over time, is plausible but imprecise. In fact, it is nearly useless for anyone who wants to explain the growth of support. To explain it, we must be able to measure it consistently over the entire period when EEO bills were being considered. This need implies quantitative measurement of congressional support.

Unfortunately, there is no standard way to measure support for innovative legislative proposals that have not been voted on.[18] When analyzing the process leading to the passage of innovative legislation, even statistically inclined social scientists measure only two levels of support: not enough for passage and enough for passage (see Walker 1977 for a good example).

Nevertheless, those studying legislatures have frequently, though unsystematically, employed an intuitively appealing quantitative indicator of legislative support for proposals: sponsorship of bills. Historian C. Van Woodward, for example, uses as an indicator of the "mounting crescendo of enthusiasm and pressure" for civil rights laws the fact that the number of bills introduced favorable to civil rights rose steadily from ten in the 1937–38 Congress to seventy-two in 1949–50 (1966, 127). Similarly, when discussing the consequences of the 1963 civil rights demonstrations in Birmingham, political scientist James Sundquist states: "Unmistakably, the nation as a whole responded. In the House of Representatives, 127 civil rights bills were introduced between May 13 and June 20 alone" (1968, 260–61). Those studying other issues and other legislatures have also used sponsorship as an indicator of activity and support.[19]

Can sponsorship be used as a systematic indicator of the general level of congressional support for EEO legislation? Probably it can, provided two conditions are satisfied. First, we would expect legislation to pass when support for it is at a maximum. Consequently, if sponsorship is a satisfactory indicator of support, legislation should pass when sponsorship is at a peak. Second, if sponsorship is an adequate indicator of support, the specific proposals that are most popular among sponsors should be the ones actually incorporated in the legislation.

Table 2.1   Number of Sponsors of Enforceable EEO Bills

Years	Congress	Senators	Representatives	Total
1941–42	77th	0	1	1
1943–44	78th	1	4	5
1945–46	79th	7	11	18
1947–48	80th	8	10	18
1949–50	81st	9	9*	18
1951–52	82d	23	9	32
1953–54	83d	23	8	31
1955–56	84th	18	11	29
1957–58	85th	11	11	22
1959–60	86th	12	8	20
1961–62	87th	19	17	36
1963–64	88th	21*	18*	39*
1965–66	89th	2	25*	27
1967–68	90th	31	22	53
1969–70	91st	45*	41	86
1971–72	92d	35*	59*	94*
1973–74	93d	0	1	1

*Bill passes.

Table 2.1 shows how many senators and representatives sponsored enforceable EEO bills during each congress from the seventy-seventh (1941–42) through the ninety-third (1973–74). In general, the first condition for a good indicator is satisfied. The House passed EEO bills in 1950, 1964, 1966, and 1972; in the 1964, 1966, and 1972 congresses, more representatives sponsored EEO bills than in any congress up to that time; only at the time of the 1950 passage was support not at a historic high, and the bill passed then provided for no enforcement.[20] In the Senate, too, bills passed when support was at a relatively high level—in 1964, 1970, and 1972.[21] Both houses passed bills together in 1964 and 1972, and each of these congresses saw sponsorship at a historic high point. Bills thus pass when sponsorship is at a high level.

Assessing the utility of sponsorship as an indicator of support by the second criterion, the passage of the most popular proposals, presents a less tidy picture. On two of the dimensions—which employment practices were declared unlawful and what the penalties were to be—there was very little disagreement among sponsors, and the proposals most popular with sponsors were adopted.

As to which groups were to be protected, the adoption of the sex discrimination provision in 1964 was a surprise to everyone—no one had sponsored a bill proposing such a prohibition. Nevertheless, groups defined in the way most popular with sponsors—in terms of race, religion, and national origin—were included in the legislation, and in 1972 the most popular proposal—including race, religion, national origin, and sex—was kept in the law.

Predicting whom the law would prohibit from discriminating based on the popularity of different proposals would have been difficult, because different proposals received virtually identical levels of support both in 1964 and 1972. In 1964 approximately the same number of bills (in the House and Senate together) proposed covering employers and labor organizations as proposed covering both of them and employment agencies as well. The more inclusive proposal, which had also been the more popular in the years before passage, was enacted. In 1972 three proposals were equally popular: no change, adding state and local governments, and adding the federal government as well. The most inclusive proposal, which had little support before 1972, and little in the House even in 1971–72, was the one enacted.

On enforcement, most sponsors wanted to let individuals initiate proceedings, to permit class action suits, and to create a special federal agency. All three proposals were enacted. The proposal that enforcement be administrative was the only one on which most sponsors were clearly defeated, both in 1964 and in 1972. The EEOC was given the power to initiate proceedings, however, though not until 1972.

On the whole, Congress acted on EEO as if sponsorship of bills was a reasonable indicator of congressional support in general. Houses of Congress pass laws when the level of sponsorship is especially high, and they frequently, though by no means always, vote for the proposals most popular among sponsors.

Accepting sponsorship as an adequate indicator of congressional support, probably the most important thing table 2.1 shows is that support tended to increase gradually over time. Between 1941–42 and 1971–72, support in the House and Senate stayed the same or increased between congresses twenty-one times, and it decreased nine times; most of the increases and decreases were relatively undramatic.

What does this suggest about the kind of causal process probably involved in the passage of EEO legislation? The trends are generally consistent with the hypothesis that Congress responded over the years to variables that similarly changed steadily, gradually increasing the pressure on Congress to act: increasingly favorable attitudes toward Jews, blacks, and other minorities (see, e.g., Simon 1974, chaps. 3–4; Schwartz 1967; Burstein 1979b); more egalitarian attitudes toward women (Ferree 1974; Oppenheimer 1970); increasingly well organized lobbying by civil rights organizations; the liberal trend in Supreme Court decisions (Berger 1967); and so on. Such factors are probably not sufficient to explain passage, particularly in 1964 when sponsors were only a small proportion of all members of Congress, but it is likely they were necessary. The dramatic civil rights demonstrations of the early 1960s may have speeded up the legislative process a bit, but they took place in an environment in which support for legislation had been growing—albeit slowly—for over twenty years.

The End of Legislative Activity

Public concern with EEO did not end in 1972. Nevertheless, sponsorship of new bills dropped virtually to zero right after Title 7 was amended. Why? There are several possibilities. Members of Congress may like to give a law a chance to work before trying to amend it. But this hypothesis is inconsistent with the fact that many proposals to amend Title 7 were made immediately after it passed, long before evidence about its effectiveness could be compiled. Alternatively, new proposals may be unnecessary because the law succeeded in ending employment discrimination. But almost all the evidence indicates that discrimination is still pervasive in the labor market (see, e.g., Jencks et al. 1979; Masters 1975, chap. 1; Featherman and Hauser 1976). Another possibility is that the public has turned against equal treatment in the labor market, creating a political environment hostile to EEO. But that would not prevent individual members of Congress from proposing legislation, and, besides, polls indicate that the public is becoming more tolerant and egalitarian, not less (e.g., Taylor, Sheatsley, and Greeley 1978; Mason, Czajka, and Arber 1976).

So why did congressional action cease? Perhaps the most likely answer is this: members of Congress ran out of ideas. A burst of conceptual innovation in the early 1940s presented Congress with a set of ideas about ending discrimination in employment. These ideas were embodied in what Senator Javits called the "classic" EEO bill and were institutionalized in a small number of disagreements about its content (Javits 1964, 37). Once the terms of debate were set, the debate continued to be organized around the same issues through the early 1970s.

Between the 1940s and the 1970s, there were three changes of potentially great consequence in EEO bills and, eventually, in the law. The two of obvious importance—a ban on sex discrimination and coverage of governments—were simply tacked onto the basic bill. There was not even any serious discussion of whether differences between race discrimination and sex discrimination called for different legal treatments (see Chafe 1977; Ratner 1979). Only the shift from administrative to judicial enforcement occasioned significant rethinking of the bill.

Ferment continues around implementation of the law, but even the most radical members of Congress show no sign of developing new legislative ideas to hasten the end of employment discrimination. And there is little pressure on them to do so. Battles continue to be fought in the courts and the administrative agencies, but these proceed in the context of Title 7. The agenda set forth in the 1940s has been completed.[22]

Conclusions: The Legislative Process

Title 7, today's central EEO law, prohibits discrimination in employment on the basis of race, religion, national origin, or sex by most private employers with fifteen or more employees, labor unions with fifteen or more members, employment agencies, and local, state, and federal governments, with some relatively minor exceptions. It prohibits discrimination in a wide array of employment practices, including hiring, training, pay, promotion, benefits, and firing. The enforcement procedures it sets forth are extremely involved, but it provides government assistance to individuals who feel they have been discriminated against, makes it possible for individuals who are dissatisfied with the government's assistance to proceed on their own, allows the federal government to initiate charges of discrimination on its own, and permits class as well as individual actions against alleged discriminators. Organizations the court finds have discriminated may have to provide jobs, promotions, back pay, and the like to victims of discrimination and may have to make major changes in their personnel practices (for the text of Title 7, related laws and relevant administrative regulations and executive orders, see, for example, Jones 1979).

This chapter has shown that the thirty-year congressional debate on EEO was organized around proposals made in the 1940s, that the growth of support for legislation was gradual, and that congressional action ceased when the original agenda had been completed. Five conclusions seem especially important.

First, the model EEO bill drafted in the mid-1940s was both innovative and conventional. The basic idea behind it—that the federal government should intervene in the private labor market to end discrimination—represented a definite break with the past. The actual language of the bill, however, drew heavily on other statutes, particularly the National Labor Relations Act and the developing New York EEO law, and therefore was quite conventional in many respects. In terms of structure, content, and the political climate that led to its introduction, Title 7 is essentially long-delayed New Deal legislation.[23]

Second, we are all aware of the conflict generated by the struggle for EEO, but the degree of consensus is also striking. The data presented above and the record of hearings and debate show that congressional proponents and opponents of EEO legislation and representatives of unions, of business, of religious and civic groups, and of blacks, women, Jews, Hispanics, and other minorities all generally agreed that if there was to be an EEO law it would be very much like the one introduced in the 1940s. Shared understandings of what proposals would be legitimate doubtless played a role in creating this consensus. A great deal of importance must also be attributed, however, to what may be called "the power of the first draft." Proponents saw their critical problem as winning support for an enforceable EEO law rather than as reassessing the content of the proposed law, even in the face of increasing evidence that similarly structured state laws were ineffective (see Blumrosen 1971). Those who formulated the first proposal, therefore, determined the structure of debate and the essentials of the final product.

Third, today's EEO law is a manifestation of the fixity of ideas in the midst of social change. Since the introduction of the first EEO bill, the United States has changed in ways that could have influenced both the content of the law and congressional action on EEO. Members of the labor force are now more likely to work for giant corporations, to be highly skilled, to be female or members of minority groups. The civil rights and women's movements rose, racial and religious prejudice declined, and attitudes about women's roles changed. The federal government has become vastly larger and more powerful while accumulating experience in regulating the economy. And ideas about discrimination and government's power to deal with it—as expressed by the Supreme Court, for example—have changed as well.

Nevertheless, although the text of today's EEO law differs in many ways from that of the earlier bills, most of the changes were of the sort that nearly always occur as a bill moves from introduction to passage— changes that make the drafting more precise, resolve issues the original sponsors did not think of, and so forth. The overall structure has remained the same and thus reflects what seems to be a common phenomenon in the development of public policy. After examining the history of a variety of American domestic and foreign policies, Nelson Polsby (1984, 112) concluded that "The amount of recycling we have seen—in which proposals are made, defeated, and reemerge later on— . . . suggests that at any point in history there is a limited stock of ideas that provide an agenda for policymakers."

Fourth, it was thus the interaction of ideas and organizational needs that led to the adoption of legislation that said one thing and not something else. Widely accepted theories of democratic politics and decision-making hypothesize that limits on decision makers' resources and analytical capacities will induce them to consider only a small number of solutions to any problem and to settle on a solution similar to others they are already familiar with (Simon 1957, chaps. 14–15; Braybrooke and Lindblom 1963, chaps. 4–5; Wilensky 1967, chap. 2). The ideas in the "classic" bill were embodied in Title 7 because they were familiar and available to the increasing number of members of Congress who came to support EEO legislation as the civil rights movement reached its climax (cf. Heclo 1972).

Finally although this chapter has not considered why EEO legislation passed when it did, the analysis does provide a guide for explanation. Because of the power of the first draft, it would be difficult to argue that Congress adopted EEO legislation when it did because it was swayed by the power of new ideas. And it would be difficult to argue that the law was simply the product of the dramatic events of the 1960s. Attempts to explain the passage of EEO legislation should be guided by the notion that Congress responded primarily to social and political forces, including slowly changing ones, when it passed EEO legislation. It is to explanation that I now turn.

3 Public Opinion and Congressional Action

Any attempt to explain congressional action should begin by considering how it is affected by what the public wants, because the idea that democratic governments are supposed to do what their citizens want them to do is so central both to political scientists' normative theory of democracy and to the public's commonsense conception of democracy. Most studies of democratic politics are, indeed, ultimately concerned with this question: Do democratic governments do what their citizens want?

Many people think not. When Americans were asked in the late 1970s, "Over the years, how much attention do you feel the government pays to what the people think when it decides what to do—a good deal, some or not much?" 28 percent replied "not much" (Miller 1979). Agreeing with this point of view, many social scientists believe that the government responds primarily to the demands of economic, military, or social elites, or to particularly well-organized segments of the business and professional communities, rather than to the wishes of ordinary citizens. Ira Katznelson and Mark Kesselman (1975, 313–14) present a common view when they write that "As the most important representative institution in the United States, Congress in action provides a key test for American democracy . . . yet . . . the influence exerted on representatives by their constituents is weak. . . . congressmen tend mainly to represent the interests of small capital and the defensive goals of the corporate complex . . . popular government has become a set of formal procedures, not an open arena of substantive representation" (see also Mills 1956; Pilisuk and Hayden 1965; Domhoff 1967; Page and Shapiro 1983, 175).

Opposed to this conclusion, however, is a considerable body of evidence, consistent with major theories of democratic representation, that legislators try to vote according to their constituents' wishes, at least on issues important in their districts, because their primary goal is reelection and they believe they must satisfy their constituents to achieve this (Mayhew 1974; Fiorina 1974; Kingdom 1977; Backstrom 1977; Burstein and Freudenburg 1978; Monroe 1978; Page and Shapiro 1983; Tufte 1978). No one expects Congress to respond instantly to majority opinion on every issue, because of uncertainty about what the public wants, the problems involved in reconciling diverse views on many issues, the complexities of congressional organization, and other factors, but reasonably prompt responsiveness is expected to be the norm. Apparently agreeing with this point of view, 13 percent of Americans believed in 1978 that the government pays "a good deal" of attention to what the people want (most of the remaining 59 percent felt that the government pays "some" attention). The public and social scientists, evidently, are divided on whether the legislature represents its citizens.

What about congressional support for EEO legislation? Was congressional action on EEO legislation consistent with what the public wanted, or did Congress respond to other forces?

Probably most people would say Congress did *not* respond primarily to public opinion. Congressional action on EEO legislation has not been studied much, but congressional action on civil rights in general has been, particularly passage of the Civil Rights Act of 1964. Most analysts suggest that Congress responded primarily to dramatic events—violent attacks on civil rights demonstrators, for example—rather than to public opinion when it passed civil rights legislation.[1] Others conclude that the popular will was stymied by antimajoritarian features of congressional organization, particularly the filibuster rule in the Senate and seniority rules in both houses, which gave disproportionate power to southerners adamantly opposed to civil rights legislation (Sundquist 1968, chap. 4). There is some evidence that Congress has responded at times to public opinion on civil rights (Burstein 1979b; Miller and Stokes 1966), but the conventional wisdom is that congressional action was not strongly related to public opinion.

In fact, all conclusions about the relation between public opinion and congressional action on EEO have been premature because no one has ever systematically analyzed the available evidence. This chapter is devoted to that end. It begins by considering the relationship between public opinion on equality and congressional action and goes on to analyze in detail some factors that may have affected the timing of the congressional response.

What the Public Wanted: Data

What did the public want Congress to do about discrimination in employment from 1942 on? This is not an easy question to answer. People's feelings about complex issues like EEO are apt to be ambivalent and inconsistent. Americans often favor democratic or egalitarian principles in the abstract but are frequently much less positive when asked about applying them in their own lives. People may favor equal treatment in principle but oppose laws to guarantee it, object to paying the costs of enforcement, or fail to understand the problems implied by a favored course of action. Attitudes about specific proposals are often unstable, and intensity of feeling on an issue and willingness to translate feelings into political action are often difficult to gauge.

In order to form a satisfactory picture of what the public wanted on EEO, members of Congress would, ideally, want to know about three aspects of constituents' attitudes: first, whether their constituents favored EEO; second, whether they wanted the government to do anything about it; and third, whether they felt strongly about the issue. In addition, members of Congress would want to have some idea about how volatile constituents' attitudes were; they would want to be reasonably sure, before acting on behalf of a majority of their constituents, that the majority would remain a majority for some time in the future. To respond too quickly to a transitory majority would be to risk defeat.[2]

Two kinds of reliable, objective data are available about what the public has wanted on EEO since the early 1940s. The first is from public opinion polls. National polls that can be considered reasonably respectable by modern standards were first regularly carried out in the United States in the mid-1930s, so potentially useful data are available for the entire period when Congress was considering EEO legislation. Relevant data were sought, therefore, in a number of the most comprehensive collections of survey data available.[3]

The second kind of data concerns state EEO and equal pay laws. One way legislators try to find out what the public wants is by watching each other, seeing which approaches, positions, and tactics work for other similarly situated politicians and which do not (Mayhew 1974). Because EEO and equal pay legislation was being debated in many state legislatures while it was being debated in Congress, members of Congress could have watched politics in their home states to see what local politicians concluded about public support for EEO legislation. The adoption of legislation there might indicate to them that it was safe or desirable to support such legislation in Congress.

Thus, public opinion and the adoption of state legislation will be used as indicators of the public's preferences on EEO. Like any attempt to gauge the public's preferences on complex issues, this study confronts at least two major problems requiring that the data be interpreted cautiously. First, there are not enough data; polling agencies asked few relevant questions over the years, and they asked even fewer repeatedly, making changes in attitudes difficult to gauge. Second, as noted above, attitudes are very complex, and their political implications may be difficult to assess even when a great deal of information is available—a problem faced by politicians as well as others interested in the political process.

Public Opinion and Congressional Support for EEO

Public Opinion on EEO

When EEO bills were first introduced, there was apparently little congressional support for them—one sponsor in the Seventy-seventh Congress (1941–42) and five in the Seventy-eighth. Some evidence why this was so may be found in table 3.1, which describes public opinion on all the earliest questions relevant to EEO asked of the American public.[4] During the late 1930s and 1940s, Americans did not generally favor EEO, as far as we can tell. More than half with opinions thought that whites should be preferred over blacks when they applied for jobs; almost half admitted it would make a difference to them if a potential employeee was a Jew. The public was not asked specifically about EEO for women but was asked two related questions. Most people believed women should be paid the same wages as men if they did the same work, but because less than a quarter of the public approved of a woman's working at all outside the home if her husband could support her, we may surmise that few people expected women to do the same work.

Given the pervasiveness of prejudice, it would be surprising if most people had favored EEO legislation (which was not seen at the time as potentially covering women). In fact, certainly less than half, and probably no more than a third, of the public favored the passage of EEO legislation. And even for most of those who favored legislation, the

Table 3.1   Blacks, Women, and Jews in the Labor Market, 1930s and 1940s

Item	Year	Response
EEO in principle		
Do you think Negroes should have as good a chance as white people to get any kind of job, or do you think white people should have the first chance at any kind of job? (whites only)	1944	As good—42%
If you were an employer hiring a new employee, would it make any difference to you if he were a Jew?	1940	Yes—43% No—51% No opinion— 6%
If women take the place of men in industry should they be paid the same wages as men?	1942	Yes—78% No—14% No opinion— 8%
Do you approve of a married woman working in business or industry if she has a husband capable of supporting her?	1938	Approve—22% Disapprove—78%
EEO legislation		
Do you favor or oppose a law in this state which would require employers to hire a person if he is qualified for the job, regardless of his race or color? (entire sample)	1945	Favor—43% Oppose—44% No opinion—13% Favor, by region: Northeast—58% Midwest—41% South—20% West—41%
Would you favor or oppose a state law which would require employees to work alongside persons of any race or color?	1945	Favor—34% Oppose—56% No opinion—10%
How far do you yourself think the federal government should	1948	All the way—32% None of the way—45%

(continued)

Table 3.1   *Continued*

Item	Year	Response
go in requiring employers to hire people without regard to race, color, or nationality?		All of the way, by region: South— 9% Non-South—36%
Intensity What do you think is the most important problem facing the country today?		Civil rights, tolerance
	1939	less than 3%
	1945	5%
	1947	less than 3%

Sources: "Do you think Negroes should have . . . ," National Opinion Research Center (NORC) poll 225, reported in Schwartz 1967, 133; "If you were an employer . . . ," Stember et al. 1966, 92; "If women take the place . . . ," American Institute of Public Opinion (AIPO-Gallup) poll 259K, in Gallup 1972; "Do you approve of a married woman . . . ," AIPO poll 136 in Gallup 1972; "Do you favor or oppose a law . . . ," AIPO poll 349K, in Gallup 1972; "Would you favor or oppose a state law . . . ," AIPO poll 349T, in Gallup 1972; "How far do you yourself . . . ," AIPO poll 414K, in Gallup 1972; "What do you think . . . ," AIPO polls 176A, 342K, 401K, in Gallup 1972.

issue was probably not especially salient—only a very small fraction of the public believed that civil rights, tolerance, discrimination, or related issues were among the most important problems facing the country.

The first serious congressional floor debate over EEO took place as World War II ended and concerned the continuation of the president's Fair Employment Practices Committee, the group created to enforce the executive orders prohibiting discrimination in defense industries and government. The debate was quite heated at times, but the committee was eventually deprived of funds because a Senate filibuster prevented a vote to provide them. This has been cited as a case where archaic Senate rules blocked progressive legislation, but it has also been noted that the attempt to invoke cloture and end the debate seemed rather lackadaisical (Maslow 1946). Given the public acceptance of discrimination, opposition to an EEO law, and lack of interest in the issue, the lukewarm quality of congressional support for EEO does not seem to have been greatly at variance with public opinion.

Much of the public opposed EEO in the late 1930s and early 1940s, but public attitudes toward the principle of equal treatment for minorities and women have become steadily more favorable since then. Figure 3.1 presents public opinion on the only three questions related to EEO asked repeatedly since the 1940s. The question about giving blacks an equal chance at jobs (the exact wording is in table 3.1) was asked in virtually identical form six times since 1944. The proportion of the population (black and white) stating that blacks should have equal opportunities for jobs rose from 42 percent in 1944 to 47 percent in 1946 and 1947, 83 percent in 1963, 87 percent in 1966, and 95 percent in 1972. It is unfortunate that the question was asked so seldom, and not at all from 1947 to 1963, but the trend seems clear enough to support the conclusion that

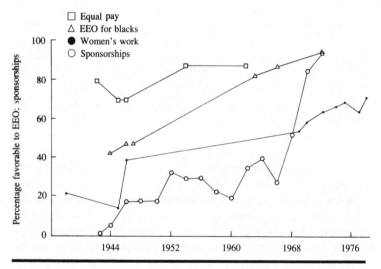

Fig. 3.1   Public opinion on EEO and congressional support for EEO legislation.
Sources: Equal pay: January 1942, AIPO Survey 259; September 1945, AIPO Survey 356; April 1946, RFOR Survey 54; April 1954, AIPO Survey 530; June 1962, AIPO Survey 660 (Hastings and Southwick 1974). EEO for blacks: May 1944, NORC Survey 225; May 1946, NORC Survey 241; April 1947, NORC Survey 150; December 1963, NORC Survey 330; June 1966, SRS Survey 889A; March 1972, NORC Survey 9001 (Hastings and Southwick 1974; Schwartz 1967, 133). Approve of married women working: October 1938, AIPO Survey 136; October 1945, AIPO Survey 359; April 1946, RFOR Survey 54; September 1969, AIPO Special Survey 55; June 1970, AIPO Survey 808; June 1972, NORC Survey 9001; 1974, 1975, 1977, 1978, Davis 1978. Sponsorships: table 2.1.

public attitudes toward blacks became steadily more favorable; there is now virtually unanimous agreement that, in principle, blacks and whites should be treated equally.

Attitudes about women in the labor force are more ambivalent and may be seen as less egalitarian than attitudes about blacks. Most Americans have long been willing to have women paid as much as men for doing the same work—the principle behind the Equal Pay Act of 1963. Until recently, however, most people were opposed to women's doing the same work, or any paid work at all—only since 1969 has more than half the public approved of a married woman's working outside the home if she had a husband who could support her (with approximately equal proportions of men and women approving).[5]

Figure 3.1 also shows how congressional sponsorship of EEO bills, taken as an indicator of congressional support for EEO legislation, changed as attitudes changed. The number of senators and representatives sponsoring enforceable EEO bills generally increased as attitudes became more egalitarian. This relationship will be discussed in detail shortly.

Unfortunately, the public has not regularly been asked any questions about its prejudices toward other groups—Jews, Catholics, Asians, Hispanics, and so on—in the labor market; in fact, few questions have been asked repeatedly about attitudes toward other groups in general. The small amount of information we have, however, indicates that prejudice toward other groups declined as well. The proportion of the public for whom it would "make a difference" if a prospective employee was a Jew (for exact wording, see table 3.1), for example, fell from 43 percent in 1940 to only 6 percent in 1962 (Stember et al. 1966, 94).

Probably the best repeated question relevant to tolerance in the American public is the one that asks whether people would vote for a qualified member of a particular group for president of the United States. Responses to this question have been interpreted as indicators of the symbolic acceptance of members of particular groups and of willingness to treat group members on their merits rather than as members of a social category (see Ferree 1974; Taylor, Sheatsley, and Greeley 1978).

Figure 3.2 describes public attitudes toward women, blacks, Catholics, and Jews as possible presidential candidates. The trends for the different groups are not precisely parallel—blacks were the least favored group in the mid-1950s, but their rating has increased the most since then, while the proportion willing to vote for a woman increased very

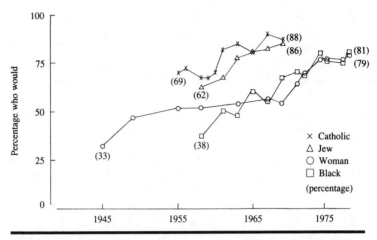

Fig. 3.2   Would vote for woman or minority group member for president. Sources: woman for president: 1945, AIPO Survey 360K; 1949, AIPO 448K; 1955, AIPO 543K; 1958, AIPO 604K; 1963, AIPO 676K; 1967, AIPO 744K; 1969, AIPO 776K; 1971, AIPO 834K; 1972, 1974, 1975, 1977, 1978, NORC General Social Surveys (Hastings and Southwick 1974; Gallup 1972; Davis 1978). Black for president: 1958, AIPO 604K; 1961, AIPO 649K; 1963, AIPO 676K; 1965, AIPO 714K; 1967, AIPO 744K; 1969, AIPO 776K; 1971, AIPO 838K; 1972, 1974, 1975, 1977, 1978, NORC General Social Surveys (question asked only of whites in 1972, 1975, 1977) (Hastings and Southwick 1974; Gallup 1972; Davis 1978). Catholic for president: 1955, AIPO 542K, 1956, AIPO 565K; 1958, AIPO 604K; 1959, AIPO 612K; 1960, AIPO 628K; 1961, AIPO 649K; 1963, AIPO 676K; 1965, AIPO 714K; 1967, AIPO 744K; 1969, AIPO 776K (Hastings and Southwick 1974; Gallup 1972). Jew for president: 1958, AIPO 604K; 1961, AIPO 649K; 1963, AIPO 676K; 1965, AIPO 714K; 1967, AIPO 744K; 1969, AIPO 776K (Hastings and Southwick 1974; Gallup 1972).

slowly until the mid-1960s, when it began to rise very rapidly, possibly owing to the influence of the women's movement—and blacks, Catholics, and women have experienced declines in public favor at times.[6] Nevertheless, the most obvious points made by the figure are that the public is much more willing than it used to be to vote for presidential candidates without regard to race, sex, or religion and that the trend has been indisputably upward for all groups. This conclusion is made more precise by simple regression equations statistically estimating the strength of the relationship between the proportion of the public willing to support members of different groups and the passage of time (treating the year each question was asked as a variable). The equations show that the increase in tolerance is so steadily upward that the proportion of the population willing to vote for a particular type of candidate could be predicted with great accuracy just by knowing what year it was. If all the variance in tolerance could be explained just by the passage of time, the proportion of variance explained (R^2) would be 1.00. As it is, the actual proportions are:

Jewish president	.95
Black president	.92
Woman president	.86
Catholic president[7]	.74

Both these data and considerable data on related issues—integration in housing and education, women's roles—indicate that Americans' attitudes about blacks, women, and other groups have become steadily more universalistic since World War II, at least on questions of principle. These trends continued during both the period between the mid-1940s and early 1960s, when no questions specifically about EEO were asked, and the period since the last questions about EEO for blacks were asked in the early 1970s (see Taylor, Sheatsley, and Greeley 1978; Mason, Czajka, and Arber 1976; Stember et al. 1966; Schwartz 1967; Simon 1974; Burstein 1979b). In addition, though not all demographic groups favor equal treatment to the same degree, the trend toward greater universalism has generally been the same for all groups—men and women, northerners and southerners, the more educated and the less educated.

Although there is little data available on Americans' attitudes about the principle of EEO, trends in attitudes on related subjects are so consistent that it seems reasonable to take seriously the trend lines on EEO attitudes drawn in figure 3.1 despite the gaps in the data.

This conclusion makes it possible to fill in the gaps and to use the resulting complete time series to relate public support for EEO more precisely to congressional support for it.

Because more data for longer time series are available for blacks and women than for other groups, while trends in attitudes toward all groups are parallel, data on blacks and women can be used as indicators of public opinion on EEO in general. Attitudes toward blacks as members of the labor force and as presidential candidates became favorable at approximately the same rate over the entire period for which data are available—at a rate of about 1.9 percent per year with regard to EEO and about 2.2 percent with regard to the presidency—and both changes are simple time trends. Consequently, the time series for describing attitudes about EEO for blacks can be completed by using the trend line, changing at just under 2 percent per year, to estimate the proportion of the public favoring EEO for blacks every year, using the 42 percent favorable in 1944 as the base point.

Changes in attitudes toward women followed a slightly different pattern. Attitudes toward women both as members of the labor force and as presidential candidates became more favorable fairly rapidly before the late 1940s, as far as we can tell, at a rate of about 2.2 percent per year on labor force participation (data available for 1938–46) and 3.8 percent on the presidency (1945–49). The rate of change then slowed dramatically for both attitudes until the late 1960s, to 0.7 percent on labor force participation (1946–69) and 0.3 percent on the presidency (1949–69). At the beginning of the 1970s attitudes on both questions, again moving in tandem, started rapidly becoming more favorable again, at an annual rate of approximately 1.9 percent on labor force participation (1969–78) and 2.8 percent on the presidency (1969–75). The similarity of both the trends and the changes in the trends on the two issues is evidence, I believe, that change in attitudes about treating men and women equally really did slow in the 1950s and 1960s and speed up in the 1970s. Estimates of attitudes toward EEO for women were therefore based on responses to the question about women's labor force participation, and estimates for missing years were derived by simply interpolating between years for which data were unavailable.[8]

Using these estimates of attitudes toward blacks and women in the labor force, the association between EEO attitudes and congressional support for EEO may be estimated in a regression equation relating number of sponsors to the percentage of the public having favorable attitudes. The number of sponsors is for each two-year Congress, of course, and the percentages with favorable attitudes are the average for the two years of each Congress (1941–42, 1943–44, etc.).[9]

Figure 3.1 showed that support for EEO tended to increase over time both in Congress and among the public, and table 3.2 confirms this impression. The data indicate that for the period after 1941:

—An increase of 10 percent in the proportion of the public favorable to blacks in the labor force was associated with an additional eleven members of Congress sponsoring EEO legislation. (The regression co-

Table 3.2   Public Opinion and Congressional Support for EEO Legislation, Seventy-seventh to Ninety-second Congresses, 1941–72: Regression Coefficients (and Standard Errors) for Two Equations

(1)   Sponsorships = 1.13 (% favoring EEO for blacks) − 43.
                (.20)   (14.)
                R^2 = .67 (adjusted for degrees of freedom)

(2)   Sponsorships = 2.53 (% favoring women working) − 84.
                (.36)   (17.)
                R^2 = .76 (adjusted)

N = 16.

efficient in equation 1 means that every 1 percent increase in the proportion favoring equal treatment for blacks is associated with an increase of 1.13 in sponsors.)

—An increase of 10 percent in the proportion of the public favorable to women in the labor force was associated with an additional 25 sponsors (equation 2).[10]

The results are consistent with the hypothesis that congressional support for EEO legislation was a function of public opinion on EEO. There are two major departures from the general pattern. The decline of sponsorships in 1965–66, while attitudes continued to become more favorable, was a temporary response to the passage of the 1964 Civil Rights Act. The decline in sponsorship in the late 1950s is more difficult to explain. It may have been due to changes in committee assignments in the Senate (see chap. 2), but it is also worth noting that the decline coincided with the slowdown in changes in attitudes about women (this explains why the R^2 for the equation concerning women is higher than the R^2 for the equation concerning blacks). EEO legislation was not seen as relating to women by most people in the 1950s, so it is not obvious why there should be a link between attitudes about women and sponsorship of EEO legislation. The question about women's labor force participation may perhaps be an indicator of other attitudes about equal treatment that did affect Congress. Now it is time to consider how Congress responded to the public on specific aspects of Title 7.

Congressional Voting on Specific Issues

As described in chapter 2, Congress made three especially important changes in the classic EEO bill when enacting it into law—prohibiting

discrimination on the basis of sex, forbidding discrimination by governments, and opting for judicial rather than administrative enforcement.
Did Congress respond to public opinion when it made these changes?

This question cannot be answered directly, because the public has
never been asked specifically about these issues. We can gain a rough
idea of the forces behind congressional action, however, by looking at
how congressional delegations from different regions of the country
voted. If Congress was responding to public opinion, we would expect
that the higher the proportion of people in a region favoring EEO, the
higher the proportion of that region's members of Congress who would
vote for the proposals seen as more "liberal" at the time—prohibiting
sex discrimination, covering governments, and enforcing the law
administratively.

The most relevant roll calls in 1964 were those in which the Senate
rejected a motion to delete Title 7 from the bill and the House passed the
Civil Rights Act; there were no roll calls on any of the more specific
issues.[11] Table 3.3 shows how voting by members of Congress from the
different regions of the country related to public attitudes about EEO for
blacks and to the adoption of state EEO laws in the same regions (which
are assumed to be indicators of the acceptability of EEO legislation in
the particular states; more on state laws below). In general, the more the
public in a region favored EEO, the higher the proportion of members of
Congress from that region who voted for it. All the states in the Pacific,
Mid-Atlantic, and East North Central regions had adopted EEO laws by
1964, for example, and all the senators from those states voted for Title
7. Approximately 90 percent of the public favored the principle of EEO
for blacks in the Pacific, Mid-Atlantic, East North Central, New England, and Mountain regions, and about the same proportion of senators
and representatives from those regions voted for civil rights, except for
Mountain state senators. The rank ordering of regions in each column of
the table is approximately the same; the major exception is the Mountain
region, which seems to have fewer states with EEO laws than might be
expected on the basis of public opinion.[12]

The pattern in the 1971–72 voting is a bit less tidy, as table 3.4
shows. Virtually everyone in the country claimed to favor EEO in principle, so that question cannot be used to distinguish between regions,
and attitudes toward women show a different pattern than attitudes toward blacks (the question about women was not asked in 1964). On the
whole, the relations among the regions were the same in 1971–72 as

Table 3.3 1964 Voting on EEO: Percentage of Senators and Representatives Voting for Title 7, of Those Voting, and Public Opinion and State EEO Laws, by Region

Region	Public Favors EEO[a]	Representatives from EEO States[b]	Senate, Keep Title 7		House, Pass Bill	
Pacific[c]	90%	100%	100%	(9)[d]	89%	(43)
Mid-Atlantic	91	100	100	(6)	99	(80)
East North Central	88	100	100	(9)	92	(85)
New England	91	80	92	(12)	96	(24)
Mountain	92	35	75	(16)	87	(23)
West North Central	82	62	69	(13)	76	(34)
West South Central	79	0	38	(8)	18	(38)
South Atlantic	74	0	25	(16)	27	(55)
East South Central	63	0	12	(8)	10	(29)
Outcome of vote			64–33		289–126	

Sources: Public opinion data, Hastings and Southwick 1974, and special tabulations; EEO states, Bonfield 1967; Senate vote, Congressional Quarterly 1964, 677, roll call 71; House vote, Congressional Quarterly 1964, 636–37, roll call 63.
[a]Public favors EEO: percentage of whites stating blacks and whites should have equal chance at jobs, December 1963.
[b]Representatives from EEO states: percentage of United States representatives from region elected from states with EEO laws, 1964.
[c]Pacific: Alaska, California, Hawaii, Oregon, Washington; Mid-Atlantic: New Jersey, New York, Pennsylvania; East North Central: Illinois, Indiana, Michigan, Ohio, Wisconsin; New England: Connecticut, Maine, Massachusetts, New Hampshire, Rhode Island, Vermont; Mountain: Arizona, Colorado, Idaho, Montana, Nevada, New Mexico, Utah, Wyoming; West North Central: Iowa, Kansas, Minnesota, Missouri, Nebraska, North Dakota, South Dakota; West South Central: Arkansas, Louisiana, Oklahoma, Texas; South Atlantic: Delaware, Florida, Georgia, Maryland, North Carolina, South Carolina, Virginia, West Virginia; East South Central: Alabama, Kentucky, Mississippi, Tennessee.
[d]Numbers percentages are based on are given in parentheses.

they were in 1964, which is what we would expect if the trends in public opinion were the same in all the regions, as Taylor, Sheatsley, and Greeley (1978) have shown that they were, at least with regard to general measures of tolerance. In addition, the 1976 ranking of regions on racial tolerance by the National Opinion Research Center is in line with regional rankings on EEO voting in Congress.

Probably the major anomaly in the table is the weakness of support

Table 3.4   1971–72 Voting on EEO: Percentage of Senators and Representa-

Region	Public Favors EEO (1972)	Public Approves Women Working (1972)	NORC Racial Tolerance Scale (1976)	Passage Senate	
Pacific	98%	62%	3.79	100%	(9)
Mid-Atlantic	98	70	3.50	100	(6)
East North Central	94	65	3.23	100	(8)
New England	100	71	3.76	100	(11)
Mountain	98	52	3.18	87	(15)
West North Central	96	55	3.40	88	(9)
West South Central	92	67	3.12	50	(6)
South Atlantic	98	72	2.28	72	(18)
East South Central	95	61	2.10	29	(7)
Outcome of vote				73–16	

Source: NORC Racial Tolerance Scale, Taylor, Sheatsley, and Greeley 1978; Senate voting, Congressional Quarterly 1972, roll calls 49, 16, 8, 39; House voting, Congressional Quarterly 1972, roll call 40, and Congressional Quarterly 1971, roll call 174.

for administrative enforcement in the Mountain region, compared with its strong support for passing amended legislation and for covering state and local governments. Before 1964, few of the Mountain states had passed EEO laws, as noted above, and table 3.4 also shows that those states rank rather low on the proportion of the public approving of women working and on the racial tolerance scale (Taylor, Sheatsley, and Greeley 1978). The data are extremely sparse, but they may indicate that attitudes toward equal treatment were less coherent or more ambivalent in the Mountain states than elsewhere, and that this quality of the attitudes was reflected in inconsistencies in the region's support for the more liberal alternatives presented. Alternatively, members of Congress from the Mountain states may have opposed administrative enforcement for reasons having little to do with civil rights, or because of their desire to maintain, at least in part, their traditional alliance with Southern delegations.[13] With only the available data, it is impossible to tell.[14]

Thus there is some ambiguity in the few data pertinent to congressional voting on specific issues. But members of Congress from the more liberal regions were more likely to support the alternative seen as

tives Voting for EEO, of Those Voting, and Public Opinion, by Region

House	Senate, for Including State and Local Governments	For Administrative Enforcement		
		Senate Vote 1	Senate Vote 2	House
90% (51)	100% (6)	100% (8)	100% (5)	61% (46)
99 (81)	83 (6)	100 (5)	83 (6)	75 (75)
84 (80)	100 (7)	77 (9)	72 (7)	53 (83)
96 (23)	100 (10)	75 (12)	60 (10)	87 (23)
81 (16)	93 (14)	40 (15)	38 (13)	38 (16)
81 (36)	78 (9)	62 (13)	58 (12)	52 (31)
46 (37)	25 (4)	12 (8)	14 (7)	29 (35)
22 (63)	57 (14)	25 (16)	26 (16)	24 (63)
34 (26)	40 (6)	0 (8)	0 (8)	7 (27)
303–110	59–16	48–46	39–45	197–202

more liberal—a result consistent with the hypothesis that public opinion on EEO had a strong influence on congressional action.

The data thus show that congressional support for EEO legislation rose as public opinion became more favorable to EEO, that EEO legislation passed when the proportion of the public favoring EEO rose higher than it had ever been before, and that specific liberal provisions were supported disproportionately by members of Congress from more liberal regions of the country.

Passage did not occur, however, when the proportion of the public favoring EEO reached a figure with any special significance, such as half the population. In fact, Title 7 did not pass until approximately 85 percent of the public favored EEO for blacks, 90 percent favored equal pay for women, and 50 percent approved of labor force participation by women whose husbands could support them. By the time the 1972 strengthening amendments passed, opinion in favor of EEO for blacks and equal pay for women was probably close to unanimous, and almost two-thirds of the public approved of labor force participation by married women. Why did Congress wait until far more than half the public favored equal treatment for women and blacks (and, presumably, for members of other minority groups as well)?

There are four plausible hypotheses. First, although the public favored EEO in principle, it may have been much less favorable to the passage of laws to bring about EEO in practice. Second, the passage of legislation may require that people feel strongly about a policy as well as favoring it. Third, members of Congress may have been hesitant to act because they were uncertain about what people wanted and how stable their desires were. And fourth, American government may be structured so that it is extremely difficult to adopt a major policy unless it has majority support in all regions of the country, not just overall. Each of these hypotheses will be considered in turn.

What the Public Wanted the Government to Do

Little information is available on what, if anything, the public wanted the federal government to do about EEO, or on how the public's desires have changed since the 1940s. Table 3.5 shows how the public responded to all the questions I could find about EEO laws. The data may be sparse, but they form a clear pattern: for most of the period since World War II, a considerable proportion of the public has favored the passage of EEO laws, but except during 1945 it has been a substantially smaller proportion than that favoring EEO in principle, and until the late 1960s the proportion in favor was nearly always less than half.[15] In addition, the proportion favoring a law seems to have increased only very slowly over time.

The data may also suggest two additional things about public attitudes toward EEO. First, the greatest proportion of people respond positively to questions that emphasize that the EEO law would prohibit discrimination only against those who are *qualified* for jobs—only in response to such questions does a majority of the public favor EEO laws (July 1947 and April 1968). Emphasizing that the people protected by the laws would have to be qualified may seem unnecessary, since no legislator who proposed an EEO law ever suggested otherwise, but such assurance may have been important to the public.

Second, although the data on EEO are inadequate for describing public attitudes while Congress was actually debating the bills that became the Civil Rights Act of 1964, some interesting data are available on attitudes toward that part of the act that gave blacks the right to equal

Table 3.5   Attitudes toward EEO and Other Civil Rights Laws

Item	Date	Response	
EEO			
Do you favor or oppose a law in this state which would require employers to hire a person if he is qualified for the job, regardless of his race or color? (entire sample)	1945	Favor—43% Oppose—44% No opinion—13%	
	1947	Favor—51%	
Would you favor or oppose a state law which would require employees to work alongside persons of any race or color? (entire sample)	1945	Favor—34% Oppose—56% No opinion—10%	
	1947	Favor—45%	
How far do you yourself think the Federal Government should go in requiring employers to hire people without regard to race, religion, color, or nationality?		All the way	None of the way
	March 1948	32%	47%
	December 1948	34	44
	March 1949	34	47
	November 1949	34	41
Some people say we should have a national law requiring employers to hire people without regard to race or color. Other people say that it should be left up to each state to decide on this for itself. With which side do you, yourself, agree?		National law	States
	1952	32%	44%
	1953	31%	47%
		Neither	No opinion
	1952	16%	8%
	1953	22%	
Do you favor or oppose making it against the law to discriminate against Negroes in employment? (whites only)	1966	Favor—45% Oppose—49% Don't know— 6%	
How do you feel about fair employment laws—that is, laws that make white people hire qualified Negroes, so that Negroes can get any job they are qualified for—do you favor or oppose such laws? (whites only)	1968	Favor—83% Oppose—15% Don't know— 2%	

(continued)

Table 3.5   *Continued*

Item	Date	Response		

Public accommodations

		Yes	No	No opinion
How would you feel about a law which would give all persons—Negro as well as white—the right to be served in public places such as hotels, restaurants, theaters, and similar establishments—would you like to see Congress pass such a law, or not?	June 1963	49%	42%	9%
	Mid-August 1963	54	38	8
	January 1964	61	31	8

Sources: "Do you favor or oppose a law . . . ," AIPO surveys 349K and 400K; "Would you favor or oppose a state law . . . ," AIPO surveys 349T and 400T; "How far do you yourself . . . ," AIPO surveys 414K, 433K, 439K, 450K; "Some people say . . . ," AIPO surveys 495K and 510K; "Do you favor or oppose making it . . . ," SRS survey 889A; "How do you feel . . . ," NORC survey 4050; "How would you feel about a law . . . ," AIPO surveys 674K, 676K, 683K (Hastings and Southwick 1974; Gallup 1972; Davis 1978; and special tabulations by the Roper Center through Yale University).

treatment in public accommodations (symbolically an extremely important part of the act). The last entry in table 3.5 shows public opinion becoming rapidly more favorable toward a law protecting blacks' rights to equal treatment in the months just before enactment. *If* public attitudes toward civil rights laws in different areas were correlated with each other (and we know that attitudes toward the rights themselves are), then the period just before the passage of Title 7 may have seen a crucial rise in the proportion of the public favoring an EEO law. Even if that was the case, however, the proportion of people favoring an EEO law was almost certainly much lower than the proportion favoring EEO in principle.

Another aspect of public attitudes toward government action on behalf of blacks is pictured in figure 3.3. The figure shows the proportion of people who felt that the Kennedy and Johnson administrations were pushing integration too fast or not fast enough; it seems reasonable to view the responses as indicators of public attitudes toward government actions on behalf of blacks.

Public attitudes toward government action are much more volatile

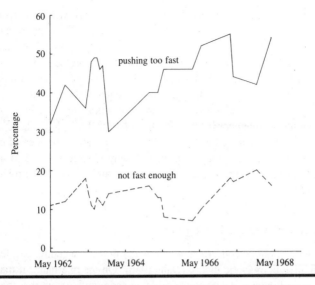

Fig. 3.3   Opinions on administration's push for integration. Sources: AIPO Surveys 658, 644, 673, 674, 675, 676, 677, 678, 679, 684, 708, 709, 714, 716, 730, 734, 748, 749, 760, 761, 769 (Gallup 1972).

than opinions about the principle of equal rights. In general, Congress acted as if it took attitudes on the speed of integration into account when voting on civil rights laws. The Civil Rights Act of 1964 passed when the proportion believing that government was moving too fast was at a historic low point—less than 30 percent—and the 1968 open housing law passed just after resistance had fallen substantially, whereas both open housing and EEO legislation were voted down in 1966, when resistance was at a peak. The major exception was the passage of the Voting Rights Act when public resistance was rising; that this was really regional legislation affecting mostly the South may have made passage easier, but we cannot be sure.

Unfortunately, there are no comparable time-series data on attitudes toward government action on behalf of women. The most relevant data concern the Equal Rights Amendment (ERA). In 1975, 1976, and 1977 people were asked if they had heard or read about the amendment, and if they had they were asked whether they favored or opposed it (AIPO survey 925K, March 1975; AIPO 947K, April 1976; NORC General Social Survey, 1977). About 90 percent of the public knew of the ERA each year; of the 90 percent, the proportion in favor was 58 percent in 1975, 57 percent in 1976, and 66 percent in 1977. These approval figures were somewhat lower than those concerning approval of married women's working when their husbands could support them (12, 8, and 6 percent lower, respectively) and were almost certainly quite a bit lower than the proportion favoring equal pay for equal work.

The data on attitudes toward government action are exceedingly sparse, but they remain consistent with the notion that people are less favorable to government action for equal treatment than to the idea of equal treatment itself. This may help explain why Congress failed to adopt EEO legislation as soon as a majority of the public favored the principle of EEO.

The Intensity of Public Concern

Intensity of public concern about particular issues is a central problem in normative democratic theory (Dahl 1956). On the one hand, it may be seen as a fundamental principle of democratic government that the majority should rule; on the other hand, it does not seem fair that a narrow majority that cares little about an issue should be able to get its way over the opposition of a substantial minority that cares very much indeed. As Robert Dahl has written, "a modern [James] Madison might argue that government should be designed to inhibit a relatively apathetic majority from cramming its policy down the throats of a relatively intense minority" (1956, 90). As a practical matter, it is widely believed that a minority that cares very much about an issue is likely to get its way disproportionately often because its members will work much harder to accomplish their ends than will the members of the majority.

The issue of civil rights may be an example of what Dahl has called (1956, 102) "severe asymmetrical disagreement," that is, a situation in which a majority slightly prefers one policy and a minority strongly prefers a mutually exclusive alternative. It is a historical truism that the South was able to impose Jim Crow laws and maintain segregation after Reconstruction because most northerners cared relatively little about race relations in the South, while southern whites, of course, cared a great deal. Thus it could be that the passage of civil rights legislation became a possibility only after the intensity of feelings in the South was matched, at least to some degree, by like intensity in the North.

The best information we have on the intensity of concern about public issues is the response to the question frequently asked by the Gallup poll: "What do you think is the most important problem facing the country?" The question is completely open ended, and people could presumably provide answers having little to do with politics. Ever since World War II, however, the most common answers have concerned the economy and war or the threat of war, and the government has responded by taking these issues very seriously indeed when planning and implementing public policy (see Tufte 1978; Burstein and Freudenburg 1978).

EEO has seldom been described as being among the most important issues facing the country, but civil rights, race relations, and discrimination frequently have. Figure 3.4 shows how the intensity of public concern about civil rights was related to sponsorship of EEO legislation and to the passage of all the civil rights laws that may be seen as the products of the civil rights movement: the Civil Rights Act of 1957 and 1960, which dealt with voting rights, the Civil Rights Act of 1964, the Voting Rights Act of 1965, the open housing law of 1968, and the Equal Employment Opportunity Act of 1972.

The figure makes three main points. First, there was almost no relation between the intensity of public concern and congressional support for EEO legislation as gauged by sponsorship. Congressional support

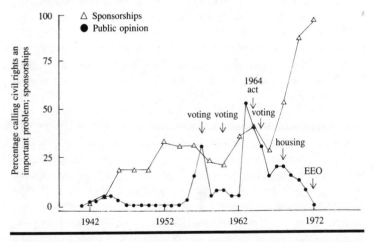

Fig. 3.4   Intensity of concern about civil rights, sponsorship of EEO legislation, and passage of civil rights laws. Sources: Gallup 1972, vols. 2–3; *Gallup Opinion Index,* reports 86, 88, 100, 104, 111, 112, 117, 125, 127, 131, 137.

rose in the late 1940s and early 1950s despite the lack of public concern, and it did so again during the late 1960s and early 1970s in the face of declining public concern.

The *passage* of legislation, however, *was* related to the salience of civil rights to the public. Laws seen as "breakthroughs"—the first legislation dealing with a particular problem, or major legislative innovations—tended to pass when public concern was especially intense or shortly thereafter. This was the situation when Congress passed the Civil Rights Act of 1957 (the first civil rights law since Reconstruction), the Voting Rights Act of 1965 (adopting a new approach to voting rights), and the open housing law of 1968.

Legislation that simply modifies existing civil rights laws, strengthening them without changing their structure or defining new rights, may, however, be adopted by Congress even when the level of public concern is not high. Congress passed the Civil Rights Act of 1960 (a minor amendment to the Civil Rights Act of 1957) and enacted the Equal Employment Opportunity Act of 1972 at times when relatively few people felt very strongly about the issues.

Adopting innovative legislation when its importance to the public is high and extending it when public concern is less intense is apparently a common pattern (Walker 1977). The pattern is what we would expect to find if the intensity of public opinion on an issue is positively correlated with the "magnitude" of the legislation subsequently passed, perhaps conceived of as a measure of innovativeness combined with scope. Unfortunately, there is no way to make this statement more precise, because we do not know how to measure the magnitude of legislation. Nevertheless, the evidence is consistent with the proposition that relatively intense public concern is necessary for the passage of breakthrough legislation, though not for the more routine modification of statutes already on the books.

A second way of gauging intensity focuses on a matter of great concern to members of Congress—whether constituents care enough about EEO so that it affects their decisions at the ballot box. The only available data on precisely this point are the results of the Gallup poll of August 1972 (AIPO 856K). Members of the public were asked, five months after the passage of the Equal Employment Opportunity Act but before the succeeding election, whether they would be more likely to vote for a candidate if he or she favored improving opportunities for minority groups. Two-thirds of the people said they would, and virtually the same proportion felt the same way toward candidates committed to greater equality for women. In 1972, anyway, most members of Congress had reason to believe that voting for EEO would help them at election time.

Uncertainty, State Laws, and Congressional Support for EEO

Members of Congress trying to decide whether to support EEO legislation will ultimately be concerned with the effective balance of political forces on the issue—not just with what constituents say they want or say they will do, but with what they actually do in response to legislative action on EEO. One way to discover what constituents will do while minimizing uncertainty and risk is to see how they react to what other legislators do. Looking at state legislative debates on EEO and their consequences would be a good way to accomplish this. If members of Congress let state legislators absorb some of the risks of action on EEO, Congress might be expected to adopt EEO legislation shortly after the states from which a majority of senators and representatives were elected. (The same logic would encourage members of Congress to vote for legislation very similar to the state laws, because it is public and legislative reaction to such laws that they have information about. This is consistent with the argument in chapter 2.)

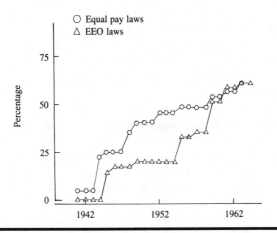

Fig. 3.5 **Percentage of United States representatives from states with EEO and equal pay laws.** Sources: State equal employment opportunity laws, Bonfield 1967; state equal pay laws, U.S. Women's Bureau 1970.

Figure 3.5 shows what percentage of representatives in each Congress were elected from states with relatively broad, enforceable EEO laws. Few state EEO laws prohibited discrimination on the basis of sex before Title 7 was adopted (the first states to do so were Hawaii and Wisconsin in the early 1960s). For someone trying to ascertain public sentiment on sex discrimination, the most relevant state laws would have been those requiring equal pay for equal work by men and women, so the percentage of representatives from states with equal pay laws is included in the figure as well.

The trend in state adoption of EEO and equal pay laws is generally upward, the major exception being from the late 1940s through the mid-1950s, when few new laws were adopted. The upward trend parallels the trends in public attitudes toward the principle of equal treatment, particularly EEO for blacks. The period of little change coincides roughly with the period 1948–53 described in table 3.5, when about a third of the public favored a national EEO law and the proportion showed no sign of increasing; in addition, this was the early part of the period in which attitudes toward equal treatment for women were changing especially slowly (fig. 3.1).

The percentage of representatives from states with enforceable EEO laws reached 50 in 1961 (40 percent in 1960, 58 percent by the end of 1961), not long before the passage of Title 7. When Title 7 passed, the percentage was just over 61 (64 if states with symbolic or very restricted laws were included); 60 percent of representatives were from states with equal pay laws by then. Various provisions of Title 7 encouraged states to adopt EEO laws, so after Title 7 was passed, it was not activity in the states that affected Congress, but more the reverse; the data are therefore presented only through 1964.

The percentage of senators from states with EEO laws was always lower than the percentage of representatives, because the states that passed EEO laws tended to be those in which liberalism, industrialism, and relatively large minority group populations were associated with the large total populations that entitle states to many representatives—New York, New Jersey, California, Pennsylvania, for example. The general trends in adoption were of course the same; the correlation between numbers of senators and numbers of representatives from states with EEO laws was over .9, and the same was true for equal pay laws. When Title 7 passed, 42 percent of United States senators were from states with EEO laws (50 percent if symbolic or narrowly restricted laws are included), and 48 percent from states with equal pay laws. The states with no laws were those in the South and in the thinly populated parts of the West.

Table 3.6 describes how congressional sponsorship of EEO legislation was related to the adoption of state EEO and equal pay laws. The number of members of Congress sponsoring EEO legislation was fairly strongly associated with state adoptions.[16] Very roughly, every time the percentage of representatives from states with EEO laws increased by two, one more member of Congress sponsored an EEO bill, and the association between state adoption of equal pay laws and congressional support for EEO was considerably stronger. These results are consistent with the estimates presented in table 3.2, which showed that congressional support for EEO legislation was more strongly associated with attitudes toward women in the labor force than with attitudes toward blacks. This may imply that attitudes about women's roles may have been of more significance in the postwar debates on equality than has been generally acknowledged, or it may simply mean that questions about women's place somehow act as indicators of attitudes relevant to government action on equality or discrimination generally.

We have no evidence whether state legislatures really reflected public opinion on EEO, but we do know that congressional support for EEO laws increased as states adopted EEO and equal pay laws, and that Congress passed Title 7 shortly after half the population of the United States was covered by state EEO and equal pay laws. The data are consistent with the idea that members of Congress looked to their states for guidance on the issue and then passed EEO legislation when state-level outcomes indicated it was safe to do so.

Table 3.6   **Congressional Support for EEO Legislation, 1941–64, and Percentage of United States Representatives from EEO and Equal Pay States: Regression Coefficients (and Standard Errors) for Two Equations**

(1) Sponsorships = .45 (% from EEO states) + 9.9
            (.11)   (3.9)
            R^2 = .57 (adjusted for degrees of freedom)
(2) Sponsorships = .72 (% from equal pay states) +3.4
            (.14)   (4.2)
            R^2 = .69 (adjusted)

$N = 12$.

Concurrent Majorities

The final potential impediment to an immediate congressional response
to the majority of the public's favoring the principle of EEO may be the
idea of "concurrent majorities" promulgated by John C. Calhoun in the
first half of the nineteenth century as part of his defense of the sov-
ereignty of the southern states (Dahl 1956; Levine 1972). Concerned,
like many framers of the Constitution, about the power of an overall
majority to completely override minority interests, Calhoun wanted to
limit the power of government by requiring that a majority of every
group importantly affected by a proposed policy be required before the
policy could be adopted—that is, policies would be adopted by "concurrent majorities" of all the groups involved. It has been argued that
American government is structured to require concurrent majorities on
divisive issues through the many requirements for greater than simple
majority votes—in amending the Constitution, overriding a presidential
veto, and ending a Senate filibuster, for example. The question arises,
Might the passage of EEO legislation have been delayed until the group
that saw itself as likely to be most adversely affected, namely southern
whites, had come to favor EEO, at least in principle?

Only a tidbit of data relevant to this question is available, but it is
worth mentioning. Although the South lagged far behind the rest of the
country in its movement toward positive attitudes on equal rights, table
3.3 shows that by 1964 a majority of whites even in the Deep South
favored EEO in principle. It is impossible to rule out the possibility that
it was necessary for a majority in all regions to favor EEO before an
EEO law could be passed.

Conclusions

Congressional *support* for EEO legislation, as indicated by sponsorships, was strongly related to public attitudes about the treatment of
minorities and women in the labor force and to state adoption of EEO
and equal pay laws; as attitudes about blacks, Jews, women, and other
groups became more egalitarian and as more laws were passed, congressional support increased. Congressional support was possibly related to
public attitudes about the passage of EEO laws and candidates who
favored helping women and minorities, but it was not related to intensity
of public concern about EEO.

Congress first *passed* EEO legislation in 1964 when the proportion of the public favoring EEO and the public's intensity of concern had reached historical high points, the proportion of the public covered by state EEO laws had just exceeded half for the first time, the proportion of the public believing the government was moving too fast on integration had fallen to a low point, and a majority of whites in all regions favored EEO.

Congress adopted the *1972 amendments* to Title 7 when almost everyone favored EEO for blacks in principle, two-thirds of the public approved of women's working outside the home, two-thirds of the public said they would be more likely to vote for a candidate if he or she favored improving opportunities for blacks and women, and relatively few people felt intensely concerned about the issue.

It would thus be fair to say that Congress responded strongly, perhaps primarily, to the public's preferences when it considered EEO legislation. It did not, it is true, adopt EEO legislation as soon as a majority of the public favored EEO. But as soon as it was clear that the public favored EEO, was increasingly favorable to legislation on the subject, and felt strongly about it, Congress adopted legislation that was a breakthrough in the struggle for equality of opportunity.

Both public opinion favorable to EEO and intensity of public concern were probably necessary to the passage and strengthening of Title 7, but it is doubtful that either was sufficient. Favorable public opinion would have been necessary because EEO bills were proposed on behalf of weak minority groups and faced intense opposition from large and powerful groups, particularly southern whites. It is hard to imagine the weak defeating the strong in such circumstances without the support of favorable public opinion.

Passage of legislation probably could not have been brought about by public opinion that was merely favorable, however; concern had to be intense as well, because of the intensity of the opposition. During most of the period from 1942 to 1972, almost all southern members of Congress could have been certain that voting for a civil rights bill would lead to defeat at the polls. Lukewarm feelings in other parts of the country, unlikely to have a serious influence on election day, would probably not motivate many members of Congress to expend the energy needed to overcome the southern opposition.

The rise in public concern would not have led to passage by itself either. Intensity of feeling about civil rights could lead to the passage of

civil rights laws only in a favorable atmosphere—had the public opposed rather than favored civil rights for minorities in the early 1960s,
the arousal of intense concern about the issue could have led to repression of those making the demands rather than to the passage of liberal
legislation.

Americans' attention was on civil rights in general, of course, not for
the most part on EEO, and certainly not on any particular EEO bill. In
this policy area, as in most others, people have only very general notions
about what they would like to see done in broad, conventionally defined
policy domains, rather than having specific ideas about legislation
(Weissberg 1976). Strong and pervasive public interest in an issue on
the legislative agenda is probably perceived by both citizens and their
representatives as indicating that the public wants the government to do
something, but not as defining precisely what. Faced with insistent but
vague demands from constituents for action on civil rights, what could
legislators who were not already active supporters of legislation do?

Probably the most obvious and least risky thing to do would be to
vote for bills already supported by everyone who had an interest in
enacting legislation—other members of Congress, the groups whose
rights were to be protected and their allies, and so on. By voting for a
collection of classic civil rights bills joined together by a Civil Rights
Act, a member of Congress could thus satisfy constituents, colleagues,
and interest groups, all with very little effort (cf. Polsby 1984; Downs
1972). It was the combination of public attitudes favorable to EEO,
intense concern about civil rights, and prior drafting of bills and coali-
tion building by sponsors that made possible the enactment of today's
EEO law.

Contrary to what is widely believed about congressional action in
general and with regard to civil rights, congressional action on EEO was
quite consistent with what the public wanted. But did forces other than
public attitudes affect congressional action? Might the relationship between public opinion and congressional action have been spurious, with
the changes in both being due to other factors? And why did public
opinion change after World War II? These are the concerns of the next
two chapters.

4 The Civil Rights Movement and Congressional Action

From the very beginning, the forcefulness of federal action on civil rights seems to have been linked to the ability of supporters of civil rights to mobilize social protest against discrimination. In 1941 the threat of a protest march on Washington by ten thousand people was followed by President Roosevelt's signing of a precedent-shattering but essentially toothless executive order banning employment discrimination in defense industries and federal employment. In 1957 an actual demonstration in Washington by twenty-five thousand people was followed by passage of the first civil rights law since Reconstruction. And the 1963 March on Washington by over two hundred thousand people was associated with the passage, a few months later, of the sweeping Civil Rights Act of 1964.

A link between organized protest and congressional action is central to most accounts of the passage of civil rights legislation (for example, Schlei 1976, vii–viii; Oberschall 1973; Lawson 1976; Garrow 1978). Yet participants in the civil rights movement and interested observers both knew that most Americans disapprove of social protest, and they often came to conflicting or uncertain conclusions about whether protest helped the cause of civil rights or hurt it. When it reported on the 1963 March on Washington, for example, the *New York Times* concluded that "the civil rights demonstration that swept more than 200,000 people through the capital today appeared to have left much of Congress untouched . . . there was very little evidence that the demonstration . . . would play a material role in advancing civil rights legislation" (29 August 1963, 1). Senator George Aiken of Vermont, a senior Republican whose vote was considered important, was reported as warning that a major demonstration in Washington would kill the chances for civil rights legislation (*New York Times*, 18 July 1963, 18). Martin Luther King, Jr., Bayard Rustin, and other black leaders sometimes disagreed with each other and other black leaders about the effectiveness of demonstrations and felt that, at least occasionally, civil rights demonstrations hurt their cause (*New York Times,* 18 October 1963, 3; 3 August 1964, 12).

Thus, even many proponents of civil rights legislation were unsure about the efficacy of social protest. In addition, according to both the theoretical work on Congress and the data described in chapter 3, Congress seems to have acted on EEO primarily because of public opinion. Is it possible, contrary to conventional historical conclusions, that the civil rights movement played little role in the passage of civil rights legislation, or of EEO legislation in particular?

In fact, there are six ways public opinion and the social protest activities of the civil rights movement may be related to congressional action on EEO. First, the civil rights movement (and associated phenomena such as media coverage) may have *caused* public opinion to change and Congress to act. Congress may have *appeared* to follow public opinion, whereas in fact it and the public were responding primarily to the movement. Garrow claims that this is what happened when Congress passed voting rights legislation (1978, 178; cf. McAdam 1982, 178). If he is correct, then the apparent relation between public opinion and congressional action described in chapter 3 is spurious.

Second, Congress may have been affected by public opinion *and* by the civil rights movement. The relation between public opinion and congressional action may have been real, but the civil rights movement may have influenced members of Congress as well.

Third, the drama of the civil rights movement may have stimulated congressional *attentiveness* to public opinion on civil rights, thereby strengthening the link between public opinion and congressional action. If public opinion favored EEO (as it did), movement activity would thus lead to an increase in congressional support without causing such support itself (see Wirmark 1974; Lytle 1966).

Fourth, the civil rights movement may have *changed public opinion,* causing it to become more favorable to equal treatment or to legislation. Congress may have responded directly to public opinion, but the opinion itself may have been the result, at least in part, of the civil rights movement. This is what many scholars seem to believe (e.g., Dahl 1967, 419; Schlei 1976, vii–viii; Orfield 1975, 62; Lawson 1976, 348; Oberschall 1973, 217).

Fifth, the civil rights movement might have been the *product* or the manifestation of increasingly liberal public opinion on civil rights. This may have been President Johnson's view when he wrote, "The potential strength of public opinion had first been evident in the march on Washington late in the summer of 1963" (1971, 59). From this perspective, public opinion would have been the fundamental determinant of congressional action, but the fact that it was so dramatically expressed through the civil rights movement may have been important.

Finally, the civil rights movement may have been of little consequence. Just as the apparent relation between public opinion and congressional action may have been spurious, the apparent influence of the civil rights movement may also have been so. Historians, journalists, and social scientists may have been so caught up in the drama of the movement that they attributed unwarranted importance to it, ignoring, for example, the fact that the passage of the Civil Rights Act of 1964 followed not only the March on Washington, but also twenty years of congressional debate and change in public opinion.

The distinctions among these possibilities are important because they imply different interpretations of how the American political system operates. If Congress only appeared to respond to public opinion, while in fact responding to something else—social protest activities in this case, perhaps well-financed lobbying in others—cynicism about the representative nature of American government would be justified, and theories that consider public opinion of paramount importance would have to be modified. Alternatively, if Congress responds to protest activities because they are seen as manifestations of public opinion, then protest can be seen as having made Congress respond to what the public wanted, and thus as having contributed to the effectiveness of the democratic process. And if movement activities had only an indirect effect, shaping the public opinion to which Congress actually responded, the civil rights movement may be seen as an important part of a political system in which public opinion is paramount but manipulable.

Unfortunately, previous work tells us very little about the influence of public opinion and the civil rights movement on Congress. Those who systematically gather evidence about historical trends in public opinion, the civil rights movement, or Congress are overspecialized; they study social movements but not public opinion or Congress (e.g., McAdam 1982; Gamson 1975; Jenkins and Perrow 1977), public opinion and Congress but not social movements (e.g., Weissberg 1976), or social movements, public opinion, or Congress alone (also see Freeman

1975, 4–5, on this point). Obviously there is no way to show how different factors interact without having data on all of them simultaneously. There are analyses that are more comprehensive in scope, but they are much less systematic in their gathering and use of evidence. Thus, for example, Orfield (1975), Oberschall (1973), and Lawson (1976) all think that the main effect of the civil rights movement was to arouse public opinion—that is, they do think in terms of relationships among the relevant variables—but they provide little data on public opinion, movement activity, or congressional action, so there is no way to judge whether their assertions are correct. In addition, we have no idea what determined congressional action specifically on EEO because there have been no studies focusing on EEO.

This chapter, therefore, is the first attempt to use systematically gathered time-trend data to show how public opinion and the civil rights movement affected congressional action on EEO. It is also one of the first attempts to carry out such an analysis on *any* issue. Did Congress respond primarily to public opinion when dealing with EEO bills? And what role did the civil rights movement play in congressional action?

Public opinion has already been described. My first task here, therefore, is to describe the civil rights movement and associated phenomena believed to have affected Congress.

The Civil Rights Movement

How did the civil rights movement affect congressional action on civil rights? Most observers believe the movement was most effective when the American people were confronted, day after day, by intensive media coverage of peaceful civil rights demonstrators being violently attacked by those who opposed their pleas for justice, particularly if the attackers were public officials. For example, Norbert Schlei, an assistant United States attorney general involved in civil rights during the early 1960s, saw congressional action on the Civil Rights Act of 1964 as greatly affected by the 1963 civil rights demonstrations in Birmingham, Alabama, when "the people of the United States saw on their television screens night after night an unapologetic Eugene 'Bull' Connor, Birmingham's police chief, and the seemingly senseless use by forces under his command of police dogs, firehoses and other undiscriminating weapons against apparently well-behaved demonstrators. . . . Suddenly, literally overnight, the time had come for consideration by the country and by the Congress of major civil rights legislation'' (1976, vii–viii; see also Garrow 1978; Lawson 1976, chap. 11; Wirmark 1974; Lichtman 1969; Dahl 1967; Sundquist 1968).

Hypothetically, therefore, the cause of civil rights was helped by peaceful pro-rights activities, violent anti-rights activities (particularly if perpetrated by public officials), and media coverage. The cause of civil rights may have been hurt by pro-rights activities that turned violent (Garrow 1978; but cf. Button 1978) and by peaceful protest by those opposed to the extension of civil rights. Thus, if we are to understand how the civil rights movement affected public opinion and Congress, we must take into account peaceful and violent pro- and anti-rights activities, including those of public officials, and media coverage.

In addition, given our knowledge of the legislative history and our specific concern for EEO, two other factors must be considered. First, it is important to know on whose behalf pro-rights actions were carried out—blacks, Jews, another specific minority group, women, all minorities? We know that most EEO bills considered by Congress before 1964 prohibited discrimination on the basis of race, religion, and national origin, and that after 1964 sex discrimination was prohibited as well. Were particular groups covered because of explicit public demands made on their behalf or for other reasons? Second, we want to know how many pro-rights actions concerned EEO specifically. Congressional action on EEO would probably have been especially affected by actions focused on that issue, but we do not want to ignore activities related to discrimination in other areas, because the movement for EEO was inextricably linked to the general movement against discrimination.

Thus, pro- and anti-rights activities (or, rather, their public manifestations) and media coverage potentially relevant to congressional action on EEO are described in the next section. The data are taken from the *New York Times,* the best and most widely used source of information on trends of issues of national importance, and run from 1940, just before the first federal action on EEO, through 1972, when Title 7 was amended. Details about the data may be found in the Notes and Appendix.

Pro-Rights Demonstrations

According to the *New York Times,* almost 3,800 pro-rights demonstrations took place between 1940 and 1972, and the reports show the extent to which the struggle against discrimination in the mid-twentieth-century

United States was a struggle on behalf of blacks—over 95 percent of the demonstrations protested discrimination against blacks.[1] There were a few demonstrations against anti-Semitism in the 1940s (and Jews were very active in the struggle for EEO; see Kesselman 1948, chaps. 2, 6), some opposing discrimination against women and members of other minority groups in the late 1960s and 1970s, and a few against discrimination in general, with no particular group singled out, but that is all.

Figure 4.1 shows the number of demonstrations each year (because there were so few demonstrations on behalf of groups other than blacks, all demonstrations are described together). The boycott of public buses in Montgomery, Alabama, by blacks protesting segregation, which began in December 1955, has been seen as signaling the beginning of the modern civil rights movement, and in fact pro-rights demonstrations

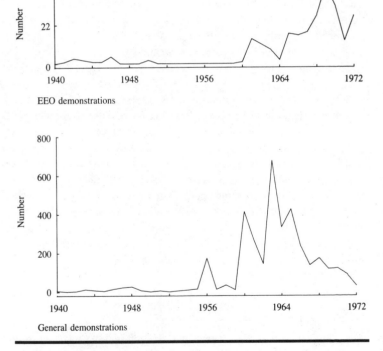

Fig. 4.1   Pro-civil rights and EEO activities. Source: *New York Times,* 1940–73; see Appendix.

rose dramatically from 10 in 1954 and 15 in 1955 to 173 in 1956. Although the level of protest fell off in the late 1950s, the decline was brief, and the resurgence of activity in 1960 had clear continuities in leadership, organization, and tactics with the movement of the mid-1950s (Morris 1981).

Despite the importance of EEO to ordinary blacks and black leaders, few demonstrations specifically protested discrimination in employment until the mid-1960s. Instead, most demonstrations ("general demonstrations"; that is, demonstrations on matters other than EEO) protested discrimination in public accommodations, voting, and education, probably because the grievances were easily dramatized, were apparently easy to resolve, and involved claims that were not controversial outside the South. The passage of the Civil Rights Act of 1964 and the Voting Rights Act of 1965 resolved many of the blacks' grievances about public accommodations and voting but left the EEO law uncompleted and their economic state still relatively precarious; consequently, a greater proportion of protest activity began to focus on EEO.

Riots

Demonstrations were the peaceful side of protest against the conditions blacks faced; riots were the violent side. Riots were not, of course, planned as part of the campaign against discrimination. Most leaders of the civil rights movement agreed, as Garrow has written, that "violence by a political actor was, within the context of the American political culture, certain to rebound to that actor's disadvantage to the extent that the polity . . . perceived that actor to be the initiator of it" (1978, 159–60). Nevertheless, many riots took place while the movement against discrimination proceeded, and there is some evidence that, whatever the participants' intent, riots did lead to increased government activity on behalf of blacks, at least in the short term in some programs (Button 1978, chaps. 2, 5). It would be very interesting to see if riots were counterproductive, as conventional wisdom dictates, or if, in contrast, they helped spur Congress to action on EEO.

Almost 1,400 riots were reported between 1940 and the end of 1972.[2] Figure 4.2 shows the trends. As the figure and table 4.1 show, riot frequency was correlated with the frequency of peaceful pro-rights demonstrations—low from the 1940s until the mid-1950s, rising from then into the late 1960s, and then declining. But riot frequency rose most dramatically in the late 1960s, after participation in peaceful dem-

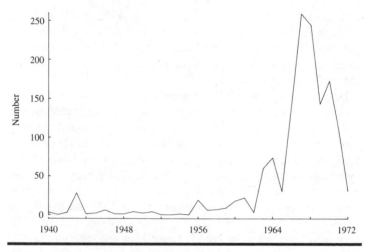

Fig. 4.2   Riots. Source: *New York Times,* 1940–73; see Appendix.

onstrations had already begun to decline. This was after two of the major victories of the civil rights movement—the passage of the Civil Rights Act of 1964 and the Voting Rights Act of 1965—had already been won but just about the time the open housing law passed in 1968. The relation between rioting and the passage of major laws is not obvious.

Anti-Rights Activities

Like those who favored the extension of civil rights, those who opposed it frequently acted on their beliefs. Particularly in the South, however, where discrimination was statutory and there was a long tradition of intimidating those seeking to end discrimination, the repertoire of collective action employed by opponents of civil rights was quite different from that used by the advocates of rights. Those opposed to the extension of civil rights sometimes expressed their views in peaceful demonstrations, as proponents of rights did, beginning in the mid-1950s in response to the Supreme Court's school desegregation decisions. But those opposed to the extension of civil rights also resorted to physical attacks on the advocates of civil rights—beatings, firebombings, shooting, and the like.

Figure 4.3 and table 4.1 describe four types of anti-rights activities: peaceful demonstrations, killings of proponents of civil rights by people

Table 4.1   Pro- and Anti-Rights Activities and Media Coverage, 1941–72

A. Basic Statistics

Variable	Annual Minimum	Annual Maximum	Mean	Peak Years
EEO demonstrations	0	44	7.7	1969, 1970, 1972
General demonstrations	1	677	111	1963, 1965, 1960
Riots	0	259	44	1967, 1968, 1970
Anti-rights demonstrations	0	62	16	1960, 1964, 1956
Injuries	1	99	21	1964, 1965, 1957
Official violence	0	22	1.8	1963, 1965, 1964
Killings	0	13	2.9	1963, 1969, 1966
New York Times coverage	0.3%	3.1%	1.0%	1964, 1965, 1963
Salience of civil rights	0%	52%	9.7%	1963, 1964, 1965

B. Correlations

EEO demonstrations	.84								
General demonstrations	.26	.55							
Riots	.73	.28	.82						
Anti-rights demonstrations	.14	.68	.19	.36					
Injuries	.07	.63	.20	.75	.69				
Official violence	.16	.86	.16	.41	.52	.26			
Killings	.49	.57	.47	.32	.37	.66	.31		
New York Times coverage	.41	.82	.57	.60	.81	.72	.64	.83	
Salience of civil rights	.26	.78	.42	.59	.78	.79	.69	.88	.65

Note: First-order serial correlations on diagonal.
Sources: All variables except "salience of civil rights," *New York Times,* 1941–72; see Appendix. For "salience of civil rights," see figure 3.4. missing years interpolated; for years with more than one survey, average of all surveys used, except 1963, when highest percentage used.

other than public officials, other "unofficial" attacks on proponents of rights, and violent attacks on peaceful protesters by public officials.

Anti-rights demonstrations were defined analogously to pro-rights demonstrations; almost all of them were directed against blacks.

Violent incidents were counted when the violence was directed against members of a minority group or other people associated with minority group members in the campaign for civil rights (such as whites participating in a civil rights demonstration). To be counted, an attack

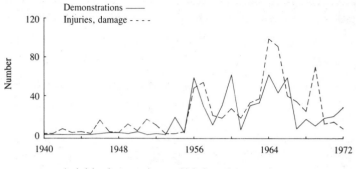

Anti-rights demonstrations, and injuries and property damage
to pro-rights forces

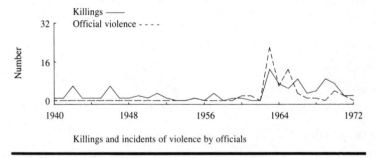

Killings and incidents of violence by officials

Fig. 4.3   Anti-rights activities. Source: *New York Times,* 1940–73; see Appendix.

had to appear politically motivated—that is, to be directed at someone
because of his or her support of civil rights.

It is difficult to gauge the amount of violence directed at blacks,
particularly in the South, because such violence was routine and long-
standing. Beatings and lynchings of blacks were widespread long before
the rise of the modern civil rights movement, but most incidents were
known only locally, and they seldom made the papers (see Shay 1938).
Such incidents were part of the structure of informal social control that
kept blacks in their place, and as such they were essentially political.
Nevertheless, it is important to try to distinguish "routine" violence
from violence that had meaning in the context of the modern civil rights
movement. In a sense the press makes this distinction; as the civil rights
movement became stronger, violent incidents were probably more likely

to be reported and to be attributed a political meaning, and it is these incidents that are reported in figure 4.3. Media sensitivity to violence and conventional definitions of what constituted political violence had probably crystallized by the late 1950s or early 1960s, but it is important to remember that the distinction between "routine social control" and "violent attacks on those supporting civil rights" developed to some extent out of the interaction between the movement and the media early in this period.

Two types of attacks on proponents of equal rights are included in figure 4.3—those involving killings and those involving injuries or property damage but no deaths. Killings were counted individually because they were relatively rare and hypothetically had the greatest impact on the public. Injuries and property damage were counted by incident—an event was recorded once, even if it involved multiple injuries and property damage. When an incident involved both killings and injuries or property damage, only the killings were counted.

The second type of violence against proponents of equal rights was that perpetrated by the police or other agents of social control (such as the National Guard) on peaceful protesters. Such attacks emphasize the "victim" position of minorities, making them seem to be the objects of excessive or illegitimate force, and have been hypothesized to arouse sympathy for their plight.[3]

Figures 4.1–4.3 and table 4.1 show that as pro-rights activities increased in the mid-1950s and thereafter, anti-rights activities increased as well. Anti-rights demonstrations increased in tandem with pro-rights demonstrations, rising from two in 1955 to fifty-nine in 1956. Attacks on the supporters of civil rights also increased.

This pattern of pro- and anti-rights activities moving roughly in parallel continued right through the early 1970s. The correlations among different aspects of pro-rights activity and anti-rights activity are all positive, and many are very strong. In addition, many aspects of pro- and anti-rights activity all reached their historical peaks at the same time—1963 saw almost seven hundred pro-rights demonstrations, twenty-two violent attacks on supporters of civil rights by public officials, and thirteen killings of people associated with the civil rights movement, and nonfatal attacks on supporters of civil rights peaked the following year. These trends paralleled those in the final component of the conventional explanations of congressional action—media coverage.

Media Coverage

"If protest tactics are not considered significant by the media," Lipsky
has written, "or if newspapers and television reporters or editors decide
to overlook protest tactics, protest organizations will not succeed"
(1968, 1157). Martin Luther King, Jr., is said to have realized that the
route to civil rights legislation "lay through the national news media and
the audiences to which they could convey the movement's pleas for
assistance and reforms" (Garrow 1978, 221–22). Many members of
Congress and of the public were apparently affected very strongly by
newspaper and television coverage of dramatic events in the civil rights
movement, particularly the attacks on demonstrators in Selma in early
1965 (Garrow 1978, chap. 5); among newspapers the *New York Times*
seems to have had an especially great influence on members of Congress, at least at dramatic moments.

To determine how public opinion, pro- and anti-rights activity, congressional action, and media coverage were related, not just at particularly dramatic moments but over the entire history of the movement for
civil rights and EEO, the proportion of total space in the *New York
Times Index* devoted to civil rights, minorities, women, employment
discrimination, and related issues was tabulated for each year from 1940

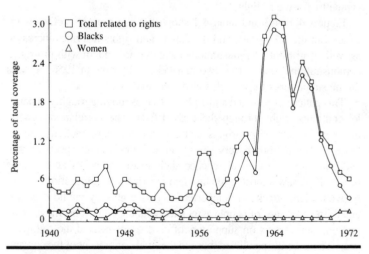

Fig. 4.4   Coverage of blacks, women, civil rights, and related issues in the *New
York Times.* Source: *New York Times Index,* 1940–73; see Appendix.

on. The most salient aspects of the results are presented in figure 4.4 and table 4.1.

First, there has never been much coverage of employment discrimination; it has never received more than a tenth of the total space devoted to discrimination and therefore is not analyzed separately.

Second, before the mid-1950s, considerable attention was paid to minority groups other than blacks, particularly Jews, whose confrontation with anti-Semitism was a major issue in the 1940s. Beginning in the mid-1950s, however, an increasing proportion of media attention to civil rights was devoted to blacks, and by 1961 coverage of civil rights and of blacks had become virtually synonymous. At least through the beginnings of the 1970s, neither women nor minorities other than blacks had succeeded in gaining much attention from the *New York Times*.

On the whole, trends in press coverage of civil rights and EEO paralleled trends in pro- and anti-rights activity. When pro- and anti-rights demonstrations increased dramatically in 1956, press coverage of civil rights, which had been sparse and had even declined a bit in preceeding years, more than doubled, from 0.4 percent of all coverage in 1955 to 1.0 percent in 1956. Press coverage of civil rights peaked in 1964, the year after the peak in pro-rights demonstrations, and the same year as the peak number of nonfatal attacks on supporters of civil rights. As pro- and anti-rights activity began to decline in the late 1960s, so did media coverage.

Thus pro- and anti-rights activity and media coverage all increased dramatically in the mid-1950s, declined a bit, rose to historical highs in the mid-1960s, and gradually declined together in the late 1960s and early 1970s. An important aspect of what happened, however, is not captured by the idea of a large number of phenomena simply moving in tandem. There are a number of reasons to think that the "basic" variable among those described, the variable responsible for the others, was general pro-rights demonstrations, at least until the late 1960s. First, many anti-rights actions were attacks on demonstrators and civil rights activists and so were obviously stimulated by the rise in movement activity. Second, the number of killings and attacks by officials did not increase much until the early 1960s, when the movement's confrontation tactics had been perfected and the movement was seen as a more serious threat to the established order. Third, although media coverage of civil rights increased as soon as demonstrations became frequent in 1956, the changes in coverage did not become really proportionate to the changes in movement activity until such activity peaked in the early sixties. Media coverage followed upon movement activity rather than preceding it.

Unfortunately, it is not possible to use annual data to examine the precise sequence in which different events occurred and then make inferences about causation, because each type of activity usually responded to the others in less than a year—if police respond to demonstrators they do so immediately. Nevertheless, the correlation coefficients do provide some evidence that anti-rights activities were a response to general demonstrations. Panel B of table 4.1 shows the relationship between anti-rights activities and general demonstrations and also shows the first-order serial correlations of each variable—the correlation of the variable with its own value for the previous year. Were anti-rights activities generated by a social process independent of general demonstrations, their occurrence would not be highly correlated with general demonstrations, but their serial correlations and correlations with each other would be relatively high. Instead, anti-rights activities were generally more highly correlated with general demonstrations than with each other, and the serial correlations for anti-rights demonstrations, official violence, and killings are lower than their correlations with general demonstrations. Thus, anti-rights activities are closely linked to general demonstrations—that is, the civil rights movement—but not to an independently organized anti-rights movement.

Thus, a wave of civil rights activities accompanied by media coverage began in the mid-1950s; it rose until the mid-1960s and then started to decline. The riots of the late 1960s brought a resurgence of popular attention to minorities, and the number of demonstrations focused on EEO rose as well. How did Congress respond to this activity as it rose, receded, and changed direction?

Collective Action, Media Coverage, and Congressional Action

We already know that congressional support for EEO legislation, as gauged by sponsorship of EEO bills and passage, was strongly related to public opinion on equal treatment of blacks and women in the labor force and that there are six ways public opinion and the civil rights movement together *could have been* related to congressional action. How did the movement, anti-rights activity, media coverage, and public opinion actually affect Congress?

The Congressional Response

The first possibility is that Congress responded directly to pro- and anti-rights activity and media coverage, and that the apparent relationship between congressional action and public opinion is in fact spurious. This possibility would have to be taken seriously if congressional action were strongly related to pro- and anti-rights activity and media coverage. Was it?

Table 4.2 shows how strongly congressional support for EEO was related to its possible determinants for the sixteen Congresses during which EEO legislation was considered, 1941 to 1972. Congressional support for EEO was related most strongly to pro-EEO attitudes and only weakly to media coverage and most types of collective action, quite contrary to what one would expect were the relationship between congressional support and public opinion spurious. The only other variables strongly related to congressional support were EEO demonstrations and riots, neither of which is typically thought of as at the core of the civil rights movement. Both were highly correlated with congressional support because they peaked so late, as congressional support rose dramatically in the late 1960s. Pro-EEO attitudes rose most consistently along with congressional support for EEO and therefore had the highest correlation with it.

Table 4.2   Correlates of Sponsorship of EEO Bills, Seventy-seventh to Ninety-second Congresses, 1941–72

Variable	Correlation with Sponsorship
Pro-EEO attitudes[a]	.85
EEO demonstrations	.81
Riots	.62
Killings	.32
New York Times coverage	.25
Anti-rights demonstrations	.23
General demonstrations	.19
Salience of civil rights[b]	.17
Official violence	.14
Injuries	.05

[a]Measured as average percentage favoring equal treatment for blacks and labor force participation of women.
[b]Measured as percentage of public calling civil rights one of the most important problems facing the country.

Nor does the relationship of collective action and media coverage with the *passage* of EEO legislation suggest that public opinion was unimportant. Title 7 passed when a lot was happening at once—a majority of the public favored EEO for blacks, other aspects of tolerance were at a historical peak, the intensity of public concern was extremely high, and general demonstrations, anti-rights demonstrations, injuries, killings, official violence, and media coverage were all at or near historical high points (table 4.1). It is hard to decide what was crucial. When the 1972 amendments passed, however, only positive attitudes toward EEO and EEO demonstrations were at a peak; activity of all other sorts had declined. There is thus not much reason to think that Congress was responding to something other than public opinion.

Although Congress may not have responded to collective action and media coverage, they may have some direct influence, even after public opinion was taken into account. Table 4.3 presents one way of determining whether they did. The table shows how much influence media coverage and each type of pro- and anti-rights activity had on congressional support for EEO, once pro-EEO attitudes were taken into account.[4] The most significant result in the table is the overwhelming importance of pro-EEO attitudes. Most of the other variables have no influence on congressional support at all once attitudes are taken into account. Only two factors other than pro-EEO attitudes appear to have affected Congress, and neither their identity nor the nature of their influence is what might be expected from a reading of the standard accounts of the civil rights movement. It is not media coverage or pro-rights activities that affected Congress, but nonfatal attacks on blacks and their allies ("injuries") and anti-rights demonstrations. Not only are they the only factors to have an influence, but the influence is negative; that is, they reduced congressional support for EEO, as their perpetrators presumably intended. Though this is somewhat surprising, it is actually reasonable that anti-rights demonstrations, in particular, could have been interpreted just as pro-rights demonstrations might have been—as indicators of attitudes and depth of feeling about a political issue—and that such demonstrations could therefore have led Congress to move more slowly on civil rights than it might have otherwise. When anti-rights activity declined, members of Congress would have felt less pressure to oppose EEO legislation, so support would increase.

Table 4.3 and the earlier figures also show that neither collective action nor media coverage seems to be necessary for the passage of EEO legislation. Title 7 passed when collective action and media coverage

Table 4.3   Determinants of Congressional Support for EEO Bills, Seventy-seventh to Ninety-second Congresses, 1941–72

Variables (attitudes and)	Unstandardized Regression Coefficients			R^2	D-W d
	Attitudes	Other Variable	Constant		
Pro-EEO attitudes only	1.58** (6.1)	—	−56.2** (−3.7)	.71	.75
Injuries	1.98** (10.2)	−.56** (−4.4)	−67.8** (−6.6)	.87	1.9
Anti-rights demonstrations	2.15** (9.2)	−.75** (−3.9)	−76.4** (−6.5)	.86	1.7
General demonstrations	1.91** (4.2)	−.053* (−2.0)	−66.0** (−3.4)	.70	GLS
New York Times coverage	1.91** (5.5)	−7.9* (−1.6)	−68.8** (−4.2)	.60	GLS
Salience	1.84** (7.0)	−.61 (−2.1)	−65.2** (−4.6)	.77	1.5
EEO demonstrations	1.04** (3.0)	.88 (2.1)	−32.6 (−1.8)	.76	.98
Official violence	1.75** (6.6)	−1.60 (−1.7)	−63.4** (−4.3)	.74	1.1
Killings	1.59** (5.4)	−.14 (−.10)	−56.5** (−3.6)	.69	.76
Riots	1.47** (4.1)	.031 (.4)	−51.5* (−2.8)	.69	.78

Note: t-statistics in parentheses; R^2 adjusted for degrees of freedom; D-W d is Durbin-Watson d-statistic.
*Significant at .05 level, two-tailed test.
**Significant of .01 level, two-tailed test.

were at high points, but the 1972 Equal Employment Opportunity Act passed when there was relatively little collective action or media attention. It remains plausible, as so many have argued, that a law as sweeping as the Civil Rights Act of 1964 could not have passed in the absence of social upheaval—and there is no way to prove otherwise—but the consistent influence of public opinion, and the passage of the 1972 law at a time of relatively little protest, should warn against exaggerating the extent to which Congress was directly influenced by collective action and media coverage.

Of course, pro- and anti-rights activities and media coverage may influence Congress indirectly as well as directly. One way would be by sensitizing members of Congress to public opinion. To consider this possibility statistically, one can add an interaction term—a variable created by calculating the product of the two independent variables already in an equation—to equations like those reported in table 4.3. For example, to determine whether Congress was more sensitive to public opinion when EEO demonstrations were frequent and less sensitive when demonstrations were few, one would use an equation including public opinion and demonstrations (as in table 4.3) to predict congressional support, *along with* an interaction term representing public opinion and demonstrations simultaneously.

That is what the equation in table 4.4 does. The table shows how pro-EEO attitudes and demonstrations interacted to influence congressional support for EEO. The influence of each independent variable at any particular time depends upon the coefficient of the interaction term and the value of the other independent variable as well as upon its own coefficient (Stolzenberg 1980). For example, in a year when there were two EEO demonstrations, the effect of pro-EEO attitudes on support would be the coefficient of attitudes (that is, .68), plus the coefficient of the interaction term (that is, .16) multiplied by the number of demonstrations (that is, 2), or .68 plus .32, or 1.00; that is, each 1 percent increase in the proportion of the public favoring EEO would be associated with one additional sponsor of EEO legislation. In a year when there were ten EEO demonstrations, however, the effect of pro-EEO attitudes on support would be greater, that is, .68, plus .16 multiplied by 10, or 2.28; thus, an increase in demonstrations from two to ten would mean that each 1 percent increase in pro-EEO attitudes would be associated with an additional 2.28 sponsors rather than 1.00.

Table 4.4 tells us that the influence of attitudes upon Congress *is* affected by the number of EEO demonstrations, and the influence of demonstrations is affected by attitudes. Because both attitudes alone and the interaction term have a positive impact on Congress, we can say that EEO demonstrations *enhance the influence of attitudes* on Congress; demonstrations sensitize Congress to public opinion. Because the coefficient for demonstrations is negative while that for the interaction term is positive, we can say that the effect of EEO demonstrations is sometimes negative and sometimes positive, depending upon what public opinion is. As a matter of fact, the total effect of EEO demonstrations on Congress would have been negative until about 68 percent of the public had

Table 4.4 **Public Opinion and EEO Demonstrations: Interactive Influence on Congressional Support for EEO Bills, Seventy-seventh to Ninety-second Congresses**

Support = .68*(Pro-EEO attitudes) − 10.9** (EEO demonstrations)
     (2.8)   (−3.9)
     +.16** (attitudes × demonstrations) − 9.1
     (4.2)   (−.7)
     R^2 = .90   Durbin-Watson *d* = 2.2

Note: t-statistics in parentheses; R^2 adjusted for degrees of freedom.
*Significant at .05 level.
**Significant at .01 level.

pro-EEO attitudes. This occurred in 1965. There is therefore every reason to believe that by 1972, when the EEO amendments passed, EEO demonstrations were sensitizing members of Congress to public opinion, while public opinion was so favorable that EEO demonstrations themselves had a positive influence. That the proportion of variance explained by this equation is higher than in any other is further indication of the importance of interactions between public opinion and other variables.

Unfortunately, it is impossible to determine whether other variables interact with public opinion in the same way, because of multicollinearity among the variables (Belsley, Kuh, and Welsch 1980, chap. 3). This does not mean there was no interaction, only that we cannot gauge it statistically. I think that pro- and anti-rights activity and media coverage did in fact sensitize Congress to public opinion, but this conclusion must remain somewhat speculative for now.

Thus far, public opinion remains the crucial determinant of congressional action. Might pro- and anti-rights activities and media coverage have affected Congress indirectly, by influencing public opinion?

Collective Action and Public Opinion

In one crucial way, the answer is no. As the figures presented earlier show, pro- and anti-rights activities and media coverage did not start to increase significantly until years after pro-EEO attitudes began moving in a more egalitarian direction. Collective action and media coverage moved more or less in tandem with attitudes during the late 1950s and early to mid-1960s but then fell off dramatically, while attitudes continued to change. It is fairly obvious (and statistical analysis confirms) that over the entire period the relation of collective action and media coverage to pro-EEO attitudes is zero.

Intensity of concern about civil rights is a different matter. In fact, as table 4.5 shows (and the earlier figures indicated), the salience of civil rights was very much a function of the violence that so many accounts of the movement emphasize.[5] Official and unofficial violent attacks on proponents of civil rights, as well as riots, all contributed to public feeling that civil rights was one of the most important issues facing the country.

As table 4.3 showed, salience itself had no direct influence on congressional support for EEO. The analysis of intensity in chapter 3 showed, however, that increasing public concern about civil rights *may* have been an important prerequisite for *passage* of the Civil Rights Act of 1964 (though not the Equal Employment Opportunity Act of 1972). *If* this were the case, the effect of violence on salience may suggest, as many analysts have, that attacks on demonstrators "aroused" the public, which in turn got Congress to respond to the by then favorable public attitudes on EEO. The social protest activity of the civil rights movement may thus have affected Congress indirectly by influencing the intensity of public concern; but the evidence that intensity itself influenced Congress is far from conclusive.

If the civil rights movement did not cause attitudes about EEO to change, might changes in attitudes have been responsible for the rise of

Table 4.5   Determinants of Salience of Civil Rights, 1941–72

Independent Variable	Unstandardized Regression Coefficient	t-Statistic
Injuries	.24	5.4**
Official violence	1.17	4.6**
Riots	.037	2.3*
Killings	.71	1.9
Constant	−.97	−.6
R^2 = .81		

Note: Estimated using generalized least squares; R^2 adjusted for degrees of freedom.
*Significant at .05 level, two-tailed test.
**Significant at .01 level, two-tailed test.

the movement? Might pro-rights activities therefore have been seen as manifestations of public opinion? This chapter analyzes the determinants of congressional action, not the rise of the civil rights movement (or the women's movement). Yet the possibility that attitudes led to movement activity must be considered, however briefly, for the sake of a full understanding of how social factors led to congressional action.

It would be hard to argue with the proposition that the civil rights and women's movements were, in a very general way, the product of the "climate of opinion" in the country at the time they were organized. Organizations will find it easier to recruit members and avoid repression if increasing numbers of people favor their goals. As an explanation for the rise of movement activity, however, this does not amount to much because it is too vague; it ignores the concrete problems of organization, communication, and resources that must be overcome if a group is to gain members and become politically consequential. Studies of the civil rights movement, women's movement, and other recent American social movements have shown that changes in public attitudes may help make organization possible but do not inevitably lead to organization and certainly do not guarantee a movement's success (McAdam 1982; Freeman 1975; Jenkins and Perrow 1977; see also Mason, Czajka, and Arber 1976). The civil rights and women's movements were neither a major cause nor a direct consequence of changes in public opinion.

The *interpretation* of the civil rights movement may have been another matter. As I noted above, President Johnson at some point concluded that major civil rights demonstrations were a manifestation of public opinion. Politicians are always trying to discover what public opinion is. For them the question about civil rights demonstrations would have been whether they represented the opinions of a lunatic fringe or of the majority of American citizens. As the number of demonstrators who were well educated, "respectable," professional, middle-aged, and members of the clergy increased, the "lunatic fringe" interpretation would have been less and less tenable. The civil rights movement was not, in any direct way, the product of public opinion. But it may have come to appear so.

The final way the social protest activities of the civil rights movement could have affected Congress is not at all. Just as it was possible for the relation between public opinion and congressional action to have been more apparent than real, it is also possible that the civil rights movement had no effect.

This possibility has been considered implicitly in the preceding analyses. The civil rights movement did have some influence on Congress, but its role was a secondary one. The primary determinant of congressional action was public opinion. The civil rights movement (and the associated anti-rights activity and media coverage) seems to have had only a slight direct effect on congressional support for EEO and little or no effect on pro-EEO attitudes. It is true that the Civil Rights Act of 1964 passed about the time movement activity peaked, but the Equal Employment Opportunity Act of 1972 passed years after most movement activity had drastically declined.

What the social protest activity of the civil rights movement did was this: it impressed upon the public the seriousness of the struggle for civil rights, and it sensitized Congress to public opinion. This was important. Congress sometimes ignores public opinion, especially on issues most people care little about (Weissberg 1976; Page and Shapiro 1983). But it is more difficult to ignore public attitudes when they are strongly held and brought forcefully to one's attention.

Public opinion remains the primary determinant of congressional action, however. The movement's arousal of public opinion and sensitization of Congress could have led to pro-rights legislation only in a climate of opinion favorable to civil rights. Had Congress and the public been aroused much earlier than the early 1960s, back when the public was fundamentally hostile to minorities, the result might very easily have been violent repression of the movement, a phenomenon not uncommon in American history (see Gamson 1975; Jenkins and Perrow 1977). It is hard to believe that it was a coincidence that the civil rights movement won so many of its legislative goals shortly after a majority of Americans had come to favor them.

This conclusion and the preceding chapters raise three further questions: First, how can one explain the divergence between this conclusion and the conclusion of most other people who study the civil rights movement and attribute critical importance to particular dramatic events, like the 1963 March on Washington and the brutal attacks on demonstrators in Birmingham and Selma? Second, if the changes in public opinion about civil rights necessary for congressional action were not the result of movement activity, what were they the result of? And third, what was the relation between the determinants of congressional action examined in this chapter and the specific content of today's EEO law?

Drama and Social Organization as Determinants of Congressional Action

Certain events that took place at the height of the civil rights movement—the March on Washington, brutal attacks on peaceful demonstrators—had a tremendous impact on almost everyone old enough to follow public events in the United States during the early and mid-1960s, and they have been seen as critical to the passage of civil rights legislation. My conclusion is not nearly so dramatic. I suggest that those events, and other less dramatic pro-rights activities, may have speeded up the passage of legislation by making Congress and the public more aware of the intensity of the struggle over civil rights, but that the slow, relatively steady changes in public opinion that had been continuing for many years were more crucial. Who is right?

If one's goal is to explain the passage of a single law, at a particular moment, there is literally no way to be sure who is right. A great deal was happening when the Civil Rights Act of 1964 (or the Voting Rights Act of 1965) was passed—there were peaceful demonstrations, violent demonstrations, attacks on demonstrators, changes in public opinion and media coverage, election campaigns, and so on. With so many things occurring at once, there is no way to determine how important each one was in affecting the passage of legislation. In such circumstances it seems almost natural, at least in the American mainstream, to explain what appears to be an extraordinary outcome—the first civil rights legislation in almost one hundred years—in terms of extraordinary causes, such as demonstrations of unprecedented size and violent lawlessness by the police in full view of reporters and television cameras. This way of thinking is almost irresistible, given the drama of the moment, and is also oddly comforting, in that it allows observers to think of social protest and political violence as aberrations, not as part of the normal American political process (Gamson 1975).

Analyses carried out further from the heat of the moment and with the guidance of theories of democratic politics and social organization are likely to lead one in a different direction, however. One begins to notice that a whole series of civil rights laws were passed over a fifteen-year period, some right after dramatic events, but some when the nation was relatively calm. In addition, public opinion had been moving in a direction favorable to legislation for many years; the dramatic events

were simply manifestations of a long-developing movement (as dramatic events related to other issues often are; see Morris 1981; McAdam
1982; Jenkins and Perrow 1977; Gamson 1975); and Congress responded to events in ways similar to its responses on other issues (Burstein and Freudenburg 1978). The leaders of the civil rights movement
may have been good dramatists (Garrow 1978), but they prepared their
public performances through years of backstage organizing and planning, and their success depended upon the receptiveness of their audience (see Schattschneider 1960). No one can prove that the Civil
Rights Act of 1964 passed because public opinion changed rather than
because of the March on Washington, or the reverse. Nevertheless, the
weight of the evidence indicates that civil rights legislation in general,
and EEO legislation in particular, passed as the result of long-term social
changes manifested in public opinion and forced upon everyone's attention by the civil rights movement.

Why Did Public Opinion Change?

Changes in attitudes on sex roles and race are widely considered to be of
great social and political importance, and they certainly seem to have
affected congressional action on EEO. Why do such attitudes change?
This was an issue that mystified Gunnar Mydral, writing about race
prejudice in the 1940s. Rational analysis told him that it was much
easier to increase prejudice than to decrease it, yet prejudice seemed to
be decreasing. How could this be explained? He believed that there were
two basic answers (1962, 78–80; see also 383–85). First, the "American Creed of Progress, liberty, equality, and humanitarianism" would
gradually influence people's attitudes and turn them away from prejudice (1962, 80). Second, some major American institutions, particularly
schools and churches, tended to operate on a somewhat higher moral
plane than the rest of the society and brought constant pressure to bear
against prejudice.

Myrdal may have been correct. Many of the proponents of civil
rights legislation testifying before congressional committees were
church leaders, and what schools teach about race and gender has
changed greatly over the past century. Nevertheless, Myrdal's ideas
have never really been put to the test, particularly if one wants to know
why specific attitudes have changed at specific rates at particular times.
For example, to assess the influence of schools on prejudice, it would be

important to know what schoolchildren have been taught about race, how their courses have changed over time, and how effectively the lessons are actually communicated to them. In fact, little is known about any of these things.

The research we do have on attitude change touches on points Myrdal raised but ignores the essence of what he had to say. It has been shown that the better educated have more liberal attitudes on sex roles and race than the less educated in the contemporary United States, and that those who have attitudes that are egalitarian in general tend to have attitudes that are egalitarian toward blacks and women specifically (Taylor, Sheatsley, and Greeley 1978; Mason, Czajka, and Arber 1976). Yet we have little idea of why this is so. Historically, the "best" minds have sometimes propounded "scientific" racism and sexism in the universities, and the "most advanced" countries have adopted genocidal racial ideologies (Gould 1981). There is no necessary relation between education and egalitarianism. The American creed may be of crucial importance, but so far no one has managed to capture it and see how it works. There are studies that agree with the conclusion reached above that social protest has not had a significant influence on recent attitude changes in the United States (e.g., Mason, Czajka, and Arber 1976; cf. Jenkins and Perrow 1977, 266), but at the moment we have few ideas and even less evidence about what *has* caused attitudes to change. This is an area that demands further research.

What Congress Did

Congress was stimulated by public opinion and social protest to do something about employment discrimination. But we cannot say from this analysis that either public opinion or the civil rights movement caused Congress to pass Title 7 in 1964 and the Equal Employment Opportunity Act in 1972. That is, the public may have wanted Congress to do *something,* but neither public opinion nor public protest provides much of a guide as to what, specifically, to do. Most citizens do not know anything about the details of specific bills, nor do they care. And demonstrators rarely if ever present drafts of actual bills to legislators. So how did Congress decide what to do?

One thing can we be sure of was that there was little relation between immediate public or movement concerns and the content of the legislation eventually passed. This is best demonstrated by considering what social groups Title 7 protects. It prohibits discrimination on the basis of race, religion, national origin, and sex. An analysis of the factors immediately surrounding passage—public opinion, demonstrations, and the like—provides no reason why this should be so. As the description of the civil rights movement earlier in this chapter showed, almost all of the public civil rights activity of the 1950s and 1960s was by or on behalf of blacks. Public protest against anti-Semitism had almost disappeared, the women's movement did not really get organized until later, and there was never very much protest against national origin discrimination. So if they were included in the law, it was obviously not due to either public protest or intense public concern.

Most of the answer was really provided in chapter 2. What members of Congress were responding to by the mid-1960s was the demand that something be done about employment discrimination. They knew that few people cared much about what specifically should be done, so long as whatever action was decided upon was plausible. As Nelson Polsby has written (1984, 169), "In crisis situations publics may express generalized needs to be led, but evidently care less about the contents, direction, or consequences of the policies pursued." In such a situation it makes perfectly good sense to vote for the bill supported by the members of Congress and interest groups who have wanted legislation all along. Even though the "classic" EEO bill had its genesis in the distant past and had been drafted in response to ideas and demands quite different in some ways from those important in the 1960s and 1970s, there was no reason not to vote for it. As seems to happen fairly frequently (see Polsby 1984; Heclo 1972), contemporary political demands were satisfied by taking old ideas "off the shelf." The possible differences between sources of political demands and sources of political ideas must be taken into account in any good analysis of the determinants of public policy.

Conclusions

The passage of Title 7 in 1964 and the Equal Employment Opportunity Act in 1972 was the result of the conjunction of three forces—public opinion on EEO and civil rights, the civil rights movement, and the ideas that led to the drafting of the law in the particular form it took. Public opinion and the civil rights movement caused Congress to act; the ideas caused Congress to act in the particular way it did.

Public opinion appears to have been the fundamental determinant of congressional action; it seems extremely unlikely that Congress would have passed legislation strongly opposed by virtually all the members from a major region of the country without majority support elsewhere. The civil rights movement also appears to have affected Congress, however, in two ways. First, it probably drew the attention of members of Congress to the issue of civil rights, leading them to monitor public opinion more closely than they might have otherwise, and strengthening the link between public opinion and congressional action. Second, the civil rights movement also provoked a violent response that increased the salience of the issue for the public, which then demanded congressional action.

Anti-rights activity seems to have had two consequences. On the one hand, anti-rights demonstrations and injuries to supporters of civil rights had, to some degree, the intended effect; they reduced congressional support for EEO. On the other hand, violent anti-rights activity increased the salience of civil rights for a public coming to favor federal action on EEO; this would have worked to the advantage of the proponents of civil rights. Neither effect was very large, and it is impossible to say who gained the most, though conventional wisdom is that it was the proponents of civil rights who gained (at a price paid in blood). I think that in an environment becoming steadily more favorable to civil rights, it was the proponents of rights who gained.

Media coverage had no independent effect on the outcome. That is not to say that the media were not important. It is very plausible, as so many have suggested, that media coverage of the activities of the civil rights movement was necessary if the movement was to succeed in getting the public concerned about the issue. But the media did not play an independent role. Coverage followed upon events; it did not, in the aggregate, precede them.

One important part of the public is missing from this picture: women. Before the adoption of Title 7, there was almost no public demand that women be protected by the EEO law. In fact, the passage of Title 7 probably did more to create the women's movement than the women's movement (barely present in 1964) did to influence passage (Freeman 1975). Though the inclusion of women was not entirely fortuitous, as some have suggested (see chap. 2), there was a considerable element of chance involved. We have no theory that can account for this.

This chapter has several implications for theories of democratic pol-

itics. First, the views of those who see public opinion as the chief determinant of legislative action have been vindicated but have also been
shown to be incomplete. Public opinion was crucial, yet what happened
could not be explained without taking into account both social movement activity and the ideas that went into the legislation.

Second, those who see social movements as a critical part of democratic politics have likewise been partly vindicated and partly shown
wanting. The social context, particularly as manifested in public opinion, clearly must be taken into account if we are to understand how
social movements work their effects; but studies of social movements
rarely take the social context seriously enough.

Finally, the conclusions force us to move back a step and ask: If
public opinion is so important, what causes public opinion? There are,
of course, many attempts to discuss how very broad trends in opinion
are affected by global changes in economic, social, and political structures. What we need for the explanation of specific political outcomes
are detailed explanations of changes in opinion in specific areas. These
we do not have.

A piece is still missing from this explanation of congressional action
on EEO: conventional politics. So far we have not considered the role
that elections, political parties, lobbying, and leadership play in congressional action. Chapter 5 deals with their influence.

5 Elections, Lobbying, and Leadership

This chapter is motivated by a question central to the study of democratic politics: Do democratic institutions aggregate the public's preferences and transform them straightforwardly into public policy, or are the preferences seriously misunderstood, distorted, or even manipulated along the way?

However important public opinion and protest groups may be in democratic politics, they can affect the content of bills and the adoption of legislation only when communicated to members of Congress, translated into specific proposals, and acted upon by the entire House and Senate. Broad trends in public opinion are supposed to be communicated to politicians through elections. The specific desires of organized groups are conveyed through lobbying. And Congress as a whole is brought to act by those members whose job it is to decide what Congress does, particularly those in formal leadership positions. This chapter therefore concludes our analysis of congressional action on EEO by showing how it was influenced by elections, lobbying, and leadership. It also considers the possibility that public opinion, shown in previous chapters to be the major determinant of congressional action, was itself produced by the manipulations of political leaders.

Elections

Congressional support for EEO legislation grew as the public's attitudes toward EEO became more favorable. Why?

The most likely reason is elections. Competitive elections are the fundamental institution of democratic politics, the "critical technique," Robert Dahl has written, for ensuring that government leaders will be responsive to the public (1956, 125; see also Lipset 1981, 27–28). Elected officials are believed to do what the public wants because they want very badly to be reelected and think that conspicuous failure to please their constituents will lead to defeat (Mayhew 1974).

The claim that elections are crucial is important but vague. We still need to know *how,* specifically, elections affect congressional action. The conventional view focuses on changes in the party balance. At election time, parties are supposed to provide voters with a choice between alternative sets of policies. The party with the more popular proposals will win, and its victory will ensure that the proposals most closely tied to public opinion will be enacted into law (see, for example, Sullivan and O'Connor 1972; Weissberg 1976). From this perspective, changes in congressional support for EEO legislation would have been related to changes in the party balance. In fact, given today's common view of the Democratic party as more liberal than the Republican party and as the party of minorities, we might expect that congressional support for EEO was correlated with the strength of the Democrats in Congress.

There is an alternative point of view, however. It may be the electoral competition itself rather than the victory of one party that links public opinion to congressional action. Competition between parties motivates them to try to please the public. If a particular policy is clearly desired by a majority, both parties will favor it, and the public will get what it wants no matter who wins. Thus congressional action may have little to do with changes in the party balance (on this view see Downs 1957; Fiorina 1974; Mayhew 1974; Burstein 1981; Page 1978).

Sometimes the parties will disagree, however, and then congressional action may yet depend on shifts in the party balance. This is especially likely when the parties are not sure what people want, when no particular policy has majority support, and when party leaders feel they can do what they want because most people do not care about an issue (Ginsberg 1976; Fiorina 1974; Tufte 1978; Stigler 1972).

Elections may lead to policy change in yet a third way—through the infusion of newcomers into Congress, regardless of party. Incumbents running for reelection are difficult to defeat for reasons only partly related to their policy stands, including visibility, experience in campaigning, and access to campaign funds and the mass media. They also tend to be very cautious about changing their stands on issues, partly because consistency is seen as a virtue (Downs 1957; Mayhew 1974, 67; Burstein 1980). Thus the reelection of incumbents is likely to mean slow congressional adaptation to changing circumstances. When a challenger beats an incumbent, the victory will sometimes be due to his or her greater sensitivity to public opinion and will be likely to lead to support for new, more popular policies. When no incumbent runs, both candidates have an interest in being responsive to public opinion and will be less constrained by prior stands than an incumbent would be. Thus, changes in public policy may be disproportionately due to newly elected senators and representatives.

If the conventional view is correct, therefore, change in congressional support for EEO legislation would have been related to change in the party balance. If the alternate views are correct, congressional support for EEO legislation *might* have been related to the party balance but was more likely related to seniority, with support found disproportionately among relative newcomers.

Previous work on civil rights provides indirect evidence consistent with each point of view but no evidence directly relevant to support for EEO legislation. Studies of the passage of civil rights legislation at the state level show that changes in the party balance may have made a difference, with Democratic legislators somewhat more likely to favor such legislation than Republicans (Erikson 1971; Lockard 1968, 46–58). A study of southern representatives voting on civil rights showed that those with less seniority were slightly more likely to vote for civil rights legislation (Feagin 1972, 495), while a study of civil rights voting by the entire United States Senate from 1957 through 1972 showed that newly elected senators were more likely to vote for civil rights legislation than the senators they replaced, regardless of party (Burstein 1980).

One thing we know with certainty: for much of the period in which EEO legislation was being considered, both parties were unsure how to deal with it or with civil rights in general. Civil rights was effectively a new issue on the national agenda in the 1940s. Most people did not care about it, but those who did—particularly blacks, Jews, and southern whites—cared very strongly, and the pro-rights forces were actively trying to get more people involved. Many people realized that attitudes about discrimination were changing but would have been unable to predict how rapidly or in exactly what direction. As blacks migrated north during and after World War II, their importance as a voting bloc increased, often in closely contested electoral districts (Lawson 1976, chap. 6), but it would have been difficult to estimate how many white votes would be lost, especially in the South, by trying to please blacks at the national level. Theory provides us with little guidance about such a confusing situation—whether the parties would agree or disagree or which would support EEO more strongly.

In fact, candidates of both parties were extremely concerned about how changing attitudes and minority voters would affect their electoral fortunes, and they devoted much effort to deciding what policy proposals would gain them the most (or lose them the fewest) votes. Thus, for example, Truman's strong pro-rights message of 1948 has been described as part of his attempt to prevent Henry Wallace from drawing off black and Jewish votes needed to defeat Dewey in the presidential election (Berman 1970, chap. 3). The situation of many representatives was exemplified by Republican Hugh Scott's 1956 note to presidential adviser Sherman Adams: "I think I ought to have the opportunity to introduce some key Civil Rights Bills. This seems desirable in the interest of the administration and for my own congressional district where I have 22,000 negro voters" (quoted in Lawson 1976, 156–57).[1]

Basically, both national parties tried to adapt to changing circumstances by proposing relatively liberal civil rights legislation, while either exaggerating or downplaying their commitment to civil rights (depending on the tactical considerations of the moment), making ambiguous statements, and behaving inconsistently. This was true even of candidates who had made genuine contributions to minority civil rights, such as Truman and Dewey, opponents in the 1948 presidential race (Berman 1970; Lawson 1976, chap. 6; Morgan 1970, chap. 2). Well into the 1960s, it was far from clear either to blacks or to the white public which party was more favorably disposed to civil rights. The liberal Democrat Adlai Stevenson was allied in 1952 and 1956 with conservative southerners, and many saw Richard Nixon as more liberal than John F. Kennedy in 1960 because of his role in securing passage of the Civil Rights Act of 1957 (Lawson 1976, chap. 7).[2] Given this confusion, it is entirely possible that changes in the party balance had no relation to congressional support for EEO legislation.

Figure 5.1 shows the relation between congressional support for EEO legislation and the percentage of members of Congress (senators and representatives combined) who were Democrats. There is essentially no relation between sponsorship and percentage Democratic; the correlation is .04. EEO legislation did pass when the percentage Democratic was above the 1940–72 mean of 57 percent—it was 61 percent in 1964 and 58 percent in 1972—but it failed to pass when the percentage of Democrats was even higher (as in 1959–60 and 1965–66).[3] Support for EEO legislation had little to do with the strength of the Democratic party in Congress.

Although sponsors of EEO legislation were not especially likely to be

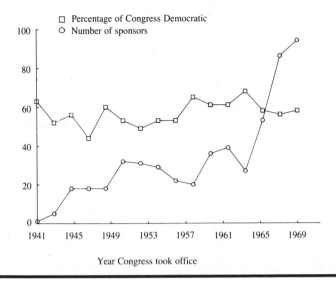

Fig. 5.1   Party balance and sponsorship. Source: *Congressional Quarterly Almanac,* various years.

Democrats, they were likely to be relatively junior members of Congress. Table 5.1 shows that representatives who sponsored EEO bills tended to have served fewer terms than the average representative. In 1964, for example, when Title 7 was adopted, the median number of terms served by all House members was five, while the median number of terms served by sponsors was three. Senators with greater than average seniority tended to be the sponsors of EEO bills in the 1940s, but by the time the number of sponsors became reasonably large, in the 1960s, the average Senate sponsor was less senior than the average senator.

Thus, during most of the period when EEO legislation was being considered, candidates of both parties moved, often hesitantly, toward supporting civil rights legislation, including EEO legislation, probably owing to fear of electoral defeat. Today's identification of the cause of civil rights with the Democratic party did not develop until the late 1960s (see Abramson, Aldrich, and Rohde 1983, 128; Weissberg 1976; Page 1978). The movement toward support for EEO legislation was disproportionately the work of relatively junior members of Congress who, not being confident that their seats were safe, were particularly sensitive to trends in public opinion. Elections affected congressional

Table 5.1   Congressional Seniority and Sponsorship of EEO Bills

Congress	House (median number of terms served by sponsor minus median number served by all members)	Senate (median rank of all members minus median rank of sponsors)
1941–42	0	No sponsors
1943–44	−1	2
1945–46	0	8
1947–48	−1	−5
1949–50	−1	1
1951–52	−1	0
1953–54	−1	1
1955–56	0	0
1957–58	0	0
1959–60	−1	3
1961–62	−1	−8
1963–64	−2*	−6*
1965–66	0*	0
1967–68	0	−1
1969–70	−1	−8*
1971–72	−1*	−4*

Source: U.S. Congress, *Congressional Directory,* various years.
Note: Positive numbers mean sponsors are more senior than average member; negative numbers mean sponsors are less senior. The most senior senator has rank 1.
*Bill passes.

support for EEO legislation by causing both parties to compete for votes in an increasingly liberal climate of opinion and by leading to the infusion of newcomers of both parties, but not by bringing into office one party that was more strongly favorable to EEO legislation than the other.

Elections motivate candidates to heed the wishes of their constituents. But as a device for communicating exactly what these wishes are or how they should be translated into public policy, elections are crude indeed. All they really communicate is which candidates are preferred and, in a very general and possibly ambiguous way, what broad policies are especially liked or disliked by the public (Dahl 1956, chap. 5; Parsons 1959; Abramson, Aldrich, and Rohde 1983). Those wanting detailed information about what policies are desired must look elsewhere. They typically look to lobbyists.

Lobbying

Lobbying, according to the Federal Regulation of Lobbying Act of 1946, is activity intended to influence the passage or defeat of any legislation by the Congress of the United States. Political scientists often define the term even more broadly, encompassing activity intended to influence all official actions of political decision makers, including members of Congress in their oversight as well as legislative capacities, judges, and members of the executive branch.

Under such broad definitions, lobbying seems almost synonymous with politics. As a practical matter, however, most people who discuss lobbying mean something more specific—namely, routine, institutionalized contact between political decision makers and representatives of organized groups who want to influence their decisions.[4] Concretely, this means that a group demonstrating outside a politician's office is involved in social protest activity, not lobbying; if representatives of the group are invited to discuss their demands with the politician and can generally count on such invitations, that is lobbying.

Lobbying is clearly indispensable to representative government. Lobbyists organize the relationship between citizens and politicians. They convey information about citizens' broad preferences to politicians, help translate general interests into specific proposals, and provide information about subtleties in the attitudes of those they represent (Wilson 1973, chaps. 15–16). Members of Congress may know in a general way that people want a law on some subject, but they may want advice on drafting a specific bill to please the greatest number. Lobbying is also vital for those trying to influence Congress. A massive civil rights demonstration may show Congress that people want a civil rights law. But only if the demonstration is combined with lobbying can demonstrators make known exactly what they want.

Despite its indispensability, lobbying is frequently viewed as a threat to representative government. This is because those who are sufficiently organized to get the attention of legislators are seen as unrepresentative of the public as a whole (in particular, they are often richer; see Schatt-schneider 1960, chap. 2) and as able, by virtue of their activities, to get Congress to act in ways opposed to public opinion or the interests of other important groups.

This section describes the lobbying concerned with EEO in particular and civil rights in general. It discusses who lobbied for and against EEO

and civil rights, and how representative of the general public they might
have been; what they lobbied for and what they got; and whether the
lobbying may be seen as having gotten Congress to follow public opinion or as having caused it to act in ways opposed to what the general
public wanted.

Who Lobbied

Analyzing lobbying on civil rights or any other issue is very difficult.
Because lobbying can be conducted almost anywhere, is often carried
out in private, may be combined with other activities, and is regulated
only very loosely, it is very difficult to gauge the amount of lobbying
any particular group does or the total amount concerned with a particular
issue, and it is therefore very difficult to assess its success (for analyses
of the difficulties involved, see Hayes 1981; Congressional Quarterly
Service 1968). What I do here is analyze some especially visible components of lobbying, understanding that doubtless much occurred that we
do not know about.

I consider three types of lobbying, defined as occurring when representatives of a group are "invited in" by decision makers to make their
wishes known. The first is testimony before congressional committees
holding hearings on EEO bills. Such testimony is often described as an
especially important and effective lobbying technique, providing information to members of Congress, legitimacy for the groups testifying,
and publicity for all concerned (Scott and Hunt 1966, chap. 4; Smith
1979; Freeman 1975, 224). Twenty-two hearings on EEO bills were
conducted by House and Senate committees between 1944 and the passage of the Equal Employment Opportunity Act in 1972. The hearings
provided groups and individuals concerned about EEO legislation with
an opportunity to try to influence both the passage of legislation and its
content, by testifying for or against pending bills and particular provisions of bills, justifying their stands, and making claims about the size
and strength of those they represented (the hearings are listed in the
Appendix).

The second type of lobbying is the presentation of amicus curiae
briefs before the United States Supreme Court on civil rights cases. The
presentation of such briefs is obviously not a way to influence legislation
directly but is seen as a form of lobbying in which groups try to influence legal trends to their own advantage and to change the legal climate
in which public opinion is formed and legislation is written. This may be

an especially appropriate technique in the period before the passage of legislation is a realistic possibility, and in fact the NAACP made extremely effective use of the amicus brief for many years before the passage of civil rights legislation (see Krislov 1963; Meek and Wade 1976, 188–90; Wilson 1973, 306).

The final lobbying technique to be described probably comes closest to the popular notion of what lobbying is—meetings between delegations from groups interested in civil rights with policymaking federal or state officials in which civil rights were discussed, as reported by the *New York Times*. As in chapter 4, the distinction is made between delegations dealing specifically with EEO and those dealing with other rights issues or civil rights in general (called "EEO delegations" and "general delegations," respectively). Almost all of the 46 EEO delegations and 193 general delegations reported between 1940 and 1972 were acting on behalf of the rights of blacks.

Table 5.2 describes who testified before Congress on EEO and presented amicus briefs to the Supreme Court on civil rights between 1940 and 1972, both for and against expansion of protection of civil rights. Private (i.e., nongovernment) pro-rights forces were basically of four types: representatives of minority groups who would be protected by civil rights legislation, particularly blacks and Jews; ministers or other representatives of Protestant churches or interfaith organizations, who typically made moral arguments against discrimination; labor unions, particularly the national office of the AFL-CIO and CIO unions, which had liberal records toward blacks; and public interest groups such as the American Civil Liberties Union, Americans for Democratic Action, and the Leadership Conference on Civil Rights (see also Congressional Quarterly Service 1968, 74; Morgan 1970; Kesselman 1948). Government pro-rights forces included pro-rights members of Congress, federal agencies, and state and local governments outside the South; federal agencies and state and local governments started to testify only toward the end of the period.

The pro-rights forces were not exactly representatives of the rich and powerful. The minority groups were, of course, relatively poor and powerless; that was, in a way, what they were complaining about in their testimony. Church groups may exercise considerable moral suasion, but they have little economic or political power. Among those involved, only labor unions would have been considered politically powerful in any conventional sense, and the labor movement itself was

Table 5.2   Pro- and Anti-Rights Interest Group Activity, 1940–72

Type of Group or Organization	Number of Witnesses Testifying before Congress on EEO		Number of Amicus Briefs before Supreme Court on Civil Rights	
	Pro	Anti	Pro	Anti
Black	69	0	9	0
Other racial	2	0	4	0
Jewish	37	0	12	0
Catholic	7	0	1	0
Nationality	9	0	4	0
Women	6	1	0	0
Protestant or nondenominational	27	0	4	0
Employers	11	11	0	2
Employment agency	1	0	0	0
Labor	54	2	14	0
Public interest	33	1	50	4
EEO	14	0	0	2
Federal government	103	41	30	1
Other government	48	8	13	34
Other covered organizations	2	0	0	2
Other	10	2	0	0
Total	433	66	141	45

Sources: Witnesses, congressional hearings: see Appendix. Amicus briefs, Berger 1967 and Mead Data Central 1976 to identify cases, U.S. Supreme Court reports for texts.
Note: Those taking no position not counted. Total number of congressional hearings = 22. Briefs are on all civil rights cases through 1964, EEO only thereafter.

divided on the issue of EEO, since many unions, particularly those in the crafts and building trades, had long histories of blatant discrimination against blacks and other groups.

Although the pro-rights lobbyists tended to represent relatively powerless groups, they appear to have had a major advantage in their attempt to influence public policy: they were not strongly opposed. Probably the most noteworthy thing about the lobbying is how one-sided it was, how dominated by proponents of minority rights. Almost all the private groups and individuals testifying or presenting briefs favored

EEO legislation or the rights of minorities. Most of the opposing witnesses at congressional hearings were government officials, and most of these were either southern members of Congress or representatives of southern state governments, whose opposition could be taken for granted anyway. Most of the anti-rights briefs presented to the Supreme Court were, similarly, from southern governments.[5]

This one-sidedness did not come about because opponents of civil rights were deprived of the opportunity to present their cases. Instead, the opponents, whoever they might have been, chose not to. No one is sure why there was so little organized opposition (it is difficult to study things that do not happen), but some people believe that opponents were sure that southern members of Congress could prevent passage of any major civil rights law (as they had in the past), making it unnecessary to spend the time and effort needed to organize or to publicly appear to favor discrimination and oppose equal treatment (Morgan 1970, 33; Dahl 1967, 425–26; Congressional Quarterly Service 1968, 76). If people were reluctant to publicly oppose civil rights laws because it was seen as awkward to oppose equal treatment, this in itself says something about how public opinion had moved away from supporting discrimination. Yet businesses could certainly have opposed EEO laws on other grounds, including the preservation of business's freedom from government intrusion. Why they did not do so no one knows.

As so often happens in lobbying, those who made their wishes known on EEO were not representative of the public as a whole. There was an effort by pro-EEO members of Congress to have pro-EEO witnesses seen as representing as large a constituency as possible; thus there was a great deal of testimony from white Protestant ministers at early hearings.[6] Nevertheless, it is clear that the movement involved neither the public at large nor many powerful groups with a strong interest in EEO (such as business organizations). The effect of the hearings and court cases, in fact, was to provide forums to groups that often had trouble making themselves heard and to grant legitimacy to their demands and arguments. That there was so little visible, organized opposition other than from the South may have contributed to their success.

What the Lobbyists Wanted

Reading the testimony of all the witnesses who testified before congressional committees shows that they generally wanted the same thing that members of Congress said they wanted during floor debate, as described in chapter 2. That is, they were for the "classic" EEO bill (usually) or against it (sometimes) but had little to say about the details of the bill. Pro-EEO witnesses tended to emphasize three themes: that discrimination was indeed a serious problem, that acting to combat it was a moral imperative, and that doing so would be constitutional.

Evidence that discrimination was a serious problem was provided by social scientists, representatives of civil rights organizations, individuals who had personally suffered from discrimination, and other experts. Discrimination was so pervasive, blatant, and public that it was easy to make this argument convincingly.

The moral argument was made by many types of witnesses but was especially emphasized by the clergymen who testified in great numbers during the early hearings (for example, the first few witnesses at the 1944 hearings of a subcommittee of the House Committee on Education and Labor were all clergymen). There were probably two reasons for this emphasis on moral arguments made by clergymen. The first was the proponents' strategic wisdom of setting up the debate in terms that put them on the side of justice. (The obvious alternative would have been for opponents to put the argument in terms of preventing the expansion of government and thereby preserving freedom.) The second reason was no doubt proponents' weakness; they probably would have preferred strong pro-EEO statements by major employers to those by clergymen, at least to some extent, but could not get any.

The constitutionality issue was a serious one. Although the Supreme Court had become much more permissive toward federal regulation of economic life since the 1930s, many people remained concerned that a federal EEO law (and other proposed civil rights laws) would go further than the Court would be willing to tolerate. Testimony arguing that the proposed law would be constitutional thus formed a frequent and important part of the legislative record (as, for example, at the 1954 and 1963 Senate committee hearings).

Only seldom did witnesses speak about the details of any particular EEO bill. Proponents simply were for the bill and stated why; opponents similarly were simply against. To the extent that there was a concern with content at the hearings, it paralleled the concern shown during the floor debate—that is, it focused on enforcement. Hostile or ambivalent members of Congress might ask witnesses about the virtues of ending discrimination through education and voluntary conciliation rather than legal sanctions; or there would be more than one bill being discussed, one the classic bill and the other a bill with weaker provisions for enforcement. The details of enforcement became a real issue beginning in the early 1960s, as support for EEO legislation grew; then a number of witnesses testified to the importance of giving the government the power to initiate action, of class action suits and, of providing back pay to victims of discrimination, all of which were proposed in the classic bill.

Thus, lobbying was not really an occasion for suggesting changes in the bills being considered. Rather, it seems to have been mostly an opportunity for groups favoring EEO to show that they all agreed that they wanted a particular bill passed. As far as we can tell from published documents, lobbying on EEO would have shown members of Congress (to the extent they took it at face value) that discrimination was widespread, immoral, subject to congressional action, opposed by few people outside the South, and best dealt with by passing the classic EEO bill. Now the question is, Did members of Congress act on this message? And if they did, were they being swayed to act in accord with public opinion?

The Effect of Lobbying

In mainstream political theory, it is not really possible for lobbying to move Congress in a way opposed to the preferences of the public. Elected officials care about reelection more than anything else, and it would be irrational and foolish to vote against the desires of their constituents at the behest of a lobbying group. In fact, members of Congress have said as much, stating that they pay no attention to lobbyists unless the lobbyists can influence voters in their districts (Kingdon 1981). Lobbyists could influence congressional voting in two circumstances: when they want something and the legislator's own constituents simply do not care, and when they manage to mislead the legislator about what his or her constituents want.

Not many people believe that lobbyists lack influence, however. The common view seems to be that lobbyists have great influence and frequently thwart the popular will (Scott and Hunt 1966; Smith 1979).

One could say that lobbying helped Congress respond to public opinion if trends in lobbying—in content and direction—were parallel to trends in public opinion, so that lobbying could be seen as the organized transmittal of public opinion. In contrast, if lobbying and public opinion were moving in opposite directions and Congress acted as the lobbyists wanted, we might have to conclude that the lobbyists were effectively acting against the wishes of the majority, as they are often accused of doing.

Table 5.3 describes trends in five types of lobbying from 1941 through 1972. Witnesses are recorded biennially because each Congress is a single unit of time, legislatively; there is typically one set of hearings (in each house) on an issue in each two-year Congress. Government amicus briefs are included because they can represent attempts by the executive branch of state governments or the federal government to influence the legal climate and indirectly affect congressional action. Table 5.4 shows how lobbying was related to pro-EEO attitudes and congressional support for EEO bills.

Both congressional testimony and private amicus briefs reached high points very early in the struggle for EEO, during the 1940s; they do not show a steady pro-rights trend as attitudes did. In fact, trends in testimony and private amicus briefs are not significantly correlated with either pro-EEO attitudes or congressional sponsorship of EEO bills.[7] Testifying and presenting briefs may have served the purposes of the pro-rights forces, by making their demands known and legitimating both the demands themselves and the arguments made on their behalf, but they were not able to get Congress to act in the absence of supportive public opinion.

The other forms of lobbying—EEO and general delegations, and government amicus briefs—did move in parallel with public opinion and were also correlated with congressional support for EEO bills. General delegations and government amicus briefs both peaked just before the passage of the Civil Rights Act of 1964, and EEO delegations (though very few) did reach their high point while amendments to Title 7 were being debated (though not the year they passed). Lobbying appears to be more highly correlated with pro-EEO attitudes than with congressional sponsorship, however, and of course sponsorship is much more highly correlated with pro-EEO attitudes than with any form of lobbying. In fact, once attitudes are taken into account, the intensity of lobbying has no independent effect whatever on congressional action.[8] In the struggle for EEO legislation, lobbying may have helped to communicate what trends in public opinion were and what actions would satisfy those most concerned about the issue, but it did not get Congress to act in opposition to the desires of the mass public.

Combining this conclusion about lobbying with our understanding of

Table 5.3   Trends in Pro-Rights Interest Group Activity, 1941–72

Year	Witnesses Testifying	EEO Delegations	General Delegations	Private Amicus Briefs	Government Amicus Briefs
1941	0	0	0	0	0
1942		0	0	0	0
1943	45*	2	3	3	0
1944		0	1	12	2
1945	32	3	0	1	0
1946		1	2	2	0
1947	33	1	1	0	0
1948		0	1	40*	3
1949	36	0	1	3	1
1950		2	1	14*	2
1951	0	0	2	0	0
1952		1	2	0	0
1953	26	0	0	7	0
1954		0	0	8	2
1955	8	0	2	1	0
1956		1	11	0	0
1957	0	0	0	0	0
1958		0	2	0	1
1959	7	0	2	0	0
1960		0	4	0	1
1961	57*	1	10	2	2
1962		2	12	0	0
1963	32	4	33*	4	26*
1964		0	30*	3	10
1965	7	5	24	4	0
1966		1	9	0	20*
1967	13	2	6	4	3
1968		7*	12	8	8
1969	33	8*	6	2	5
1970		4	9	4	1
1971	10	0	5	8	8
1972		0	2	4	3

Source: Delegations, *New York Times,* 1941–72; see Appendix.
Note: Peak years starred. Witnesses biennial.

Table 5.4   Lobbying Correlates of Sponsorship and Public Opinion, Seventy-seventh to Ninety-second Congresses, 1941–72

Variable	Correlation with	
	Pro-EEO Attitudes	Sponsorship
Witnesses	−.09	.00
EEO delegations	.48	.48
General delegations	.50	.23
Private amicus briefs	−.15	−.01
Government amicus briefs	.51	.30

the role played by the civil rights movement in the fight for congressional action, we can infer that getting legislation passed can involve a complex division of labor within and among the groups involved. If Congress is to act, its attention must be drawn to an issue; sometimes highly public demonstrations of protest are necessary for this. Then members of Congress must be advised about what to do. Sometimes the same group can play both roles—organizing demonstrations and testifying before Congress. Often, however, the skills and resources needed for the two tasks are different and will be provided by different groups (cf. Sabatier 1975; McCarthy and Zald 1977). Whether the establishment and activities of different groups—for example, the lobbying-oriented NAACP and the demonstration-oriented Southern Christian Leadership Congress—are consciously coordinated or not, all may play important and complementary roles in the ultimate achievement of shared goals (see, e.g., Wilson 1973, chap. 9).

After public opinion became more favorable to minority rights, the civil rights movement grew, and lobbyists made their wishes known, the stage was set for congressional action. Setting the stage does not produce legislation, however. That requires coordinating the activities of the members of two complex organizations—House and Senate—and of the president. This takes organization and leadership.

Leadership

The modern American legislative process is extremely complex. Thousands of bills are introduced in each house during every Congress, many of them involving highly technical subjects, vast amounts of money, or highly controversial issues. The fundamental rules for deciding which bills become law—number of votes needed for passage, possibility of presidential veto, origination of revenue bills in the House, and so on— are established by the Constitution. The rules of everyday operation that enable both houses to deal with the vast amount of business that comes before them, to approve bills and come to agreement with each other, are established by each house. Smooth day-to-day operation depends upon organizational mechanisms for dividing labor among committees, establishing priorities among bills, enforcing rules for debate, and the like.

The formal and informal rules that organize the activities of the House and Senate are implemented by the leaders of both houses. They manage the process in which bills are referred to and considered by committees, given high or low priority, amended, debated, and adopted or rejected. They help maintain party discipline, build coalitions to support favored bills, and try to influence the content of the laws eventually adopted.

A critical issue for those concerned about the democratic political process is the influence of leaders on legislative outcomes. Clearly leaders are necessary if an organization as large as Congress, operating in a complex environment, is to succeed in legislating at all. But there has been considerable debate on whether leaders merely organize Congress so that it can respond effectively to public opinion (or maybe other external influences) or whether they lead Congress to act in ways they desire, without regard for or perhaps even in opposition to what the public wants. House and Senate majority and minority leaders, whips, committee chairs, and other leaders may use their power over the flow of legislation, pork barrel projects, committee assignments, and other matters of concern to members of Congress to influence action in line with their own ideological preferences or desires of special interest groups. So may the president (see the discussions in Kingdon 1981; Jackson 1974; Ferejohn 1974).

Particular political leaders have sometimes been described as having had substantial influence on congressional action on civil rights—Senate minority leader Everett Dirksen on the passage of the Civil Rights Act of 1964, particularly Title 7, and Vice-President Richard Nixon on passage of the Voting Rights Act of 1957, for example (Berman 1966, 77–80; Lawson 1976, chap. 7). In addition, the southern Democrats who disproportionately occupied major committee chairmanships in the House and Senate owing to their seniority have been seen as having slowed the progress of civil rights legislation (Dahl 1967, 416–29; Shuman 1957; Morgan 1970, 1–2).

Probably the most common contemporary opinion about the power of congressional leaders and the president, however, is that they have the power to sway the votes of members of Congress whose constituents do not care very much about an issue and to·arrange vote trading and build coalitions across issues so that those members of Congress whose constituents care strongly can gain the support of those whose constituents do not. They do not seem to have the power to get members of Congress to oppose their constituents' strongly held preferences very often (see Kingdon 1981; Jackson 1974).

Technically, this implies that the influence of leaders upon congressional support for EEO legislation should depend upon how favorable public opinion is toward EEO, and the influence of public opinion should depend on the actions of leaders. If the public opposes EEO, support by leaders will have little or no influence on other members of Congress, who could not typically be swayed to support legislation their constituents opposed. As public opinion shifted in favor of EEO, however, leaders could come to have a substantial influence, as they organized Congress to respond to the changes in public opinion and got apathetic members to support EEO in return for favors on other issues. Similarly, as leaders get involved in a climate becoming more favorable to EEO, the influence of public opinion on Congress could increase, because the leaders help Congress as a whole respond to it effectively.

Figure 5.2 shows the relation between sponsorship of EEO legislation by congressional leaders and total sponsorship, where leaders are defined as House and Senate majority and minority leaders, whips, committee chairs, and ranking minority members of committees.[9] The figure shows that there was an initial rush of enthusiasm for EEO legislation among congressional leaders, which was not shared by other members of Congress; in the late 1940s and early 1950s, a relatively high number of leaders sponsored EEO bills, but few others did.[10] Their lack of ability to get others involved makes sense in light of the fact that the public as a whole was not enthusiastic about EEO at this time. In the mid-1950s, sponsorship by leaders fell to a level more in line with the overall level of congressional support, and, as the figure shows, thereafter support by Congress as a whole moved fairly closely in parallel

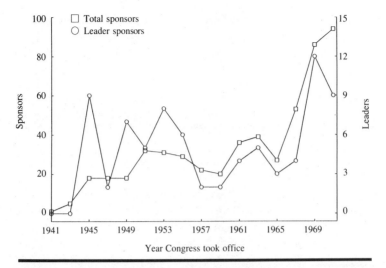

Fig. 5.2   Sponsorship by leaders and total sponsorships. Source: *Congressional Quarterly Almanac,* various years, and U.S. Congress, *Congressional Directory,* various years.

with support by leaders (we know who the formal leaders were, but in the circumstances it appears that they were more like followers at some points). In fact, the correlation between sponsorship by leaders and total sponsorship for the entire period was fairly high at .70 (compared with a correlation of total sponsorship with public opinion of .85).[11]

Presidents did not have a great influence on congressional support for EEO legislation, so far as we can gauge their level of support. Presidents Truman, Johnson, and Nixon publicly favored passing or strengthening EEO legislation, whereas Roosevelt and Kennedy were neutral and Eisenhower was opposed. Sponsorship rose under Truman, but he was unable to get legislation passed; it also rose under Kennedy, who saw congressional leaders press for EEO legislation almost against his opposition (he was sure it could not be passed). Title 7 was adopted under Johnson, but he was unable to get a bill passed mandating administrative enforcement. Overall, the correlation between presidential support for EEO legislation and congressional sponsorship was .42.[12]

Congressional support for EEO legislation was correlated with sponsorship by leaders, but it was also correlated with pro-EEO attitudes. The real question is what influence leadership had on congressional support for EEO legislation once attitudes are taken into account.

The equation in table 5.5 shows that leadership and public attitudes do indeed interact, as suggested above, in their influence on congressional support for EEO legislation. (Anti-rights demonstrations are also included because they too were found, in chapter 4, to affect congressional support.)[13] The positive coefficients for both the attitude and the interaction terms mean that the influence of public opinion on Congress was enhanced by leadership support for EEO legislation. The coefficient for the leadership term is negative, but as noted in chapter 4 (and Stolenzberg 1980), the total effect of a variable in an equation like this depends on the coefficients of both the variable alone and the interaction term, along with the value of the other variable in the interaction term (pro-EEO attitudes here). Taking both coefficients and the values of the variables into account, it turns out that leadership too had a positive effect on congressional support for EEO, and the more strongly the public favored EEO, the stronger the influence of congressional leaders. These statistical results are consistent with the idea that leaders help make Congress sensitive to public opinion but cannot have much effect if they try to move Congress to oppose the public.

Congressional leaders are sometimes thought to be especially influential while a bill is being debated and voted upon; they can determine what amendments will help make the bill acceptable and can collect the votes needed for passage. Unquestionably they do this, and their activities are indispensable if Congress is to act. The question here is whether they can independently shape legislative outcomes, apart from the effect of other factors.

This is, in fact, very difficult to ascertain. At one level, congressional leaders must have an effect, because the public, for example, has no

---

Table 5.5   Determinants of Support for EEO Legislation

$$\text{Sponsors} = -33.0** + 1.03** \text{ (pro-EEO attitudes)}$$
$$(3.3) \qquad (4.6)$$
$$-.36** \text{ (anti-rights demonstrations)} -3.9* \text{ (leader sponsors)}$$
$$(-3.1) \qquad\qquad\qquad\qquad\qquad\qquad (-2.8)$$
$$+.11** \text{ (attitudes} \times \text{ leader sponsors)}$$
$$(4.5)$$

Adjusted $R^2 = .96$ Durbin-Watson $d = 2.8$

*Significant at .05 level, two-tailed test.
**Significant at .01 level, two-tailed test.

opinion on most of the details of particular bills. Somebody has to take care of them, and to the extent that leaders do this, they can have a significant influence on the outcome. If they favor a particular proposal and it is subsequently adopted, however, we cannot conclude that it was their support that made the difference between adoption and rejection. Instead, they may simply have discovered, by gauging the strength of those for and against legislation and the opinions of other senators and representatives, which proposals would be most popular and then proposed them formally themselves. The only way to see if leaders have a real effect on adoption would be to find instances where the same proposal was made twice within a short time (short enough so that the balance of forces would not change), once opposed by the leaders and once supported, and see if their support carried any votes with it other than their own.

Unfortunately this rarely happens, and one is left simply knowing that popular proposals tend to have the support of the leaders, without knowing whether leaders caused the support or were simply acting in response to the same factors as everyone else. Thus, for example, the Senate majority and minority leaders and whips all voted against deleting Title 7 from the 1964 Civil Rights Act, and the overall Senate vote against deletion was 64–33; the leaders and whips all voted for passage of the Civil Rights Act of 1964 as a whole, and it passed 73–27. When the balance of forces is less clear and the House or Senate is divided, the leaders tend to be divided among themselves as well. The House voted for court rather than administrative enforcement in 1971 by the very close vote of 202–197. The House minority whip (Representative Arends) and President Nixon favored this result, but the majority leader and whip and the minority leader (Representatives Boggs, Ford, and O'Neill) all voted against it. When the Senate first opposed court enforcement in 1972 by a vote of 46–48 (preferring administrative enforcement) and later changed its mind and supported court enforcement 45–39, it did so with the majority and minority whips (Senator Byrd of West Virginia and Senator Griffin) and the president favoring court enforcement on both votes, the minority leader (Senator Scott) opposing it on both votes, and the majority leader (Senator Mansfield) opposing it on the first and not voting (but paired against) on the second. It is very difficult to tell whether the leaders are reflecting divisions in the Congress or Congress is reflecting divisions among the leaders, during the actual voting on a bill.

Thus, congressional leaders had an influence on the growth of congressional support for EEO legislation in conjunction with public opinion. The more favorable public opinion was to EEO, the greater the leaders' influence.

It is also difficult to find evidence that leaders could effectively oppose public opinion (at least using the kind of data analyzed above). Such a conclusion seems problematic, however, because it ignores one of the most famous elements of the debate over EEO legislation: the use of the House and Senate rules by prominent congressional leaders—the senior southern Democrats—to delay the passage of civil rights legislation, seemingly for many years. Didn't they cause Congress to oppose public opinion?

A Note on the Structure of American Government

From the very beginning of the congressional debate on civil rights, certain aspects of the rules under which the House and Senate operated were seen as preventing the will of the majority from being enacted into law. The filibuster rule in the Senate required a vote of two-thirds of the senators present and voting to end debate on a bill. This meant that a minority of the Senate—one-third plus one—who opposed a bill could prolong formal debate indefinitely and prevent the bill from ever being voted on, even if a majority (but less than two-thirds) favored it. As early as the 1940s it was claimed that a majority of the Senate favored EEO legislation, and that only the filibuster rule prevented Senate passage of an EEO bill.

In the House, civil rights progress was slowed by the Rules Committee, which essentially serves as a major organizer of the proceedings of the House by establishing priorities among bills on almost all subjects and determining when and how they will be debated. For much of the period when civil rights legislation was being considered, the committee was dominated by southerners adamantly opposed to such legislation, who used their power to keep the House from formally considering civil rights bills on the floor. House and Senate rules (including the seniority system, which gave great power to southerners from the 1930s through the 1960s) were therefore seen as making Congress itself a "formidable obstacle" to civil rights progress (Dahl 1967, 417).

But how great an obstacle did these rules really present? Could civil rights legislation have been adopted much earlier had congressional rules not placed impediments in the way of rule by simple majorities?

There is little doubt that EEO legislation could have been adopted somewhat earlier if the sentiment of simple majorities were all that mattered. It is obviously more difficult to get a two-thirds vote in favor of a measure than a simple majority. Public opinion was gradually but steadily becoming more favorable to EEO, so it is easy to imagine legislation passing earlier had it not been stymied by the rules.

How much earlier is less obvious. Early attempts to overcome civil rights filibusters have been described as relatively lackadaisical and even as a "sham, if not a fraud" (Maslow 1946, 440; see also chap. 3 above). Those favoring EEO legislation acted as if they wanted an EEO bill adopted, but not badly enough to organize a serious fight against determined opposition by southern Democrats. As noted in chapter 3, this level of commitment seems reasonable, given that most Americans did not care much about EEO and, to the extent they did care, were about as likely to oppose it as to favor it. Some of the supporters of EEO legislation were probably doing something that is quite common in Congress—taking a stand on a moral or good government issue, out of either sincere belief or a desire to impress the relatively few constituents who would care, without really expecting anything to come of it (see, e.g., Hayes 1981, 119; Mayhew 1974, 132–36). Their support for EEO legislation was real, but in a situation in which most voters were indifferent at best and many congressional colleagues were opposed, EEO legislation was not important enough to fight for seriously.[14]

Until the early 1960s there would have been little reason to believe that a majority of Americans wanted an EEO law. The congressional failure to enact a law may not have been morally praiseworthy, but it was probably not out of line with public opinion. Even if by the late 1940s a majority of people favored EEO for blacks in principle (without necessarily wanting a law), the issue was important mainly to the southern opponents of civil rights; thus an apathetic majority confronted a passionate minority on the issue. Philosophical debates about the role played by intensity of preferences in a democracy will go on forever, but there is no doubt that much of the formal structure of American government is designed to protect the rights of minorities who feel intensely about an issue (for example, the need for greater than simple majority votes to amend the Constitution, and there being two senators from every state regardless of population). Probably minorities who care intensely about an issue will tend to get their way disproportionately in any political system, and the structure of American government enhances this possibility. Given the intensity of southern opposition to civil rights laws, it is difficult to imagine an EEO law's being adopted until at least a fair proportion of those outside the South came to feel intensely about the issue. This certainly did not happen until the late 1950s, and maybe not until the early 1960s. I would say that the filibuster rule, the power of the House Rules Committee, and other impediments to majority rule may have delayed the passage of Title 7 by three or four years at most. This is not a trival amount of time for those involved, but it is not the fifteen- or twenty-year obstacle to progress that some have suggested. As Louis Kesselman discerned in the late 1940s, shortly after the initial disappointments with congressional inaction, an explanation for the failure to pass on EEO law "should be centered largely upon the forces which sought to persuade Congress to enact the desired legislation, rather than upon parliamentary maneuvers" (1948, x–xi).

This conclusion may apply to the adoption of new policies generally, not just to EEO or civil rights. In his study of policy innovation, Nelson Polsby concluded that leaders are often given more credit for the adoption of policies than they deserve, simply because they are so prominent in the discussions taking place right before enactment, when more people are paying attention to policy debates than at any other time. What leaders really do, Polsby writes, is act as political brokers, selecting from among alternative possible policies the politically viable proposal and then "channeling energies that were too strong for them to resist. Thus politically neutral—even mildly unfriendly—politicians can be enlisted to the cause of policy innovation when forces in the political system come together to demand that the search for a policy outcome bear fruit" (1984, 128).

What Caused Public Opinion to Change? (Reprise)

Even after taking into account elections, lobbying, and leadership, public opinion remains the paramount determinant of congressional action, albeit transformed and organized into support for specific bills by lobbying and leadership. As in chapter 4, it is necessary to ask at this point whether public opinion itself was created by other forces, particularly lobbying and leadership.

Political opinions in general are shaped by a society's elites and domi-

nant institutions. American schoolchildren are taught the virtues of representative government, the two-party system, private enterprise, and so
on. Political leaders can strongly influence perceptions about which possible policies are reasonable ways for dealing with specific issues and
which are not and thus can structure political debate (Weissberg 1976,
chap. 10; Lindblom 1977, chap. 15). Specific leaders, particularly the
president, often have the power to shift opinion on particular issues,
especially in times of crisis. And some people believe that changes in
whites' opinions about racial equality have been the product of changes in
the law and public policy, rather than the cause (e.g., Dye 1971, chap. 8).

Although people's opinions are influenced by elites and dominant
institutions, it is difficult to show that they can be systematically affected
in predictable ways, to the point where we could say that elites were
consciously and effectively creating public "demand" for policies the
elites themselves wanted in the first place. Beliefs acquired early in life
are not easily changed, particularly when people care about an issue, are
reinforced in their beliefs by their friends and acquaintances, and are
indifferent to or ignorant of views that elites are trying to disseminate
through the mass media.

Those who lobbied before Congress on behalf of EEO certainly
wanted to influence public opinion as well as the view of members of
Congress, and they were probably aided in their attempt by some of
their congressional supporters, who helped see to it that white Protestant
ministers testified and put the issue of EEO in moral terms. Those who
filed amicus briefs hoped to change the legal climate, and ultimately the
public's ideas about what constituted acceptable behavior on racial matters. In the long run, the lobbyists may have altered public opinion. In
the short run, however, hearings and court decisions have small audiences, and it is far from clear that even widely publicized decisions
like *Brown v. Board of Education* change many minds.

The influence of leaders is questionable as well. From the 1940s on,
the most conspicuous attempt by a major political figure to lead the
public on civil rights was that made by President Truman. He integrated
the armed forces, made strong public statements opposing discrimination in many areas, and sent strong civil rights bills to Congress. Yet he
was unable to sway Congress, and there is no evidence that he significantly changed public opinion (Dahl 1967, 417). Public opinion was
moving generally in a pro-rights direction during his term of office, but
the trend does not seem to have been affected by any specific actions by

Truman, or by Eisenhower, who generally opposed federal action on civil rights, or by Kennedy, who supported civil rights legislation but was hardly militant.

Something caused public opinion to change, and it is likely that elites and major institutions played a role. But we have no evidence that short-term attempts to manipulate opinion were effective or that anyone developed a long-term strategy for affecting opinion that was likely to have predictable results (see Wilson 1973, 330; cf. Berman 1970, chap. 5; Miroff 1981). Robert Dahl has written that the passage of the Civil Rights Act of 1964 "came only after a tidal change in public attitudes, brought on by a collection of events and circumstances beyond the power of any one person to shape, control, or even channel" (1967, 428). I think he goes too far. Some shaping and channeling did take place. But his essential idea—that attitudes were critical, changing, and yet not manipulable in any predictable way—seems correct.

Conclusions

The formal and informal institutions of democratic government played a significant role in the adoption of today's EEO law, but not always in the way conventionally attributed to them.

Elections increased congressional support for EEO legislation, but not because the party that favored EEO won and the other party lost. Instead, electoral competition and the fear of losing seats in a climate characterized by uncertainty and also by increasingly positive attitudes toward EEO led both major parties to favor EEO legislation roughly equally, at least through the mid-1960s. In addition, the election of new senators and representatives led to increases in congressional support for EEO, because newcomers were more likely than senior members to support EEO legislation, regardless of party.

Lobbying transformed general desires for EEO legislation into support for a specific legislative proposal, helped set the terms of the debate, legitimated the demands of pro-EEO forces and their arguments, and provided information about the breadth of their support. In the process of transforming general desires into specific proposals, lobbyists play an active role in the legislative process. The public's preferences are usually so general that they may be satisfied any number of ways; when lobbyists settle on one way in particular, they are playing a role in determining the substance of policy. There is no evidence, however, that lobbyists for EEO legislation made proposals objected to by those they were representing, or that lobbying caused Congress to act in ways opposed to public opinion.

Those in formal leadership positions in Congress played a major role in the adoption of EEO legislation, but primarily as organizers of the congressional response to public opinion rather than as actors powerful in their own right. The fairly substantial group of leaders who supported EEO legislation during the 1940s and early 1950s were unable to win over many of their colleagues, probably because they were too far ahead of public opinion. When public opinion came to favor EEO legislation more strongly, leaders were able to exert considerable influence, gaining many colleagues' support for EEO legislation. The president exerted no such power. The House and Senate rules, along with the positions of southern Democrats strategically placed to take advantage of them, may have slowed the adoption of EEO legislation, but probably only for several years at the most. For much of the period when EEO was being debated, the legislative struggle was a classic one between an apathetic majority wanting action and a determined minority opposing it. It is no surprise that the minority can slow things down a bit in such circumstances. One consequence of this is that when legislation was passed, it was at the behest of a determined majority that had devoted considerable effort to achieving its goal; victories won under such conditions are not likely to be easily reversed.

It is thus difficult to show that those in positions of leadership have the power to move Congress in ways opposed by the public for any length of time. It is also difficult to find evidence that political leaders or other elites manipulated public opinion in such a way that apparent congressional responsiveness to public opinion was actually responsiveness to the desires of elites. No doubt elites mold opinion. But many elite and nonelite groups try to do so, and it is impossible to show at this point that any particular group can do so with any assurance of how its efforts will turn out.

Congressional action on EEO was the product of a complex set of forces. The possibility of action was raised by changes in attitudes—formalized in legal doctrine—about the role of government during the 1930s. The ideas for legislation grew out of the political and legal climate of the New Deal. Congress acted on these ideas largely because of shifts in public opinion, but the congressional response was hardly automatic—it was affected by lobbying, electoral competition, the infusion of new blood through turnover, the intense feelings generated by the civil rights movement and its opponents, and the actions of congressinal leaders. The result was a piece of much-delayed New Deal legislation finally completed in the 1970s as the product of a political campaign that was both peaceful and violent, dramatic and plodding, idealistic and practical. The American political system proved to be open to change and responsive to public opinion, but also resistant to pleas from the disadvantaged.

Finally, EEO legislation seen as strong by the entire mainstream of American politics was adopted. What happened then? Was it really strong enough to end discrimination in employment? Or was it effective as symbolism, at least for a time, but ineffective as an instrument against discrimination? This is the subject of succeeding chapters.

6 Consequences of the Struggle for Equal Employment Opportunity

Equal employment opportunity legislation was adopted as the result of social changes that were manifested in public opinion, crystallized in the civil rights and women's movements, and transformed into public policy by political leaders. Once adopted, the legislation provided an enforcement mechanism through which the struggle for EEO could be pursued, and it may thereby have contributed to further changes in American society. What have been the consequences of the struggle for EEO and the passage of legislation?

There are two major approaches to answering these questions, and something near to two standard sets of answers. The first approach is that of essay writers and journalists concerned with broad social trends, who draw on a wide range of often anecdotal evidence. They frequently conclude that EEO legislation has had a radical impact on American society, dividing Americans by race and national origin into groups entitled to special privileges (White 1982, 32), destroying the autonomy of local governments (Glazer 1978, ix), and assaulting basic notions of individual worth and merit (Looking Backward 1980, 34).

The second approach is that of those who use the methods and statistical techniques of contemporary social science. This approach has been developed primarily by economists, whose statistical analyses show that the incomes of nonwhite men have risen significantly since World War II compared with those of white men. They attribute most of the income gain to increasing relative productivity, however, and see EEO legislation as having been of little consequence. Economists Richard Butler and James Heckman bluntly state, "there is no evidence that government antidiscrimination policy has had any impact on eliminating black-white wage differentials" (1977, 267). Somewhat in contrast to studies of racial income differences, a couple of analyses of male/female income differences conclude that EEO legislation may have had a modest positive effect on women's relative incomes (see Beller 1979), but these studies must confront the fact that, by some measures, women's incomes compared with men's are actually lower now than they were thirty years ago (see below). Thus, the statistical analyses hardly show the struggle for EEO as having had radical consequences; instead, it is difficult to find any effect at all.[1]

This chapter and the next reassess the consequences of the movement for EEO. The reassessment begins with both respect and skepticism toward the two approaches just described—respect for the breadth of concerns manifested in the first approach but skepticism toward its unsystematic use of evidence, and respect for the methodological rigor of the economists' approach but skepticism toward its narrow focus on economic concerns.

The reassessment also begins by examining the political and social context of the fight for EEO. Those favoring EEO wanted to end employment discrimination and thereby to improve the economic status of those who had been discriminated against. By focusing so much of their effort on the fight for EEO legislation, they were presumably operating on the basis of two implicit hypotheses about American society: first, that legislation was *necessary,* because discrimination would not disappear unless it were made illegal, and second, that legislation would be *effective,* because the allocation of rewards in society is partly political and can be changed through democratic politics.

If one views the process of income allocation as partly social and political as well as economic and sees the drive for legislation as just one possible strategy among many, five conclusions follow that have significant implications for assessing the consequences of the struggle for EEO.

First, the focus on legislation had implications for the use of resources in the struggle; devoting resources to monitoring and enforcement may mean fewer are available for applying other kinds of pressure on discriminators, such as demonstrations or boycotts. This possibility is not considered in systematic studies of the effect of EEO legislation.

Second, the hypothesis that legislation was necessary to end discrimination could be wrong. Discrimination could end because it is economically inefficient (Becker 1971), because of increasing education and the spread of liberal ideas about race and gender, or for other reasons. If this happened, EEO legislation might be unnecessary, and its passage might just represent symbolic recognition of changes taking place in the society anyway. Decreases in discrimination not caused by legislation are not analyzed in economists' work on EEO.

Third, the hypothesis that legislation can be effective could be wrong, because people find ways to evade it (Lazear 1979), because enforcement is lax, or simply because "you can't legislate morality." This, of course, is the conclusion of considerable previous work.

Fourth, though statistical analyses treat EEO legislation as hypothetically affecting the distribution of income to individuals, the legislation is in fact concerned to a large degree with group membership—male or female, black or white, and so on. It was the result of political activity by and on behalf of group members, and in the end it will affect them as group members. If the legislation leads to increases in the relative incomes of group members, part of the increase is likely to be used to further the groups' political ends and consequently may lead to additional increases in income (Lieberson 1980, chap. 3). Thus, because EEO legislation may have political as well as economic implications for groups as well as individuals, any analysis should consider the income accruing to the relevant social groups. No previous analysis does this.

Fifth, to the extent that income allocation is a process in which social groups are struggling for advantage, the relative position of all the groups must be considered simultaneously, because one's gain may be another's loss. This point has been noted by many people over the years (e.g., Stern, Gove, and Galle 1976) but has been ignored in analyses of the effect of EEO legislation. Thus we have no idea whether EEO legislation might be causing one disadvantaged group to gain at the expense of another rather than at the expense of the white men who dominate the economy.

This study draws on economists' formal models but places them in a larger context, thereby presenting what might be called a political approach to the analysis of the struggle for EEO. Adopting this approach makes it possible to go beyond past work and systematically consider the political implications of the passage of legislation, the effect of social change on the struggle for EEO, and the implications of EEO for the economic status of social groups.

Those who sought EEO had two immediate goals: the passage of legislation that would legitimate their demands and provide an institutional channel for the redress of grievances, and changes in the labor market that would end discrimination and lead to increases in the income and status of those who had been discriminated against. This chapter focuses on the achievement of those goals. Other longer-term goals, which were articulated less often and were unintended consequences of the struggle for EEO, will be dealt with in the next chapter.

Possible Immediate Political Consequences of EEO Legislation

When adopted, EEO legislation was radical in its promise. It employed the language of a traditional American value—equal opportunity—but its demand that the value be implemented in the treatment of minorities and women implied major changes in operation by employers, unions, and government. Both those who favored the legislation and those who opposed it were aware that what was being proposed was no small matter. In addition, as I just mentioned, in the years since passage some people have come to see EEO legislation as even more radical and disruptive than originally imagined.

However radical the legislation might be in some respects, it was conservative in two important ways. First, it was quite traditional in the structure it provided for achieving EEO. As a delayed piece of New Deal legislation, Title 7 created enforcement procedures closely modeled on those of other statutes, oriented toward protecting the rights of the accused, voluntary conciliation, case-by-case resolution, and heavy reliance on prosecution by individual victims of discrimination. The Voting Rights Act of 1965, with its categorical presumption of discrimination and its direct approach to enforcement, was a much greater departure from tradition. Title 7 represented no significant change in the way government went about its business.

Second, EEO legislation was conservative in that it preserved public order. By passing legislation, Congress formally legitimated the goal of EEO and established a legal framework and administrative agencies ostensibly designed to make EEO a reality. To some extent the movement seems to have responded to this action by giving up public, "disruptive," "unconventional" ways of dramatizing its demands and diverting some of its resources to working through the channels provided by Congress. As figure 6.1 shows, demonstrations for EEO and civil rights generally fell after the passage of legislation, whereas complaints to the Equal Employment Opportunity Commission (EEOC) and appeals to the courts rose. Thus was engineered a trade-off apparently common in American politics: protest groups give up disruptive protest and reaffirm the legitimacy of "conventional channels" and power arrangements in

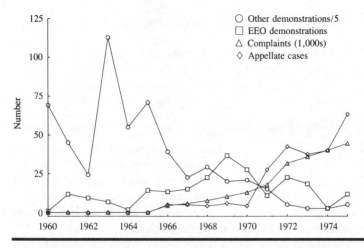

Fig. 6.1   Protests and EEO enforcement. Sources: Charges to the EEOC: from EEOC annual reports, 1967–76; reports 8 and 9 (fiscal years 1973 and 1974) use a different reporting system than the other reports, so charges were estimated by interpolation. The reporting system has changed so much in recent years that a longer time series could not be calculated. Court cases: Decisions reported in Bureau of National Affairs (1969–78) for U.S. Courts of Appeals and U.S. Supreme Court coded on an annual basis. This includes all cases decided under Equal Pay Act of 1963 and all cases decided under the following laws decided after 2 July 1965 (the date Title 7 went into effect): Title 7, Railway Labor Act, Taft-Hartley Act, the Civil Rights Acts of 1866 and 1871, and U.S. Constitution, based on complaint of discrimination on the basis of sex, race, national origin, or religion. Decisions had to have been handed down before 1 January 1978. Reverse discrimination cases were not included.

return for a grant of recognition and promise of future rewards from the authorities (McAdam 1982; Freeman 1975, chap. 6; Gamson 1975, chap. 3).

No one formally sat down and agreed to this tradeoff, needless to say. And other things, including repressive government activities, were also working to reduce the level of protest, or at least especially violent or threatening protest. Nevertheless, those involved acted *as if* such a trade-off had been arranged, as often seen in other political conflicts (McAdam 1982; Tilly 1978). EEO and other civil rights legislation apparently helped bring a return to political order at a time of crisis.

What did those in the movement for EEO receive in return for diverting their resources into conventional channels? And how successful has the movement for EEO been in changing labor market outcomes? The rest of this chapter tries to answer these questions.

The Effect on Incomes of the Struggle for EEO

Among social scientists, only economists have persistently tried to gauge precisely the effect of the struggle for EEO on the incomes of groups that have been discriminated against, and they have developed a fairly standard way of doing so.[2] They begin, naturally, by asking why blacks have lower incomes than whites and women lower incomes than men, and they posit two basic answers. The first is that their productivity may be lower; they produce less, and so, inevitably, they will be paid less. Productivity is difficult to measure, and economists (and other social scientists) try to gauge it in a variety of ways, the most common of which is education, seen as "human capital" contributing to productivity on the job. And indeed, it is plausible that blacks earn less than whites because they have traditionally had so much less education.

The second reason for intergroup income differences is discrimination (or occasionally some other aspect of the social context, such as cultural beliefs about the proper division of labor in the family that lead men but not women to devote themselves full time to careers). For example, white men may have a "taste for discrimination" that causes them to dislike being involved in certain kinds of social relationships with blacks, such as employer or fellow employee. White men might overcome this dislike, but only if they were paid to. A firm's white employees might be willing to work with a black only if he were paid less than they were, with the extra money going to them as payment for overcoming their aversion to working with him. More generally, the approach involves a formalization of the commonsense idea that prejudice against nonwhites and women in the labor market translates directly into lower incomes for them.

In addition to productivity and discrimination, two other factors may affect the relative incomes of women and nonwhites, at least in a society where discrimination coexists with attempts to reduce it. The first is the availability of jobs. Because white men can resist opening new job opportunities to nonwhites and women—through seniority rules, on-the-job hostility and sabotage, and the like—nonwhite and female progress is much more likely when many jobs are available (see, e.g., Bell 1974). Nonwhites and women are likely to gain on white men in prosperous times and to fall behind when unemployment rises.

The second additional factor possibly affecting the incomes of women and nonwhites is the enforcement of EEO legislation. Hypothetically,

EEO legislation makes it expensive to discriminate by requiring discriminators to defend themselves in costly legal cases, compensate victims of discrimination, and so forth. Employers' and unions' desires to avoid these expenses should lead them to discriminate less (see, e.g., Hill 1977, 4; Levitan, Johnston, and Taggart 1975, chap. 13).

Within this theoretical context, economists attempt to explain intergroup income differences and gauge the effect of EEO legislation by following what is to them a fairly obvious course. They find published measures of income, compute black/white or female/male income differences, and statistically analyze the effect on these differences of relative productivity, the availability of jobs, and the enforcement of EEO legislation. They leave the social context, including the "taste for discrimination," out of their analyses (more on this below).

From the political perspective referred to above, there are at least three major flaws in this approach. First, ignoring prejudiced attitudes (taste for discrimination) or other relevant aspects of the social context makes no sense at all. This neglect apparently stems from economists' reluctance to deal with noneconomic variables. But the neglect may have serious consequences for our understanding of changes in black/white or female/male income differences. Because attitudes toward blacks and women in the labor market have become more favorable at the same time as EEO legislation has been passed and enforced, black or female gains in relative income may very well be due to changes in *both* enforcement *and* attitudes. If only one of the two— enforcement—is included in the analysis, then all gains due to both may be attributed only to the one included. Previous analyses may therefore overestimate the influence of EEO legislation by attributing to it an effect that is really the result of changing attitudes, and of course they may underestimate the influence of attitudes by ignoring them entirely. Everyone studying sex and race discrimination knows this. Otis Dudley Duncan has pointed out to economists analyzing sex discrimination, for example, that they are too cavalier about the consequences of leaving out of the scope of their studies attitudes and the division of labor between husbands and wives. "Most feminists and many sociologists," he has written, "would presumably respond that with this much of the problem out of scope, what remains is likely to be misleading" (1974, S109). And Thomas Sowell has noted, in his analysis of racial discrimination, that "black income as a percentage of white income rose significantly after passage of the Civil Rights Act of 1964—whether because

of the Act or because *the changed public opinion which made the Act
possible also made possible a reduction in hiring discrimination*"
(1981, 115; emphasis added). Yet though analysts know, at some level,
that social and political factors influence income differences, they do not
act on this knowledge by taking such factors formally into account.[3]

Adding attitudes to the models may affect our interpretation of how
labor markets work, in ways going beyond estimates of the effect of
particular factors. By including enforcement but leaving out attitudes,
previous work causes us to focus on the legal and economic determinants of labor market outcomes while neglecting the social and political
factors. The importance of attitude change in causing EEO legislation to
be adopted in the first place makes this omission especially serious. As
Butler and Heckman write, "any analysis of policy impact is incomplete
and purely descriptive until some account is made of how the policy
came into existence. Virtually none of the estimates of program impact
reported [previously] can be used . . . without regard to the factors that
cause policy to be effected" (1977, 251–52).

The second flaw in the standard approach is the way income is measured. The measurement of inequality in studies of EEO has been both
eclectic and routine, using whatever data are readily available. Three
measures of income are especially popular: median wage and salary
income of year-round full-time workers, which is often seen as the best
measure of what EEO legislation was designed to affect, the opportunities available to full-time employed members of the labor force; median wage and salary income of all those with such income, which
gauges the opportunities available to everyone who is employed; and
median total money income, which includes income from social security
payments, welfare, dividends, interest, and so on, as well as wages and
salaries and is therefore seen as probably the best measure of overall
individual economic well-being (see Freeman 1973, 73; Masters 1975,
142).

These measures are of course useful (in fact, two will be used below), but their unthinking use leads to the neglect of two important
aspects of intergroup income inequality. First, the measures exclude a
high proportion of adults not in the labor force, because only those with
certain kinds of income are included in the figures. This causes us to
ignore the effect of labor force participation on economic well-being and
the possible effect of the struggle for EEO on such participation. For
example, as Butler and Heckman point out (1977, 250), if legislation

drives low-wage blacks out of the labor force (for reasons they elaborate), those who leave will not have their incomes included in the census wage and salary data. Black incomes will *appear* to rise relative to white incomes, but only because many of those with low incomes are no longer included in the figures, *not* because the income of the average black has risen.

Similarly, supporters of the women's movement often point out that women's earnings seem to be stuck at about 60 percent of men's despite apparent advances in the status of women. This apparent lack of progress can be partly explained by the entry of large numbers of women into the labor force in recent years. As inexperienced workers, they are likely to have relatively low wages and therefore drag down the average income for women as a group (Blau 1984 warns against exaggerating the magnitude of this effect, but there is no doubt it is of some consequence). Thus, if a woman is not in the labor force and her earnings are zero, she is not part of the figures on wage and salary income. If she goes to work and makes the wage typical for a new entrant into the labor force, she becomes part of those counted in the official figures and probably drags down the average. Her increase in income will be measured as contributing to a decline in the status of women. This seems absurd.

Thus, because labor force participation can affect economic well-being, it is important to take into account movement into and out of the labor force when calculating the average income of group members. What this implies, however, is that a valid measure of intergroup income inequality will take into account *everyone* in the relevant groups who *could* enter the labor force, because the decision to do so will affect measured inequality and because it will be affected, at least for some people, by EEO legislation.

This conclusion makes plain the second aspect of inequality neglected by standard measures—inequality between groups as opposed to inequality between individuals. Of course, groups are being compared with each other in standard measures—blacks to whites, women to men. The problem is that the groups are treated merely as aggregates of income-earning individuals. If there is anything to the argument presented at the beginning of the chapter, however—that income allocation is partly political and oriented to group membership—then the total resources available to groups as potential political actors must be an important concern. If a group's income may be affected by its ability to use its resources to organize politically, then analyses of inequality must consider the income accruing to entire groups, not just those fractions of them that happen to be in the labor force.[4]

The third flaw in the standard approach is its dealing separately with race and sex discrimination. Doing so may exaggerate the progress of nonwhite women by comparing them with white women who are themselves discriminated against; it ignores the possibility that nonwhites are gaining at the expense of women, or vice versa; and it tempts us to develop separate theoretical frameworks for dealing with race and sex discrimination, where a unified framework would be preferable.

The analysis presented below is guided by past work but improves upon it by taking the social context into account, interpreting income as payments to social groups as well as to individuals, and dealing simultaneously with sex and race discrimination.

What Is to Be Explained

This analysis considers the effect of the struggle for EEO on the relative incomes of different groups measured in three ways. The first two employ income measures commonly used in analyses of EEO effect: median wage and salary income of all those with such income, which measures what EEO legislation was most clearly directed at—rewards for the working—and median total money income, as a measure of general individual welfare. In contrast to most previous studies, the incomes of nonwhite men, nonwhite women, *and* white women will be compared with those of white men. White men were the implicit comparison group in the law and should be the comparison group in any study of relative incomes. The actual variables are the relative incomes of each group, measured as a percentage of the income of white men. The data run from 1948, the first year they are available, through 1978.

The third measure is less conventional but follows from the argument above that income should be seen as accruing to all those in a social group, rather than just to those in the labor force or even just those with income. It is a measure of the *proportion of total income* going to each of the four relevant groups—white men, nonwhite men, white women, and nonwhite women—relative to each group's *proportion of the total population,* taking into account everyone old enough to be in the labor force, regardless of whether they were working or had income. This is calculated by multiplying the mean income per person in each group by the total number *with income* (to get total group income), then dividing that by total group membership to get mean income for *everyone* in the group and dividing that by the mean income per person for all four groups weighted by group size. Thus, if white men constituted 45 percent of the population but received 60 percent of all income, their "group share" would be 60/45, or 1.33.

This measure may be less intuitively obvious than the first two, but it has three advantages over them. First, it avoids using an earnings measure that goes *down* as a woman's earnings *rise* from zero when she enters the labor force and that *rises* as the income of a discouraged worker goes *down* when he leaves the labor force. Second, it measures relative resources available to social *groups* (as opposed to people in the labor force), thereby defining the income distribution process as a political one oriented to groups as well as an individual-level one oriented to employment. Third, encompassing all four groups, it makes it easier to see how the relative earnings of each group are related to the earnings of all the others. One important fact this measure makes clear is that the cost of changes in intergroup inequality depends on group size, which is therefore highly relevant to an analysis of change in relative group incomes. Because black men are such a small proportion of the population in the United States, they can gain relative to white men without white men's having to give up nearly as much as the blacks are gaining, per capita. This is clearly not the case for white women. (Further implications of group size are discussed in chap. 7.) The data for this measure of group share run from 1953 through 1978.[5]

Figures 6.2 through 6.4 and table 6.1 show how relative earnings, income, and group share have varied over the years. The figures for earnings (fig. 6.2) and income (fig. 6.3), along with the table, tell a familiar story. Nonwhite men and women have made considerable gains in relative income during the past twenty-five to thirty years, but they still have a long way to go before catching up with white men. The figures and the table also show that nonwhite relative incomes were changing slowly (in the case of nonwhite male total income, even declining somewhat) before the passage of civil rights legislation but have risen more rapidly since 1964, particularly for nonwhite women. Thus, for example, relative nonwhite male earnings had their ups and downs from the late 1940s through the early 1960s but were almost the same percentage of white male earnings in 1964 as they were in 1948—58.5 percent as opposed to 59.6 percent. After the passage of Title 7, however, relative earnings rose to a peak of 73.4 percent before falling back a

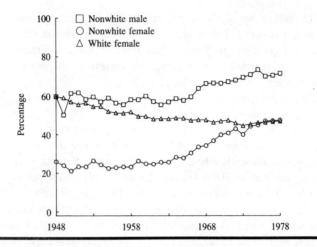

Fig. 6.2   Median earnings as percentage of white men's. Source: U.S. Bureau of the Census, *Current Population Reports,* series P-60.

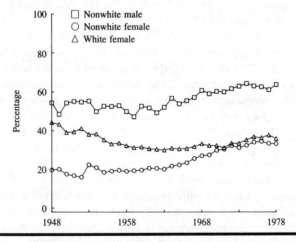

Fig. 6.3   Total incomes as percentage of white men's. Source: U.S. Bureau of the Census, *Current Population Reports,* series P-60.

Table 6.1   Minimum and Maximum Relative Group Incomes

	Minimum	Maximum
Earnings relative to those of white men, 1948–78 (%)		
Nonwhite men	50.0 in 1949	73.4 in 1975
Nonwhite women	21.0 in 1950	47.3 in 1978
White women	44.5 in 1973	59.6 in 1948
Median total income relative to that of white men, 1948–78 (%)		
Nonwhite men	47.1 in 1959	64.3 in 1974
Nonwhite women	15.9 in 1952	34.4 in 1976
White women	29.9 in 1963	44.4 in 1948
Group share as percentage of parity, 1953–78		
White men	156.2 in 1978	175.5 in 1953
Nonwhite men	86.9 in 1962	98.6 in 1974
Nonwhite women	28.5 in 1955	52.1 in 1978
White women	38.5 in 1953	55.7 in 1978

bit in the late 1970s. Relative nonwhite female earnings tell a similar story. They barely changed until the passage of Title 7, moving from 25.9 percent of white male earnings in 1948 to 28.2 percent in 1964 but advancing after passage to 47.3 percent in 1978. Trends for total income are similar.

The picture is quite different for white women. Their relative earnings fell steadily through the early 1970s, reaching their lowest level in 1973, and their relative total incomes likewise declined, though only through the early 1960s. The downward trends were reversed about the time EEO legislation was passed, but white women's relative incomes have yet to reach the peaks they attained in the late 1940s. Because the relative incomes of white women have fallen while those of nonwhite women have risen, white and nonwhite women came to have very similar incomes by the late 1970s, both earning just under half of what white men earned and considerably less than nonwhite men as well.

A somewhat different perspective is provided by considering changes in proportional group share, as shown in figure 6.4 and table 6.1. This figure highlights the gap between men and women and between white men and everyone else even more strongly than the data presented pre-

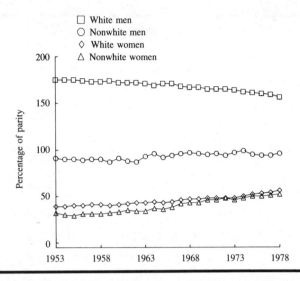

Fig. 6.4   Group share of total income. Source: U.S. Bureau of the Census, *Current Population Reports,* series P-60.

viously. Since the early 1950s, however, nonwhite men and women and white women have all gained relative to white men, whose relative incomes have fallen from 175 percent of parity (where all groups' relative share would equal 100) in 1953 to 156 in 1978. According to this measure, and in contrast to the data on earnings and income, the period since the mid-1960s has seen nonwhite and white women do especially well, while the relative incomes of nonwhite men have changed very little. The group share going to nonwhite women increased approximately 0.6 percent per year from 1953 through 1964, but slightly over 1 percent per year thereafter. Similarly, the rate of increase for white women doubled after 1964. The big losers (at least relatively) have been white men; the group share measure of inequality makes it more obvious than the others that one group's relative gain must be another group's loss.

White women's gains in group share must largely be due to entry into the labor force, since relative earnings have begun to increase only recently. Whatever the source of the increases among minorities and women, however, their fates seem to be linked. The group shares of nonwhite men and women and white women are highly correlated with each other (all correlations are greater than .69), so there is no evidence, at least so far, that the gains of one disadvantaged group are coming at the expense of another.

It would be nice if one could simply choose one of the measures and say unequivocally that it is the "best" way to describe the relative positions of the different groups, particularly since conclusions about income trends are clearly affected by the measure used. Unfortunately, that is not possible. Some measures of inequality may be better than others, and I think that the group share measure provides a very useful way of looking at income trends, but it is also true that there are often several ways of measuring inequality in a particular situation, each having a reasonable justification. Here, as in past work, the analysis will be carried out using several measures (partly so that the results may be compared with past work), and decisions about relative utility will wait until the end.

Explaining Income Differences

As I have already explained, intergroup income differences will be seen as determined mainly by four types of variables: those measuring the relative productivity of members of the different groups, discriminatory attitudes or other measures of the relevant social context, the demand for labor in the economy, and the enforcement of EEO legislation.

The variables actually used are as follows. The measure of relative productivity is median years of education completed by members of each protected group as a percentage of white male median years of education. This is a crude measure of relative productivity but is widely used because it is the best measure readily available (see Welch 1973; Aaron 1978, chap. 3).

Figure 6.5 shows how relative levels of education have changed since the late 1940s. At that time nonwhites lagged far behind whites, but they had almost caught up by the end of the 1970s. In addition, white and nonwhite men have been catching up to the women of their own races educationally. Probably the most obvious point made by the figure is that the educational levels of the four groups have virtually reached parity.

The relevant social context is measured in terms of attitudes toward nonwhites and women in the labor force. The focus is on attitudes for two reasons. First, they may be viewed as rough indicators of the taste for discrimination that plays so important a role in the economic theory of discrimination. Second, as described in chapters 4 and 5, they were

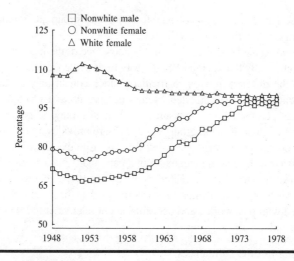

Fig. 6.5   Education as percentage of white men's. Sources: Median years of school-ing, by race and sex: for 1947, 1950, 1960, U.S. Bureau of the Census 1975, 380–81; 1952, U.S. Department of Labor 1974, 299–301; 1957, U.S. Bureau of the Census, *Current Population Reports,* 1958, series P-20, no. 77; 1958, 1961, U.S. Bureau of the Census, *Current Population Reports,* 1960–61, series P-60, nos. 33, 39; 1959, 1962, 1964–75, U.S. Department of Labor 1978, 247–249; 1976–78, U.S. Depart-ment of Labor 1980, 143–47. Beginning with 1977, data refer to blacks rather than nonwhites.

extremely important determinants of congressional support for EEO leg-islation and so constitute a critical aspect of the political and social en-vironment in which the labor market operates and EEO law is to be enforced. Since figure 6.1 and data for more recent years show that most organized effort to end discrimination has been channeled through the EEO enforcement process rather than other mechanisms, EEO enforce-ment activity (described below) is probably the most relevant additional aspect of the social context.

Attitudes toward nonwhites and women in the labor force are mea-sured in terms of the same questions used in previous chapters. (Ideally, we would like to have data about the attitudes of specific groups, such as employers, toward being in various labor market relationships with blacks or women, including working with them, being supervised by them, and the like, but the data used are all that are available.)

Figure 6.6 presents the estimates of public opinion toward blacks and

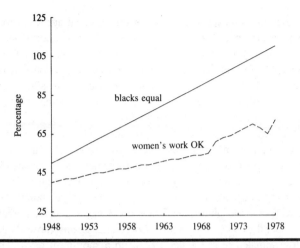

Fig. 6.6   Attitudes toward blacks and women. Source: see chapter 3.

women in the labor force through the late 1970s (estimated as before; because figures for the last few years are extrapolations of trends from previous years, among the estimates are somewhat artificial ones suggesting that more than 100 percent of the people favor equal treatment for blacks; here the percentages should just be taken as indicators of a trend, rather than literally). There now appears to be near universal acceptance of the principle of equal treatment for blacks and whites. Attitudes toward practical matters are often less liberal or egalitarian than attitudes on grand principles, of course, but there is every reason to believe that the trends in attitudes toward blacks are real and consequential (Taylor, Sheatsley, and Greeley 1978; Burstein 1979b).

Acceptance of female labor force participation is, however, still far from universal. As recently as 1978, 28 percent of the public still felt that women with husbands who could support them should not work for pay (women have been only slightly more favorable than men). There obviously remains considerable resistance to the notion that women should have the same rights as men in the labor force.

The state of the economy is measured in terms of the unemployment rate. This has ranged from a low of 2.9 percent in 1953 to a high of 8.5 percent in 1975. It was relatively low during the period right after the passage of Title 7 but rose considerably in the 1970s.

Theoretically, EEO legislation reduces discrimination because it imposes costs on employers (or unions or employment agencies) for discriminating; employers are expected to stop discriminating when they realize that it will be costly to continue doing so. Ideally, therefore, the best predictor of the effect of EEO legislation would be a measure of the costs incurred by employers who continue to discriminate after discrimination is prohibited—a measure of the probability of being caught multiplied by the penalty imposed would be best.

Such a measure is unfortunately impossible to find, and as a practical matter EEO enforcement is measured in two ways. The first involves viewing federal expenditures on EEO enforcement as an "investment" in EEO, with its effect cumulating over the years (Freeman 1973, 100). That is measured here as cumulative EEO outlays per nonwhite and female worker in the labor force. The second way to gauge enforcement is to consider the outcomes of actual proceedings against those alleged to have discriminated (e.g., Beller 1979), on a short-term basis. This is measured as the percentage of EEO court cases at the appellate level won by women and nonwhites each year. It seems plausible that the likelihood of losing in court would affect employers' willingness to change their employment practices.

Table 6.2 provides some information about the EEO enforcement effort. EEO enforcement expenditures tended to rise from the time the law was first passed through the mid-1970s, taking an especially large jump after the law was strengthened in 1972 and the EEOC was empowered to take alleged discriminators to court. The increases slowed toward the end of the 1970s, however, and expenditures per person even began to decline in real terms.

Objectively, it is not obvious what would constitute an "adequate" enforcement effort in the short term. The amounts spent are substantial, yet they do not seem great when contrasted with the amount spent on training programs (Masters 1975, 152) or the losses suffered owing to discrimination (see Jencks et al. 1979, chap. 7; Featherman and Hauser 1976). It is fairly widely agreed that the federal enforcement effort is very inadequately funded given the magnitude of its task, partly because its opponents have worked to minimize the funding available (see Levine and Montcalmo 1971; U.S. Commission on Civil Rights 1977, 329–35; U.S. Congress, Senate Committee on Appropriations 1970, 1043 ff.).

To the extent that employers' behavior will change primarily in response to the binding decisions of the courts, the changes are likely to be

Table 6.2 Equal Opportunity Enforcement Activity

Year	Total Federal EEO Outlays (millions of current dollars)	Federal Outlays per Nonwhite and Female Worker (1967 dollars)	Final Appellate Court Decisions Favoring Minorities and Women			
			Cumulative Total		Percentage Each Year	
			Race	Sex	Race	Sex
1965	0	0	0	0	—	—
1966	13.6	0.44	5	0	80	—
1967	21.9	0.66	7	0	40	—
1968	27.8	0.78	9.5	0	62	—
1969	38.2	0.98	12.5	0	60	—
1970	56.1	1.31	15	0	62	—
1971	62.2	1.38	28.5	3.5	54	58
1972	102.2	2.11	42.5	13.5	50	62
1973	154.5	2.89	55	21	54	47
1974	190.9	3.11	67	23.5	44	28
1975	239.7	3.48	80.5	34	35	41
1976	263.6	3.49	91	42.5	38	45
1977	301.1	3.60	103	49.5	29	22
1978	305.5	3.25	—	—	—	—

Sources: Total federal EEO outlays are enforcement expenditures for EEO, from U.S. Office of Management and Budget (1971–78); figure is sum of federal service EEO outlays and private sector EEO outlays by federal government. Fiscal year 1976 transition quarter is averaged in. For 1966–70, figure is calculated on basis of assumption that it equals 4.184 times EEOC appropriations for that year, which was the case in later years. Total outlays in current dollars. Federal outlay per nonwhite and female worker is figure for total federal EEO outlay, in constant 1967 dollars, divided by total number of women and nonwhites in the labor force.
Court cases: same data base as figure 6.1. Only substantially "final" decisions were counted; that is, not decisions on intermediate procedural issues, not decisions remanding to a lower court with only general guidance, and so forth, but rather decisions that would be viewed as final by the participants and the court unless appealed. Each case was counted only once. Cases in which all nontrivial points were won by women or minorities were coded 1, mixed results were coded 0.5, and cases in which all nontrivial points were lost were counted as 0.

uncertain and slow in coming. It took years for the appellate courts to resolve any substantial number of EEO cases, especially for women, and victory is clearly far from a sure thing. If employers respond primarily to the threat of financial penalties for disobeying the law, then the law could not have become effective until 1971, seven years after passage, with the first United States Court of Appeals decision that made the threat of such penalties effective (*Robinson v. Lorillard Corp.*, 44 F.2d 791; also see *Albermarle Paper Co. v. Moody*, 422 U.S. 405 [1975]). The United States Supreme Court did not decide any Title 7 cases until 1971 (see U.S. Equal Employment Opportunity Commission 1972, 23–31). Although such evaluations are inevitably somewhat subjective, the EEO enforcement effort seems slow and uncertain rather than swift and sure.

In sum, this chapter gauges the effect of the following variables on the relative incomes of nonwhite men, nonwhite women, and white women:

Education: years, relative to white men.

Attitudes: for nonwhite men, the estimated percentage of the population favoring equal treatment for blacks and whites in the labor market; for white women, the percentage favorable to female labor force participation; for nonwhite women, the average of both attitudes.

State of the economy: unemployment rate.

EEO enforcement: for all groups, cumulative federal EEO enforcement expenditures per nonwhite and female member of the labor force, in constant dollars (designated "enforcement $" in the tables below); in addition, for nonwhite men and women, the percentage of final appellate court decisions on racial discrimination decided in favor of minorities each year, lagged one year (to allow them time to affect employers' behavior); for white women, the comparable variable for sex discrimination cases (designated "% court wins").

Some Expectations

The basic hypotheses about relative incomes are straightforward. Everything else being equal, the incomes of nonwhites and women relative to those of white men should be positively correlated with their level of education relative to white men, the pervasiveness of egalitarian attitudes, and EEO enforcement effort and negatively correlated with the unemployment rate.

We already know, of course, that the incomes of nonwhite men and women have risen, and we would be rather surprised if they had not, given rising educational levels, the spread of egalitarian attitudes, *and* the passage of EEO legislation. But we do not know how great an effect each variable has had. The legislation might be purely symbolic, simply representing official notice of trends taking place in the society and having no independent effect, for example, Or changes in relative productivity and even attitudes might have had little effect on the relative incomes of blacks; discrimination may have been so deeply entrenched in economic institutions that only the power of the state could reduce it.

The incomes of white women have already confounded our intuitive and theoretical expectations to some degree because of their decline, by some conventional measures, from the 1940s well into the 1960s in the face of increasingly favorable attitudes. That white women's earnings and total incomes started to rise about the time EEO legislation was passed and amended may indicate that legislation was especially important for them. It also might be that differences between race discrimination and sex discrimination, seldom taken seriously by the early theorists (see Becker 1971, 106–7), lead to anomalies if analyzed in the context of the classic model of EEO effect.

The hypothesis about the effect of EEO legislation derived from the literature is a crude one, simply predicting that EEO enforcement will increase the relative incomes of groups that have been discriminated against. It says nothing about the magnitude of the effect, how quickly it will occur, or which aspect of law enforcement—administrative activities, court decisions, long-term investments, or short-term enforcement activities—will have the greatest influence. The effect of the law could have been dramatic and immediate—one day it became illegal to discriminate, so people simply stopped. In fact, however, the history of EEO enforcement makes one expect its influence to have been slow and modest, at least so far. Voluntary compliance no doubt took place to some degree, but court and agency records and other contemporary accounts show great resistance to the initial implementation of the law—lengthy appeals over minor technical points, refusal to keep proper records, and fairly transparent attempts to get around the intent of the law (see, e.g., Benokraitis and Feagin 1978; Abramson 1979). The prohibition against sex discrimination was simply not taken seriously in many quarters, including, some claimed, the EEOC itself (Freeman 1975, chap. 6); it took years to convince newspaper classified advertising departments that they could no longer advertise jobs as "help wanted—

male" and "help wanted—female" (Freeman 1975, 76–79). In addition, because state EEO laws had never led to the development of a significant body of case law, there was much genuine confusion about what the law required and little sense of its implications, even among its proponents (see Sovern 1966, chap. 3; Blumrosen 1971, chap. 1). In a situation characterized by resistance, misunderstanding, and confusion, it would be surprising had the law produced dramatic and significant changes in the short term. Thus we would expect the law to have had only a modest effect; we cannot predict the relative importance of the two enforcement variables, cumulative expenditures and court victories.

Findings

Tables 6.3 through 6.5 present the results of regression analyses gauging the effect of the independent variables on earnings, total income, and group share, respectively.[6]

Table 6.3   Determinants of Earnings of Nonwhites and Women, Relative to White Male Earnings: Unstandardized Regression Coefficients

Independent Variables	Nonwhite Men	Nonwhite Women	White Women
Attitudes	−.036	.049	−.23*
	(−.45)	(.48)	(−2.4)
Education	.18	.31*	.59**
	(1.2)	(2.2)	(3.4)
Unemployment	−.42	−.15	.42*
	(−1.0)	(−.49)	(2.2)
Enforcement $	.37**	.55**	.12
	(3.4)	(7.3)	(1.2)
% court wins	.082**	.084**	−.030*
	(2.7)	(3.9)	(−1.8)
Constant	49.	−2.3	−.26
	(6.0)	(−.33)	(.012)
Adj. R^2	.84	.96	.96
D-W d	2.2	1.7	GLS

Sources: All variables but unemployment, see previous tables and figures; unemployment, U.S. Department of Labor, *Handbook of Labor Statistics* 1977, 1980.
Note: t-statistics in parentheses; D-W d is Durbin-Watson d-statistic.
*Significant at .05 level, one-tailed test.
**Significant at .01 level, one-tailed test.

Table 6.4   Determinants of Median Total Income of Nonwhites and Women, Relative to White Male Income: Unstandardized Regression Coefficients

Independent Variables	Nonwhite Men	Nonwhite Women	White Women
Attitudes	−.097	.047	−.23
	(−1.6)	(.53)	(−1.6)
Education	.42**	.21*	.68**
	(3.5)	(1.7)	(2.7)
Unemployment	−1.0**	.20	.32
	(−3.3)	(.75)	(1.3)
Enforcement $	.22**	.28**	.31*
	(2.7)	(4.3)	(2.1)
% court wins	.023	.061**	.020
	(.99)	(3.3)	(.84)
Constant	34.**	−.65	−26.
	(5.4)	(−.10)	(−.87)
Adj. R^2	.86	.93	.86
D-W d	2.2	1.7	GLS

Note: t-statistics in parentheses; D-W d is Durbin-Watson d-statistic.
*Significant at .05 level, one-tailed test.
**Significant at .01 level, one-tailed test.

For nonwhite men and women education generally has the predicted effect; its effect on income, however measured, is positive in every equation and statistically significant in most. Increasing education has paid off for nonwhites.

The effect of education on the incomes of white women is less clear. Education is positively correlated with relative white female earnings and income, as predicted. The problem, however, is that white women's relative levels of education have *declined* since the 1940s, as have earnings and income. The parallel trends in education and income are in accord with theory; yet, given white women's high levels of education (even after their relative decline) and their low incomes, it seems disingenuous to argue that white women's incomes declined because their educations did. In addition, contrary to our initial hypothesis, education is *negatively* correlated with white women's group share; their group share has risen as relative education has fallen. These anomalous results are difficult to explain in conventional terms. My guess is that the rela-

Table 6.5   Determinants of Group Share of Nonwhites and Women as Proportion of All Income: Unstandardized Regression Coefficients

Independent Variables	Nonwhite Men	Nonwhite Women	White Women
Attitudes	−.19	.32	.17**
	(−1.3)	(1.6)	(2.7)
Education	.53**	.17	−.37**
	(2.6)	(.81)	(−3.7)
Unemployment	−.55	−.077	−.094
	(−1.6)	(−.27)	(−.71)
Enforcement $	−.053	.20*	.32**
	(−.66)	(1.8)	(5.7)
% court cases	.0093	.051**	−.013
	(.42)	(3.2)	(−1.3)
Constant	69.**	2.4	73.**
	(10.5)	(.004)	(5.7)
Adj. R^2	.73	.97	.96
D-W d	2.4	2.1	GLS

Note: t-statistics in parentheses; D-W d is Durbin-Watson d-statistic.
*Significant at .05 level, one-tailed test.
**Significant at .01 level, one-tailed test.

tive educational levels of white women simply have little to do with their relative incomes, because their educational level is so high, their returns to education so low, and their labor force participation rates so variable. The coefficients for education may represent the effect of education confounded by other factors.[7]

Attitudes do not have the predicted positive effect on the relative incomes of nonwhite men and women. The incomes of white women, in contrast, are affected by attitudes, but one's interpretation depends on which measure of income is used. Earnings and total incomes are negatively affected by attitude changes, whereas group share is positively affected. In this case I would argue that the results for group share are the most "real," in the sense of providing the most plausible interpretation of what has happened in American society. The effect of attitudes on earnings and total income appears negative because earnings and total income declined for part of the period, whereas attitudes were becoming more favorable to women in the labor force. As I argued earlier, though, much of the seeming decline in white women's incomes is probably due to the steady influx of relatively inexperienced female workers into the labor force. When this is taken into account, as it is in the measure of group share, we see white women's economic situation improving as attitudes toward them improve. This seems much more reasonable than the other, negative interpretation.

Unemployment does not generally have the predicted negative effect. It has a small negative effect on nonwhite male total income, but not on earnings or group share. It appears to have a *positive* effect on white women's earnings, possibly because women are less likely to be laid off than men and are more likely to drop out of the labor force when they lose their jobs. But its overall effect is small.

EEO enforcement has had the predicted positive effect on nonwhites and women, though not uniformly. Those most consistently benefiting from EEO enforcement are nonwhite women. Both EEO expenditures and court victories have a significant positive effect on their earnings, total incomes, and group share. The earnings and total incomes of non-white men have increased as a result of EEO enforcement as well, but the net effect on their group share seems to be about zero. Finally, the effect of EEO enforcement on white women, like other variables' effect on them, is less predictable and more variable than for the other groups. Enforcement expenditures have had a substantial positive effect on their group share and a lesser, though still positive, effect on their total income. Court victories have had no positive effect, however, and in fact have had a negative effect on white women's earnings. No obvious explanation for this last finding comes to mind.

The total effect of EEO legislation on the incomes of nonwhites and women is summarized in another way in table 6.6. The table provides

Table 6.6   Estimated Net Effect of EEO Legislation on Nonwhites and Women, 1965–78

Effect on	Nonwhite Men	Nonwhite Women	White Women
Relative earnings	+13.6%	+18.6%	−1.2%
Relative total income	+6.1%	+10.3%	+8.5%
Group share	0	+7.6%	+8.8%

Note: Calculated from enforcement expenditures, court victories, and effect of each estimated by unstandardized regression coefficient, summed for both variables over entire time period. Based on coefficients significant at .05 level only.

estimates of how much the incomes of women and nonwhites have been increased by EEO legislation, controlling for the effects of the other variables. The table shows that one's interpretation of the effect of EEO legislation depends strongly on which measure of income is used. If one looks at the earnings of those in the labor force—which is what EEO legislation was most manifestly intended to affect—then nonwhite men and women may be seen as having benefited substantially from EEO legislation, while white women may even have been harmed a bit. If, in contrast, one takes labor force participation to be problematic and considers the total income going to all group members whether they are in the labor force or not, then women appear to have been the main beneficiaries of the law. Both white and nonwhite women increased their group share by about 8 percent as a result of EEO enforcement, with white women gaining slightly more than nonwhite. The effect of EEO legislation on nonwhite men's group share has been zero—no effect at all. If relative total income is examined, all groups may be seen to have gained from EEO legislation.

Conclusions

With the passage of EEO legislation, the struggle for EEO shifted to a considerable degree from social protest activities to working through the administrative agencies and courts. What has happened as the struggle has continued?

Nonwhite women have clearly been helped by EEO legislation and have benefited from increased education. They apparently have not benefited directly from changes in attitudes, but they have almost certainly profited indirectly, as changes in attitude led to the passage of EEO legislation and, probably, to increased educational opportunities as well.

Part of the reason for nonwhite women's gains from EEO legislation may be their having been so badly off initially that their jobs and incomes could improve considerably without posing any real threat to the normal workings of the economy. Much of the black female economic advance over the past forty years has been, after all, from farm laborer and maid to secretary and other clerical positions. This is a real advance, but not one that threatens white or nonwhite men.

Nonwhite men have not been harmed by EEO legislation, so far as I can tell. This is not a trivial conclusion. Some economists have hypothesized, for example, that employers would be less likely to hire blacks if they had to pay them the same wages as whites. Consequently, the wage gains made possible by EEO legislation could be negated, for the black population as a whole, by more unemployment (Butler and Heckman 1977, 248). EEO legislation prohibits discrimination in hiring as well as in pay, but, realistically, those not hired are less likely to realize they have been discriminated against than those already working for a firm but being underpaid. The economists' fears are reasonable, but they have not been borne out. EEO legislation may in fact have helped nonwhite men; their earnings have risen, after all. And if black men's group share has not risen substantially, that may be because women's group share has gone up so much. It may be no trivial matter for nonwhite men to have held their own while white and nonwhite women's group shares have risen.

Like nonwhite women, nonwhite men have gained from having gotten more education and have benefited only indirectly from changing attitudes.

Outcomes for *white women* are more difficult to describe. Their earnings did not start to rise until years after the passage of EEO legislation, but the legislation has increased their group share more than that of any other group. I argue that group share rather than earnings should be the focus of interest in the short run, because EEO legislation has been associated with increased labor force participation, leading to an immediate increase in group share and, potentially, a greater increase in earnings in the long run. This will not be automatic, by any means. The seemingly negative effect of court victories on white women's incomes, along with legal scholarship suggesting that the courts resist women's claims to upper-level jobs, may imply that white female earnings may not increase readily (Bartholet 1982). But there is some sign of a turn-around, and the results certainly do not rule out earnings increases in the near future.

The effect of education on the relative incomes of white women is ambiguous, but attitudes generally have a positive effect. Increasingly favorable attitudes thus seem to help groups whose members are already well educated (white women), while increases in education are important for groups starting out with relatively little (nonwhite men and women). It may be that prejudiced attitudes are more of a barrier for those who are educationally qualified for better-paying jobs.

It must also be emphasized that, despite the implementation of EEO legislation, women's incomes remain far below those of men, including those of nonwhite men. Women have benefited from EEO legislation, but the gap between their incomes and those of men is still very wide indeed.

This analysis reaches several conclusions different from those of past work, particularly economists' time-series analyses. First, the passage of EEO legislation changed the nature of the struggle for EEO, shifting it from social protest activity to the courts and administrative agencies. Past work ignores this.

Second, none of the three disadvantaged groups loses from the passage of EEO legislation; there is no obvious indication that one group is gaining at the expense of another. Past work, by focusing on race discrimination or sex discrimination, but not both, fails to consider this possibility.

Third, group income is affected by changes in the social context relevant to the struggle for EEO as well as by EEO legislation itself. White women gain directly from changing attitudes about their labor force participation, and all three protected groups gain indirectly from changing attitudes, because of their effect on the passage of legislation. This possibility is always mentioned and almost never studied in past work.

Fourth, EEO legislation can be effective, contrary to what some previous studies imply.

Fifth, the economic status of women as a group has not been declining, or even static; viewed in terms of group share, the proportion of all income going to women has clearly been increasing.

There is no way to tell whether, in the absence of legislation, discrimination would eventually disappear for other reasons, nor do the data tell us whether the legislation plus the social changes that have taken place in the United States thus far will eventually lead to an end to discrimination. I think we can say, however, that EEO legislation is not simply symbolic; it does have real consequences, independent of the social context in which it was adopted. At the same time, however, it is difficult to imagine its having been adopted or being effective in a climate of opinion fundamentally hostile to EEO.

Some major conclusions of this analysis are new because the adoption of a political approach to EEO leads to new questions and to some changes in standard ways of seeking answers about the struggle for EEO.

The importance of taking into account the social and political context of the struggle for EEO cannot be overemphasized. The economic theory that provides the framework for analyses of EEO gives little guidance as to what factors, beyond productivity, may affect intergroup income differences. Analysts therefore have considerable discretion on what additional factors to consider. What can happen when one sticks to a narrow economic framework is shown by Butler and Heckman, who did one of the few studies to take seriously the choice of additional variables. They chose to focus on the possibility that increases in transfer payments, particularly AFDC, led black men to drop out of the labor force, and they concluded that such transfer payments, rather than EEO legislation, have most significantly affected the economic status of black men. This conclusion is clearly intended to suggest that the economic status of black men is primarily the result of their own unfettered economic decision making rather than being the result of racism, the decline of manufacturing (Wilson 1980, chap. 5), or even political manipulation of the welfare system (Piven and Cloward 1971). An approach that focuses on transfer payments without even considering the political context in which they are decided upon is naive, to say the least. And the conclusions of an analysis dealing with such a truncated set of variables are worthless.

I suggest four ways future work may improve our understanding of the struggle for EEO. First, we should continue to pursue attitudes toward minorities and women and the availability of jobs, but we should move closer to the actual employment situations of women and nonwhites by focusing on the attitudes of employers and co-workers and on job opportunities in industries, occupations, and regions where women and minorities are concentrated and in those they are entering at especially high rates. Less-educated black men and well-educated women seem to be having especially great difficulties in the labor market, so analyses focusing on them may be especially apropos in the short run (see Jencks 1983a,b; Bartholet 1982).

Second, it will be important to learn more about families and about sources of income other than employment. Particularly for women, decisions about work and decisions about family life are closely linked; effort devoted to paid work is related to family structure (including number and age of children), the division of labor in the household, and attitudes toward working women (see, e.g., Lloyd, Andrews, and Gilroy 1979; Waite 1978). As the proportion of families with two earners rises, such considerations may have a significant influence on the labor market behavior of men as well. Changes in family law and increases in the number of single-parent households may also be important. Finally, as Butler and Heckman argue, some workers will drop out of the labor force if they can get money in other ways.

The analysis reported above does not include the suggested variables because data on most are not readily available. But the data are not likely to become available unless someone suggests the need.

Third, interactions between explanatory variables should be considered. As I argued above, EEO enforcement and attitudes may affect incomes directly. But they may also affect incomes by interacting with education and unemployment. As discrimination declines, for example, women and nonwhites should ultimately be as well rewarded for acquiring education as white men have been. These and similar hypotheses could not be tested above for technical reasons (the relevant variables are so closely related that their separate effects could not be distinguished), but eventually they should be. The fact that black returns to education have increased in recent years (Haworth, Gwartney, and Haworth 1975; Jencks 1983a), as one would expect if EEO legislation had the hypothesized effect, indicates that such tests would be fruitful.

Finally, and perhaps most important, analyses of the consequences of the struggle for EEO can be improved by examining the struggle as a whole—that is, as a conflict over access to resources waged in many ways, including, but not limited to, the enforcement of legislation. Work that focuses solely on the enforcement of EEO legislation, treated as just another variable in an economic model of individual income attainment, simply misses much of what is important about the struggle—the role of social protest, changes in the social context, and the implications of the decision to work through the democratic political process. Only an approach that considers how social change and political organization impinge upon economic outcomes can hope to lead to an understanding of the struggle for EEO and where it is taking us.

7 The Future of Equal Employment Opportunity

The relative incomes of women and blacks have improved in recent years because of changes in relative educational attainments, decreases in prejudice, the enforcement of EEO laws, and other factors. Blacks and women still have a long way to go before catching up with white men, however. One way to gauge their progress is to see how long it will take them to reach equality with white men if they continue to gain at the rate they have since 1964, when Title 7 was adopted. Projecting the changes in relative income between 1964 and 1981 (the last year for which data were available when this was written) into the future, non-white men will receive the same median total income as white men in the year 2075; nonwhite women will catch up in 2060, and white women in 2114. As the top half of table 7.1 shows, no matter how income is measured, it will be well into the twenty-first century before blacks or women reach parity with white men. If present trends continue, most people in today's labor force will not live to see the day when blacks and women earn as much as white men.

Why? In a way, the projections are no surprise.[1] It typically takes a long time—usually generations—for groups that have suffered from discrimination or are newcomers to a labor market to catch up to established groups (see, e.g., Lieberson 1980; Thernstrom 1973; Featherman and Hauser 1978).

Exactly how long it takes may vary a great deal, nevertheless. Historically, some racial and ethnic groups have made economic progress much more quickly than others, and groups that have made rapid progress during some periods have seen their gains reduced or even reversed at other times (see, e.g., Thernstrom 1973; Lieberson 1980; Bonacich and Modell 1980). The rate at which blacks and women may achieve economic equality with white men has been a major concern of the struggle for EEO. The struggle is predicated, in fact, on the belief

Table 7.1   Years When Group Incomes Will Reach Parity (Parity = Equality with White Men for Earnings and Median Total Income, 100 for Group Share)

Group	Earnings	Total Income	Group Share
Projecting 1964–81 Rates of Change			
White men	—	—	2028
Nonwhite men	2044	2075	Never*
Nonwhite women	2031	2060	2032
White women	Never*	2114	2018
Projecting Rates of Change through 1964			
White men	—	—	2090
Nonwhite men	Never*	2253	1972**
Nonwhite women	2477	2617	2104
White women	Never*	Never*	2071

*Relative income was lower at end of period than beginning; simply projecting trends, parity would never be reached.
**Nonwhite male group share was actually 94.1 in 1972 and has never reached parity.

that nondiscriminatory treatment in the labor market would enable minorities and women to make gains in relative income more rapidly than they otherwise would. The relative incomes of nonwhites and women are rising more rapidly now than they were before Title 7 was adopted (compare the top half of table 7.1 with the lower half), but the projections in table 7.1 suggest that their gains remain relatively modest. Many nonwhites and women are, indeed, dissatisfied with the present rates of progress and want ever-stronger measures taken to ensure equality in the workplace.

This is just what opponents of affirmative action are afraid of. They claim that the courts, administrative agencies, some corporations, and some unions have been taking measures against discrimination that are so strong they amount to reverse discrimination, giving preference to women and nonwhites even when they are less qualified than their white male competitors.[2] These assertions, in turn, frighten some proponents of EEO, who believe that many of those claiming to oppose only reverse discrimination are in fact opposed to EEO itself (see the summary of views in Benokraitis and Feagin 1978, chap. 6, for example).

Thus there is a heated debate about whether the gains being made by nonwhites and women (on at least some measures of income) are coming "too slowly" or "too quickly" (that is, with the aid of reverse discrimination). Those involved are concerned about what is (or is not) being done to close the black/white and female/male income gaps and about what should (or should not) be done in the future.

This chapter shows why it is likely to take blacks and women so long to catch up to white men and considers what might increase or decrease their rate of progress. By extending the analysis of the factors emphasized in previous chapters—particularly prejudice and discrimination, education, the economy, and politics—I will show that the rate at which blacks and women have been gaining is more likely to decrease than to increase, but that such an outcome is by no means inevitable.

Why Income Gaps Always Close Slowly

Blacks and women have long been discriminated against. Each group is also, in its own way, a relative newcomer to the modern American labor market—women because most were not in the labor force until recently, and blacks because their entry into urban labor markets in large numbers has been more recent than the entry of the last major wave of European immigrants. Blacks and women have thus only recently begun to compete for the better jobs long available to many white men—skilled manual, professional, managerial, and technical jobs.

In such circumstances we would normally expect it to be a long time before blacks or women (or any other group of newcomers) would reach income equality with established groups, even in the absence of any discrimination.

The first, and possibly the most fundamental, reason is generational. When new opportunities become available, younger members of a group are typically far better able to take advantage of them than are older group members. Older people have completed their educations, have learned skills useful under the previous conditions but not necessarily suited to the new opportunities, have established networks of contacts who may have been useful in getting the types of jobs previously available but not the new ones, and so forth. That is, the older a person is, the more he or she will have invested in established ways of doing things and the more difficult it will be to change.

Change will also be less worthwhile for an older person. For a twenty-year-old, for example, investing time and money in the college education necessary for a newly available type of job is likely to be quite rational; a sixty-year-old approaching retirement, however, would be unlikely to recoup his or her investment.

Thus, younger group members may do as well economically as members of established groups, but older people are unlikely to. A disadvantaged or newcomer group as a whole is therefore not likely to reach economic parity with other groups until the retirement or death of all the group members who entered the labor force before the new opportunities became available. It would be likely to take until at least forty or forty-five years after 1964 before blacks or women earn what white men do even if all discrimination had stopped as soon as Title 7 was adopted. Younger blacks and women are in fact doing better economically relative to white men than older blacks and women, who are likely never to catch up to their white male age peers (Barrett 1979; Featherman and Hauser 1976; cf. Wilson 1980, chap. 8).

Income gaps between racial and ethnic groups (if not between the sexes) close slowly not only because older group members are unable to take advantage of new opportunities but because they pass on their labor market disadvantages to their children as well. Children from families that are less well off acquire less education, do worse on tests of cognitive skills, have lower occupational aspirations, and generally enter the labor force less well equipped to compete for good jobs than the children from families that are better off economically (see, e.g., Jencks et al. 1979; Featherman and Hauser 1976). If members of a particular group have done poorly in the labor market up to some point in time, their children are likely to do relatively poorly as well, though probably better than their parents (if factors other than discrimination are involved). Blacks' progress is thus likely to be slowed because black children grow up in poorer families than white children.[3]

Girls, of course, do not suffer this disadvantage compared with boys. Their incomes may suffer as the result of socialization by their parents to traditional, low-paying female jobs, but the actual effect of childhood socialization on adult female income has not been accurately gauged (Miller and Garrison 1982). Probably few people would argue, however, that the average white woman enters the labor force as well prepared for it by parents or school as the average white man.

Thus, predictions about how long it may take for women and nonwhites to reach economic parity with white men must be phrased in terms of generations. Taken to an extreme, this argument implies that groups that start out behind will never completely catch up, because each generation's disadvantages are passed on, to some degree, to the next (see Dorn 1979, chaps. 4–5). Yet we know that some minority groups, most notably Jews, have managed to catch up and even surpass dominant groups in income and returns to education within a generation or two (Chiswick 1983). Within the very important constraints imposed by aging and childhood socialization, therefore, we would expect to find that groups' progress can be affected by their ability to organize, the resistance they meet from other groups, the rate at which the economy is expanding or contracting, and other factors (Lieberson 1980; Featherman and Hauser 1978). To determine what might increase or decrease the rate at which blacks and women gain on white men, we should therefore consider how they are likely to be affected by the factors emphasized in the model described in chapter 6—the pervasiveness of prejudice, relative education, the economy, and the political struggle for EEO.

Prejudice and Discrimination

The Continuation of Recent Trends

Prejudice against blacks and women has long hurt their ability to enter many kinds of jobs and to get the same pay as white men. A decline in prejudice, as chapter 6 has shown, has directly and indirectly (through its impact on Congress) contributed to greater labor market opportunities for blacks and women and to relative increases in their incomes. Future gains in the relative incomes of blacks and women depend on continuing declines in prejudice. Will prejudice continue to decline?

Prejudice against blacks and women in the labor market and other areas has been declining fairly steadily for quite a while now, at least regarding principles of equal treatment, and there is no obvious reason why these trends should reverse or even slow down. At the same time, however, there are at least three reasons to be very cautious about predicting that the progress of blacks and women will be helped as much by declines in prejudice during the next few years as in the recent past.

First, we do not know why prejudice has declined. This means that though there is no obvious reason that recent trends should reverse, there is also no solid reason to expect them to continue. They might, or they might not. Prejudice has risen in the past after declining (see Stember et al. 1966) and could again. The continuation of recent trends could help blacks and women, but it cannot be depended upon.

Second, although more and more people accept general principles of equal treatment, such trends are less obvious when specific questions about real-life situations are asked. Whites, for instance, are much more likely to favor integrated schools in principle than they are to favor sending their own children to schools that are half black (Smith 1981). Men may favor increasing equality between the sexes in principle but resist doing what is necessary to bring it about (Thornton and Freedman 1979). Trends with regard to specific questions about concrete situations are typically in the same general direction as trends on issues of principle, but the rate of change tends to be much lower, is often close to zero, and may be easier to reverse. Thus white men may be relatively unprejudiced in the abstract but have considerable prejudice toward members of other groups in work situations (and, of course, white women may be prejudiced against blacks, black men may be prejudiced against women, etc.).

Third, prejudice that may be difficult to detect in normal circumstances may be brought to the surface if white men begin to see blacks and women competing widely and actively for the jobs normally held only by white men. Questions about feelings toward members of particular groups may evoke an unprejudiced response when they are viewed in the abstract, but the response may be quite different when a real threat of competition arises; then latent prejudice may come into the open and be translated into active discrimination (Lieberson 1980, chaps. 9, 12). It is therefore possible that if declines in prejudice lead blacks and women to become an actual economic threat to white men, the recent trends could be reversed; a decline in prejudice can lead to conditions promising its eventual increase. Such a reversal need have nothing to do with perceptions that blacks and women are receiving favored treatment from the courts, administrative agencies, or employers; it could arise as blacks and women do better than previously and thereby become a greater economic threat for whatever reason, including hard work and merit.

Possibly counterbalancing these caveats, there is also one reason to expect discrimination to continue to decline, perhaps even more rapidly than before, and that is the operation of the free market. Theoretically, as Becker and others have argued, discrimination should decline as employers striving for efficiency find themselves driven to hire the best potential employees, regardless of race or sex (see Sowell 1981). Experience has shown that the logic of the argument does not generally hold in the real world, but the argument remains a powerful one, and it could prove relevant as previous barriers begin to crumble and employers discover that blacks and women do well in jobs formerly monopolized by white men. Successful performance by some blacks and women could lead to increased willingness to hire them and a competitive edge for employers who do. (An especially well-known historical example is the admittance of black baseball players into the major leagues.) Relatively small initial reductions in discrimination, manifested in the actions of a few employers, could lead to widespread further reductions and the opening up of whole new fields.

Unfortunately, arguments about the effect of the free market on discrimination can cut both ways. Blacks and women can gain from economic rationality on the part of employers, but they can lose as well, as those who have developed the concept of statistical discrimination show.

Statistical Discrimination

Blacks and women suffer not only from discrimination based on hostility, but from statistical discrimination as well. Statistical discrimination occurs when an employer believes (correctly or not) that members of one group will be less productive on the average than members of another and uses this belief as a simple, inexpensive guide to employment decisions, enhancing the average quality of his employees by hiring only members of the more productive group (Thurow 1975; Fiss 1971). An employer who believed that blacks' education was inferior to whites', for instance, might find it cheaper to hire only whites than to carefully evaluate the educational background of each white and black applicant. Even relatively small initial differences between groups (real or perceived) may become the basis for major decisions—hire or not hire—and thus have a substantial effect on labor market outcomes.

This kind of discrimination can be very difficult to overcome, because it can be economically rational for employers as long as there are real differences between social groups; and it can be sustained by beliefs that such differences exist even after they have disappeared (see Jencks 1983a). As real differences between white men and other groups decline (educational differences between black and white men, for example), and as these changes become widely known, statistical discrimination is likely to decline. But there is no reason to expect it to decline more rapidly (or more slowly) in the future than in the past.

Reverse Discrimination

Although blacks and women have traditionally been hurt by discrimination, the claim has been made recently that now they are being helped—

being helped, that is, by reverse discrimination, in which they are given preference over better-qualified white men. If reverse discrimination is widespread, or becoming so, blacks and women could be expected to take advantage of it and to make increasingly rapid economic progress in the years to come.

Is reverse discrimination widespread? Everyone seems to know instances of it, at least from hearsay, and major newspapers, magazines, and books are full of stories about the pervasiveness of reverse discrimination and how it is radically affecting many areas of American life (see, e.g., Sawyer 1981a; Reed 1981; Glazer 1978, ix; Firms are disrupted 1981; New bias 1981; It's the thought 1981).

The stories, however, are just that—stories, not solid evidence. There is, in fact, surprisingly little systematically collected evidence about the pervasiveness of reverse discrimination (see Burstein 1985; Jencks 1983b; cf. Abramson 1977). No data have been systematically collected from employers. There have been some complaints to government agencies about reverse discrimination and some well-known court cases, but they amount to a handful compared with complaints alleging discrimination against women and minorities (Burstein 1979a, 389). No national poll data on personal experiences of reverse discrimination have been published (which seems odd, given the interest the issue arouses). A few studies provide evidence that some white men believe they have been discriminated against or may have their careers affected by affirmative action, but the proportions are always substantially smaller than the proportion of women and blacks who feel discriminated against (Hopkins 1980; Fernandez 1981, 118).

In fact there is so little direct evidence that reverse discrimination is widespread that many of those who believe it is are forced to buttress their anecdotes with descriptions not of reverse discrimination, but of *plans* for affirmative action that are *claimed* to lead to reverse discrimination (e.g., Glazer 1978, chap. 2). All that is missing is evidence that the plans are implemented, that employers are punished if the plans are ignored, and that the plans actually lead to reverse discrimination. Such evidence is surprisingly difficult to come by (see Benokraitis and Feagin 1978; Abramson 1979; New bias 1981; Looking backward 1980). There have no doubt been cases of reverse discrimination, and concern about it is understandable, but there is no evidence that it is widespread.

Blacks and women would certainly benefit if discrimination simply kept declining in American society until it disappeared completely[4] and possibly, in the short run at least, if reverse discrimination were to become common. This could happen. But there is no evidence that reverse discrimination is common, and there are at least as many reasons to expect discrimination to decline slowly (or even to increase) as to expect it to decline more rapidly.

Education

The most famous civil rights court case of the twentieth century, *Brown v. Board of Education*, was motivated by the knowledge that blacks could not achieve social or economic equality with whites as long as they were denied equal access to education. Their century-long fight for education (Lieberson 1980) has paid off. Blacks now have almost as much education as whites and have been able to translate increases in relative education into increases in relative income. These gains cannot continue indefinitely into the future, however. Thirty years ago black men had only about two-thirds as much education as white men; it would be very surprising if in thirty years they had a third more education than whites.

White women have long had more years of education than white men; their recent gains in relative income cannot be attributed to changes in the amount of education acquired, and it seems highly unlikely that future gains would be the result of acquiring more education.

Thus, if blacks and women are to utilize the educational system in their attempt to increase their incomes relative to white men, their approach will have to involve something more subtle or complex than simply acquiring more education, however important years of education might be for occupational and income attainment. Their attention is likely to focus on two aspects of education: type and quality.

Type of Education

Almost everything we know about the effect of education on occupational attainment and income focuses on the amount of education acquired—getting more education leads to higher-status occupations and higher incomes. Remarkably little is known about how *type* of education—vocational versus academic high school, college major, postsecondary technical training, field of study in graduate school, and so on—affects individuals' economic success (Kerckhoff and Jackson 1982).

The type of education that probably has the greatest effect on individuals' occupational attainment and income is advanced vocational training, including professional schools (law, medicine, business, etc.) for those with college degrees and apprenticeship programs for those without. Historically, blacks and women have suffered intensely from discrimination when they applied for admission to professional schools and apprenticeship programs, particularly those controlling access to the better-paid professions (physician as opposed to social worker, for instance).

Discrimination in access to training opportunities has declined substantially in recent years, and women in particular have taken advantage of the new opportunities to move rapidly into traditionally male fields such as law and medicine. Increased access to opportunities for training will certainly help blacks and women gain on white men in the years to come, but it is likely to account for only a modest proportion of the total income differences, for at least two reasons. First, some people, particularly blacks, argue that admissions procedures are still often discriminatory, while others argue that the steps taken to increase the number of blacks in professional schools and apprenticeship programs amount to reverse discrimination.[5] Thus, access to particular types of education has itself become an equal rights battleground, and to the extent that white male resistance slows the process of change in educational institutions, the progress of blacks and women will be more difficult.[6]

Second, because only a relatively small proportion of blacks and women (like a similarly small proportion of white men) will have access to the highest-level blue- and white-collar jobs requiring specialized training, changes in access to educational institutions alone will go only a relatively modest part of the way in eventually raising the average income of all women and blacks in the labor force. Even rapid gains in access to educational institutions would go only part of the way in closing the income gap between men and women and whites and blacks.

Other changes in the types of education required by blacks and women might also increase their relative incomes, but by how much is problematic. Men who major in business or engineering do better economically than those who study other subjects (Griffin and Alexander 1978), and so one might think that women who majored in those areas rather than in more traditionally female subjects like English or education would do better as well. In fact, however, majoring in the more "practical" fields helps women very little, so far as we can tell from the limited data available (Angle and Wissmann 1981), possibly because women are not rewarded for their education in the same way men are. There is little evidence that making the type of education acquired by blacks and women like that acquired by white men would greatly reduce the income gaps between the groups in the near future (see also Jencks et al. 1979; Kerckhoff and Jackson 1982).

Quality of Education

Differences in quality as well as type of education probably account for part of the race and sex differences in incomes, particularly the difference between blacks and whites. Until it started to become clear to southern whites that the Supreme Court would eventually require equal education for blacks and whites, the education available to southern blacks was drastically inferior to that provided to whites (Lieberson 1980). It is plausible that the education received by blacks is still inferior to that received by whites and that this affects their occupational attainments and incomes (Sowell 1981). Yet it is extraordinarily difficult to demonstrate that the differences are significant or that they have a major effect on income differences between groups. There are several reasons for this. First, whatever differences do exist in the quality of formal education available to different groups are apparently relatively subtle and difficult to document (Jencks et al. 1979; Aaron 1978, chap. 3). Second, the relation between quality of formal education and occupational attainment or income is far more difficult to document or understand than was once thought; educational credentials may be more important to most employers than anything in particular learned in school (beyond basic literacy), and most education relevant to work performance may take place on the job rather than in school anyway (Aaron 1978, chap. 3; Thurow 1975, chap. 3). Finally, so few people may receive a significantly better than average education that their higher incomes (if needed they are higher) will have little effect on the average for a entire social group (Griffin and Alexander 1978; Jencks et al. 1979, 295–96). Thus I would hesitate to argue that the quality of education available to blacks is equal to that acquired by whites, or that future increases in the quality of blacks' education will have no effect on their incomes. Yet it is also difficult to argue that the differences between groups are great or that improving the quality of blacks' education will go a long way toward closing the income gap between them and whites. (Differences between men and women would be even less significant than those between blacks and whites, because men and women attend the same schools, for the most part, and are exposed to the same educations.)

It is easy to overrate the likely gains blacks and women may make by acquiring more, better, or different types of education. Two other aspects of their educational accomplishments have major implications for their future incomes, however.

The first is rate of return to education—that is, what each additional increment of education gets one in terms of occupational status or income. Right now, blacks' and women's major educational problem is not lack of education, but a low rate of return; they are not rewarded for acquiring education to the same extent white men are (Jencks et al. 1979, chap. 7; Featherman and Hauser 1976). Changes in the rate of return to educational require reductions in discrimination and so are not an educational matter at all.

The second relevant aspect of blacks' and women's educational accomplishments is what they do educationally once discrimination declines (as it already has to a significant degree). Until recently, it has not paid blacks to acquire as much education as whites, because they would not be rewarded for it, and it paid neither blacks nor women to train for occupations dominated by white men, because their chances of doing well in those occupations were so slight. It was quite rational for many blacks to drop out of school or to major in poorly paying fields like education, and for women to study vocationally "useless" subjects, because they would not be able to make much use of other types of education. The question is, If other fields appear to be opening up, how long will it take for blacks and women to adjust by acquiring more education or education more relevant to the newly available jobs?

The answer seems to be that it does not take long. Blacks have rapidly increased the amount of education they acquire. Even more striking because less expected by many have been recent changes in the educational aspirations and accomplishments of women. Until recently it was firmly believed by many (including those on university admissions committees) that women could not do well in many fields, including the physical and biological sciences and other areas requiring logical thinking. Even those who felt that women could potentially do well in any area often believed that the early socialization of girls was such that by the time they were well along in school they had in fact become incompetent in many subjects as the result of pressure from teachers, parents, and peers. If this were true, change in women's attainment in such areas would be slow until new generations of girls were raised from infancy socialized to think they could do as well as boys. As it has turned out, however, women have moved into subjects like law and medicine very rapidly. This shows how malleable individuals' interests and competencies can be, once opportunities become available, and indicates that the occupational distribution of women and blacks can change much more quickly than many people have expected, at least among younger members of a group (see Lueptow 1981).

In sum, the relative incomes of blacks and women are likely to increase in the years ahead as the result of their gaining access to types of education formerly relatively closed to them. The total effect of changes in the education of blacks and women is not likely to be great, however. Much more important will be declines in labor market discrimination, so that blacks and women could be rewarded for the education they already have and for going into new fields with the knowledge that they will be able to compete for jobs on an equal basis. The struggle for equal access to education is far from over, but what is more important is equal access to jobs.

The Economy

The relative incomes of different social groups depend to some degree on the rate at which the entire economy is growing and on which industries are growing or declining.

Historically, newcomers to labor markets and groups that have been discriminated against do best when the economy is expanding and there are many jobs available. The sanctity of seniority systems in labor relations and in Title 7, as well as the inclination of jobholders to sabotage the work of newcomers when times are hard, makes it very difficult for newcomers to an occupation to move up very rapidly unless the number of jobs is increasing. Thus the rate at which blacks and women gain on white men depends on how rapidly the American economy grows.

The nature of the economic growth is important as well. Newcomers and groups that have been discriminated against tend to move disproportionately into sectors of the economy that are just beginning to develop or that are growing especially rapidly, because their needs force them to take greater risks than other people, especially given the resistance they are likely to face from other groups in established industries. Historical examples include the Irish going into police work and Jews entering public education and the federal government (Gorelick 1981). The economic progress of particular groups may depend upon the creation of new industries.

Conversely, particular groups may suffer if they are found disproportionately in declining industries. Black men in particular are being hurt by the decline of American heavy manufacturing (Wilson 1980), for example.

Blacks and women would therefore be likely to gain on white men more rapidly if the American economy grows rapidly in the years to come, if new industries arise that they are able to help create or move into, and if the better jobs they now hold do not disappear. Is this what is likely to happen?

Unfortunately, there is no way to tell. The American economy has been stagnating for some time, and economists, business leaders, and politicians have lost considerable confidence in their ability to bring a return to rapid growth (see Thurow 1980). Prescribing and predicting what direction the economy will take has become a small industry in itself, but so many of the predictions are so vague, mutually contradictory, and unsupported by sound theory that I would hesitate to make even broad predictions about the future of the American economy, much less try to predict with any precision how the possible changes will affect particular social groups.

Ultimately, however, changes in the economy are likely to affect blacks and women far less than changes in prejudice, education, and other factors. The American economy has grown and changed tremendously since the country began to industrialize, but the economic situation of blacks and women is still far from equal to that of men. Blacks and women are affected differently than other groups by changes in the economy, primarily insofar as they are normally treated differently in the labor market—that is, insofar as they suffer from discrimination. Economic growth or decline by itself will not change this significantly.[7]

Politics

Contemporary EEO Legal Doctrine and Enforcement

The recent progress made by blacks and women has depended upon the enforcement of EEO legislation as well as on the factors already dis-

cussed. Thus developments in legal doctrine and the strength of enforcement efforts are likely to have a significant effect on the economic status
of blacks and women for some time.

Two things are clear now about the legal doctrine on EEO established
by the federal courts: it is unsettled, and it is far from radical.

The unsettled quality of legal doctrine as manifested in court decisions may be exemplified in its interpretation by Nathan Glazer, one of
the most prominent propounders of the view that the enforcement of
antidiscrimination legislation has taken a highly undesirable turn toward
quotas and reverse discrimination. In the original, 1975 edition of his
book *Affirmative Discrimination,* he attacked the courts for their
"strange definitions of 'discrimination' . . . requiring all the major employing institutions in the country to employ minorities in rough proportion to their presence in the population" (1978, 66) and for their concept
of affirmative action, which "assumes that everyone is guilty of discrimination" (1978, 58). In the new introduction written for the 1978
edition, however, he noted that "recent decisions of the Supreme Court
have given promise that those apparently inexorable developments may
be slowed" (1978, x). The 1979 *Weber* decision, which allowed com-
panies to give preference to blacks in training programs, may have
seemed to deny that new promise. It is clear that projections of future
trends in court decisions are risky indeed; the direction is simply not
clear in many areas (see, e.g., Jones 1982; Belton 1981; "Employment
discrimination law" 1982).

What is clear is that current legal doctrine is not radical and is not
likely to become so. One way to consider current doctrine is in light of
three proposals about how the Supreme Court *might* interpret Title 7,
made early in the development of the law in a Note in the *Harvard Law
Review* (Title VII 1967). The central question is this: When an employer
or a union is shown to have discriminated, what must be done for the
victims to compensate them for the harm they have suffered? The first
possibility is the "status quo" approach (Title VII 1967, 1268). The
discriminating employer or union is simply to cease discriminating, and
those who have been discriminated against, though they may receive the
pay they were deprived of, must subsequently compete for jobs on an
equal footing with other applicants. The positions they were deprived of
are occupied, and they gain no special advantage in future competition
for similar positions, even though they might have been more qualified
than the people who got the jobs.[8]

In the second approach, "rightful place," the victim of discrimination is given some kind of advantage in applying for jobs that open up in the future, possibly by creating fictitious "seniority" equal to what he or she would have had if there had been no discrimination. Finally, in the third approach, cleverly called "freedom now," an individual who had been deprived of a job because of discrimination would be given that job, even if that meant displacing the (presumably white and/or male) incumbent.

In some ways the "freedom now" approach seems the fairest. There would be complications stemming from difficulties in identifying all victims of discrimination and in displacing workers who did not themselves discriminate but only benefited from discrimination by employers or unions, but the approach has the virtue of most completely compensating the victims.[9] Nevertheless, it has never been tried and almost certainly never will be. It is too radical and would meet too much resistance.[10]

Instead, what has happened is that the courts have cautiously adopted the "rightful place" approach, sometimes giving members of victim groups preference for new positions as they open up, provided systematic discrimination has been shown to have occurred. Then quotas—such as having to hire one new black police officer for every new white until some prescribed total is reached—may be enforced. The Supreme Court went a bit further than this in the *Weber* case, deciding that the law *did not prohibit* taking race into account when choosing among applicants to a training program, in a situation (a plant in Louisiana) where it was common knowledge that blacks had not had access to training opportunities in the past because of discrimination. There has been no indication since *Weber* that the Court is willing to go any further. The Supreme Court's approach ensures that change will be slow and incremental, and it carefully protects the beneficiaries of past discrimination (that is, people who got jobs because many of their potential competitors were discriminated against). Strong arguments have been made that this is the fairest and most expedient way to proceed (e.g., Title VII 1967, Fiss 1971; Belton 1981). That may be. But whether it is or not, it does not seem radical. It simply sees to it that employers and unions, in certain narrowly defined circumstances, compensate blacks and women for injustices they suffered previously.

Even the continuation of this doctrine and its firm enforcement cannot be taken for granted, however. The doctrine itself is continually being challenged before the courts, and there are signs that they may retreat, making it more difficult to prove that discrimination has occurred and limiting the remedies available, particularly where upper-status jobs are concerned (Bartholet 1982). The ascent of blacks and women up the economic ladder may be slowed by courts that are more sympathetic to blacks who want to be truck drivers than to those who want to be managers.

Continuing enforcement of the law is doubtful as well. Federal enforcement efforts have generally been erratic, disorganized, and underfunded, and they are now being cut back (Herbers 1982). This means that enforcement depends on private parties. An individual who feels he or she has been discriminated against faces tremendous obstacles on the road to justice, however, if it proves impossible to work the complaint out amicably with the employer or union. EEO cases often take years to resolve and require that the aggrieved party invest vast amounts of time and effort. Legal expenses can amount to many thousands of dollars, which the typical black or woman obviously cannot afford (Steel 1983; Norton 1981). Some lawyers are willing to handle EEO cases on a contingency basis, because the law provides for their being compensated for time and expenses by the defendant. They are paid only if they win, however. And because the EEO law does not provide for punitive damages (as tort law does, for example), neither the aggrieved party nor the lawyer has any hope of a large "windfall" award. As a practical matter, few lawyers are willing to handle EEO cases for individuals, and it is difficult to imagine most individuals who have been discriminated against taking legal action, because they are likely never to recoup the time, energy, or money that is involved in an EEO case.

With the EEO efforts of the federal government disorganized and those of individuals generally irrational from an economic point of view, much of the responsibility for bringing major cases and developing legal doctrine has been taken up by legal organizations that are essentially part of the civil rights and women's movements, such as the NAACP Legal Defense and Education Fund, the Lawyers' Committee for Civil Rights under Law, and the Women's Rights Project (see Belton 1978; Norton 1981; O'Connor and Epstein 1981–82). They seem to be almost the only ones capable, so far, of acquiring the resources, developing the expertise, and sustaining the lengthy involvement necessary to win cases against major employers and unions. Without their continuing involvement in EEO litigation, it is unlikely that blacks and women would have gained as much as they have from the enforcement of the EEO laws.

This is another way of saying, as I suggested in chapter 6, that the struggle for EEO in the courts and administrative agencies remains a political struggle, pursuing by legal means the goals proclaimed in street demonstrations and congressional testimony and relying on the political organization of the relevant groups and their sympathizers. This is not surprising, though we do not usually view administrative and judicial law enforcement this way. More and more, we are coming to realize that many laws aimed at reform are not self-enforcing and that, in fact, they may not help their intended beneficiaries at all unless those potential beneficiaries organize and continuously pressure the enforcement agencies (Sabatier 1975; Galanter 1974; Hayes 1981, chap. 2). Given the way today's EEO law is written, interpreted, and enforced, the magnitude of its effect depends heavily on how well organized its proponents and opponents are and will be.

The Balance of Power

If the efficacy of EEO legislation will depend on the power of its proponents and opponents, knowing who they are and assessing their power could help predict how great an effect the law is likely to have in the near future.

Presumably the law is supported, at least to some extent, by the large segment of the public that supported its passage in the first place. This widespread support is important; it prevents those opposed to EEO in principle from being very outspoken and requires them to claim (most of the time) that they are not opposed to EEO, but only to some of the supposedly outrageous methods by which it is enforced.

Degrees of support and opposition can vary among social groups, however, and their relative power and size may be important. The most obvious supporters of strong enforcement are those who stand to gain economically—members of minority groups and those women who are in the labor force or expect to be. The most obvious opponents would be those who personally have the most to lose—probably less-qualified white men whose economic success depends to a significant degree upon their not having to compete with qualified members of minority groups and women (see Villemez 1977).

Other groups might very well be ambivalent or divided. Women who are not in the labor force, and whose economic well-being depends upon their husbands' economic success, might worry about how their husbands will do in fair competition with women. Men with wives actually or potentially in the labor force might favor EEO because it would enable their wives to earn more and thereby increase the family income; or they might be made uncomfortable at the prospect of their wives' earning more than they do. Employers should favor EEO, because theoretically it will lead to a more efficient allocation of labor, more economic growth, and higher profits; but they may resent the short-run costs involved in instituting affirmative action programs, the risks of being sued for discrimination, and the loss of autonomy involved when they lose the power to choose their workers any way they want without outside interference.

On balance, the strongest supporters of EEO legislation are members of groups that have traditionally been economically deprived and politically weak. Potential opponents include the major corporations and business organizations that are in fact the defendants in most EEO litigation (see O'Connor and Epstein 1981–82). In such circumstances it is difficult to be sanguine about the prospects for EEO enforcement. Enforcement of the law could continue to be as effective as it has been; but it is hard to imagine traditionally powerless groups overcoming resistance from those who control most of the country's economic resources and imposing radically stronger enforcement mechanisms on American employers.[11]

Some Differences between Blacks and Women

There are two differences between blacks and women (with black women sometimes in an ambiguous position) that may be relevant to their relative progress in the years ahead but that have not yet been referred to. These are relative group size and the structural implications of each group's integration into the labor market on the basis of equality with white men.

Group Size

Blacks, of course, are a relatively small proportion of the population, while women are a majority. In the struggle for EEO, group size can be an advantage and a disadvantage. Because blacks are relatively few, they could fairly easily be absorbed into positions formerly closed to them. Even if many employers continued to discriminate, blacks could still make great economic progress as long as a significant proportion of employers did not. Blacks could emulate the Jewish pattern, gravitating to firms that would treat them fairly and avoiding those that would not

(Jencks 1983a; Jews, of course, were an even smaller group; cf. Lieberson 1980).

Women are such a large group, however, that it is difficult to see how they could attain economic parity with white men before all (or almost all) employers ceased discriminating (even assuming that a higher proportion of women than men choose to remain outside the labor force).

Although the fact that there are many fewer blacks than women may make their economic success easier, it may make their political success more difficult. In a democracy there is strength in numbers, so the potential political strength of women is far greater than the strength of blacks. Women are politically divided now on some equal rights issues and may very well remain so; nevertheless, to the extent they become more unified and organized politically, they represent a political threat blacks cannot match.

Structural Implications of EEO

What would universal EEO mean for American society? If it implied no more than a society exactly like the one we have today, only with more black and female managers and more male secretaries and telephone operators, one can imagine EEO arriving without much fuss as prejudice declined. If, however, it implied major structural changes in the economy or other areas of life, it might meet much more resistance and be more difficult to attain.

For many people, EEO for blacks is relatively easy to imagine, despite America's long history of racism. Blacks could occupy whatever jobs they wanted and were qualified for, and in the long run the differences for most people would amount simply to working next to some blacks as well as whites. Blacks could become like white ethnic groups, maintaining cultural distinctiveness but achieving as much economic success as anyone else.

There are those who argue that this could not happen, that American capitalism depends upon the subjugation of blacks, who represent a cheap source of labor while racism divides the working class. The bulk of the evidence is inconsistent with this, however (Beck 1980). In the short run, EEO would imply some whites' losing income to blacks, but no major structural changes would be required to bring about a truly racially integrated work force.

Sexual equality is a different matter (see Stern, Gove, and Galle

1976). Equal treatment of women in the labor force could lead to changes in many areas of life, though no one is sure what they might be. The division of labor in the family could change as women refuse to do the housework and take care of the children as well as work for pay (as is commonly the case with women in the labor force today; Vanek 1981). The division of household tasks could become more equal. Alternatively, differences between families could increase, as more men stay home to take care of the household and children while their wives work (cf. Becker 1981, chap. 2). The organization of employment might change, as more husbands and wives in two-career families demand changes that make it easier to combine work and family responsibilities—flexible hours, flexible benefit plans, employer-provided child care, more part-time but permanent positions, and the like. Many taken-for-granted aspects of day-to-day life might have to change as both husbands and wives in more and more couples are at work during the day—pediatricians could not assume that mothers are always available to bring children in for checkups during the day and might have to work on evenings and weekends; appliance repairers might have to be willing to go to customers' homes in the evening; the traditional hours and locations of many types of businesses might have to change. Sexual equality in the workplace could lead to major changes in sex roles, relationships in the family, economic institutions, and in fact throughout the society, changes not seriously considered by those who added "sex" to the types of discrimination prohibited by Title 7.

This may very well imply that sexual equality will be much more difficult to achieve than racial equality. Working next to someone whose skin happens to be a different color will probably be much easier for many people than changing their notions about sex roles and the structure of major institutions. This in turn may mean that resistance to EEO for women will be much greater than the resistance to EEO for blacks. No one can predict the relative progress of women and blacks with any certainty, or the relative degrees of resistance they will face, but the possibility that sexual equality will be resisted more strongly than racial equality must be seriously considered.

Conclusions

At present rates of change in relative incomes, blacks and white women will not catch up to white men until well into the next century at the earliest. Parity could probably not be reached a great deal sooner. Because of the importance of age and childhood socialization in labor force outcomes, large income gaps between groups cannot be expected to close in less than a generation (meaning forty to forty-five years), and more than one generation is often needed.

But could parity be reached somewhat sooner? Or might it take longer, even a lot longer?

Because the income gaps between blacks and whites and women and men are so much a function of prejudice and discrimination, the rate at which the gaps close depends strongly on how rapidly prejudice and discrimination decline. They may continue to decline as rapidly in the future as they have in the past, and the rate of decline could even increase if employers see a competitive advantage to hiring qualified individuals regardless of race or sex. The rate of decline could slow, however, if latent prejudice is aroused as blacks and women encroach more often on traditionally white male jobs, and if statistical discrimination continues to work against blacks and women. There is little reason to expect blacks and women to be helped much by reverse discrimination. So little is known about why prejudice and discrimination have declined recently that it is risky indeed to predict that recent trends will continue. In addition, my reading of history suggests that discrimination is at least as likely to increase as competition for jobs in a stagnating economy becomes more intense as it is to decrease through the workings of the free market. On balance, I would predict that discrimination may continue to decline as rapidly in the future as it has in the past, but if the rate changes it is more likely to decrease than to increase.

Educationally, blacks made the "easy" gains relative to whites in the previous generation—reaching approximate equality in terms of years completed—and future gains for blacks and women will involve aspects of education that are both more subtle and more difficult to translate into economic gains than mere quantity of schooling completed. Thus, to the extent that blacks have gained on whites economically in recent years because of increasing education, their rate of gain is likely to be slower in the future. As the type of education acquired by women becomes more similar to that acquired by men, the income gap between the two groups may close; but women's economic gains depend less on their academic abilities than on the willingness of employers and unions to reward them for the training they acquire. Thus, change in the education acquired by blacks and women is unlikely, by itself, to have a major effect on the differences in income between them and white men.

The economy could change in ways especially helpful to blacks and women, and it is even possible that the development of new institutions or new industries now barely dreamed of could contribute greatly to their economic progress. But this is guesswork; no one would want to claim with great confidence that future changes in the economy will help blacks and women significantly in their fight to earn what white men do.

The enforcement of EEO legislation may have a significant effect on the incomes of blacks and women relative to those of white men. Enforcement, in turn, seems to depend strongly on how well blacks, women, and their supporters organize to pressure employers, unions, administrative agencies, and the courts. It also depends on how well their opponents organize. Blacks and women have gotten better organized in recent years and are beginning to acquire more elective offices, administrative positions in government, and judgeships. If these trends continue, EEO enforcement could be strengthened, and income parity could be reached sooner than projected; but this depends on how intensely the efforts of pro-EEO forces are opposed by others.

Blacks could make economic progress more rapidly than women because they are relatively few and could (or at least black men could) be absorbed into positions throughout the economy without raising demands for major changes in economic institutions or the family. Women could not be absorbed so readily, and their entry into the labor force and into upper-level jobs may be strongly resisted because of the changes implied in economic institutions and the family. Politically, of course, large groups have the advantage in a democratic political system.

Thus the progress of blacks and women depends most strongly on how rapidly discrimination declines and on continuing political organization on their part. It is impossible to predict trends in prejudice with any confidence, but I would expect changes to come more slowly in the future than they have in the past, as economic competition among blacks, whites, and women increases. This would slow the progress of blacks and women. Increasing their rates of progress depends upon discovering how to reduce discrimination and upon the political balance of forces between those who favor EEO and those who oppose it.

8 Conclusions

This book has been about the promise of democratic politics and about its performance. It began with two questions about the struggle for EEO: First, why did Congress decide to prohibit employment discrimination when it did and in the way it did? Second, to what extent has the struggle for EEO, including the demand for EEO legislation, improved the opportunities available to groups that suffered from employment discrimination? Because EEO is such an important issue, answering these two questions is important for its own sake; but the attempt to answer them was also intended to help us confront a broader, more general question: Can the possibilities democratic politics seems to afford actually be used effectively by the disadvantaged in their struggle for more equal rights and opportunities? This chapter summarizes the book and shows how it helps us answer these questions; it also discusses why these questions have been so difficult to answer and describes the contributions this book makes to our ability to answer them, not just for EEO in the United States, but for other issues and other places as well.

The Struggle for Equal Employment Opportunity

Everyone who was an adult during the 1960s more or less "knows" why civil rights legislation was passed, because a standard, widely accepted account of what happened was published in the major newspapers at the time, an account that has been repeated since in major college textbooks in the social sciences and has not been substantially altered by scholarly work on the period. Congressional action on civil rights, according to this account, was the result of changes in public opinion, the marches, demonstrations, sit-ins, and other protest activities of the civil rights movement, public revulsion at the violent attacks by white southerners on peaceful civil rights marchers, media attention to the civil rights movement, and the inspired or strategic actions of political leaders inside and outside government, including Martin Luther King, Jr., Senators Dirksen and Humphrey, and President Johnson.

This "knowledge," however, is deficient in at least two ways. First, the account it provides is so vague and ambiguous that it says little about how the various factors influenced Congress or each other. The account does not tell us, for example, whether civil rights demonstrations changed people's minds about civil rights or only intensified the feelings people already had. It does not say whether congressional leaders simply organized the congressional response to public opinion or got Congress to act in opposition to public opinion or significantly influenced the content of legislation. And it leaves unanswered hosts of other questions about exactly how Congress was brought to act as it did.

Second, the standard account simply ignores many things central to the struggle for EEO—the content of EEO legislation, the role played by ideas in the fight for legislative action, the determinants of the passage of Title 7 as distinguished from the Civil Rights Act of 1964 as a whole, the 1972 amendments, the slow growth of congressional support, and the persistent lobbying efforts by a few organizations. Probably many of these factors have been ignored because the events of the early 1960s were so unusual and dramatic that they seemed sufficient by themselves to account for congressional action; there seemed to be little need to note that the struggle for civil rights legislation had been a long one, won at least as much because of persistent lobbying and gradual changes in public opinion as because of huge demonstrations and compromises between prominent senators.

This book has provided a new account of why Congress acted when and as it did on EEO. The new account is consistent in some ways with the old one, but it is also much more specific in its description of how various forces influenced Congress and each other, and it demonstrates the importance of factors previously ignored.

Before the late 1930s, it made almost no sense to think about Congress's passing EEO legislation, because federal legislation regulating either labor relations or race relations was not likely to withstand judicial scrutiny. Congress began considering EEO bills almost immediately after changes in constitutional doctrine made it plausible to expect a federal EEO law to be seen as constitutional by the Supreme Court. An essential prerequisite of congressional action, thus, was a sense of possibility.

A second prerequisite of today's EEO law was a set of ideas about how the federal government should deal with employment discrimination. Here, as in other issue areas Nelson Polsby has discussed (1984), a few ideas go a long way. The text of the classic EEO bill developed in the early 1940s was based on New Deal ideas about how the federal government should regulate business and unions and was never seriously reexamined during the thirty years it was debated, except for some aspects of the enforcement process. The two most important changes made in the bill—prohibiting sex discrimination and prohibiting discrimination by state and local governments—were made without much serious debate or much change in the basic structure of the bill. EEO legislation may have been passed as the result of social and political changes taking place in American society since the 1940s, but the legislation itself was little affected by these changes.

Proposals for prohibiting employment discrimination were developed long before most Americans were willing to accept them. People willing and able to nurture the proposals, to keep them alive, and to organize support for them were therefore an essential component of the process leading to eventual passage. This means the small group of senators and representatives who persistently sponsored EEO legislation, held hearings, and tried to gain the support of their colleagues, along with the organizations that lobbied for EEO legislation over the years, including civil rights organizations, black and Jewish groups, church organizations, unions, and public interest groups. It was they who built up a record of expert testimony, moral justification, and support for the classic bill, so that when public opinion forced Congress to act with a sense of urgency, it acted by adopting the bill that had been on the legislative agenda for many years.

The major reason Congress acted was, of course, public opinion. Congress passed EEO legislation in 1964 and amended it in 1972 primarily because it had become convinced that the public wanted it to. When EEO bills were first considered by Congress, in the early 1940s, most Americans opposed EEO for blacks and women, and many opposed it for other groups, such as Jews, as well. Even among those who favored the principle of EEO, many objected to having EEO legislated. Congressional support for such legislation was therefore just what one might expect of a legislature whose members were motivated primarily by a desire to please their constituents—namely, minimal. As public opinion gradually became more favorable to EEO and to antidiscrimination legislation during the next thirty years, congressional support for

EEO legislation increased correspondingly. Title 7 passed shortly after members of Congress could say with some confidence, for the first time, that more than half the public favored EEO and felt strongly that civil rights was a major public problem.

Both political theory and studies of members of Congress argue persuasively that legislators follow public opinion because they fear that if they do not they will lose something they want very much—reelection. Thus it is competitive politics—though not necessarily change in the party balance—that links public opinion to congressional action. But the congressional response was not automatic or mechanical; before Congress would act on EEO, it had to be shown what the public felt and how intensely the public wanted action.

The civil rights movement and its allies played a central role in this process and appear to have accomplished three things. First, public protests against discrimination caused members of Congress to monitor public opinion on EEO and related issues more diligently than they might have otherwise. Protest thus led to heightened congressional awareness of the increasingly pro-EEO trend in public opinion. Second, the violent response the protestors evoked in the South increased the intensity of public concern about civil rights; as members of Congress monitored public opinion, therefore, they found a public not only increasingly favorable to EEO, but also intensely concerned about it. This intensity may have been essential for the initial legislative breakthroughs in civil rights, because although the strong opposition of white southerners to civil rights legislation could stymie the will of an apathetic majority of the American people, it could not overrule an intensely concerned majority. Finally, as noted above, movement lobbyists and their congressional allies provided a crucial link between trends in public opinion and the adoption of specific legislation, by convincing other members of Congress that they could satisfy public demands by supporting the classic EEO bill.

A sense of possibility, a set of ideas, a group of people persistently trying to gain support for the ideas, shifts in public opinion within a competitive democratic political system, a movement heightening the public's concern—all these set the stage for the adoption of Title 7 and its strengthening amendments. The final ingredient was leadership. Congressional leaders played a significant role in the fight for legislation by seeing to it that Congress responded effectively to public opinion and by orchestrating the necessary parliamentary maneuvers.

A list of the factors that led to the adoption and amendment of Title 7 should be complemented by a list of factors Congress did *not* respond to, at least in the way suggested by some previous observers. Lobbyists had influence over what Congress did, but only in conjunction with public opinion; they did not have the power to get Congress to do anything the public did not want. Congressional leaders, likewise, apparently had little power independent of that granted them by public opinion; they could not get Congress to adopt EEO legislation when the public opposed it, and—regarding the senior southern senators and representatives—could not long delay it after the public came to favor it. Nor did the mass media have an independent role in the process leading to the passage of legislation; newspapers and television publicized the civil rights movement and the sometimes violent reaction to it but had no influence of their own on public opinion or congressional action. Finally, change in the party balance had no effect on congressional action. Congress thus responded primarily to public opinion brought to its attention and heightened in intensity by the civil rights movement; acceding to the wishes of lobbyists and its own leaders, it then adopted a bill everyone had long agreed was the way to deal with EEO, if it was to be dealt with at all.

The struggle for EEO legislation was, of course, just part of the struggle for EEO. What difference has the struggle made? Has it really helped the groups that suffered from discrimination in employment?

The attempt to answer these questions required confronting scholarly literature more developed than that analyzing the determinants of congressional action. The literature is split, however, into two parts. On one side are those technical analyses that generally conclude that EEO legislation has had little if any economic effect, especially on blacks. The rigor of these analyses is useful, in that they show how restrained the responses of government and economic institutions have been to the struggle for EEO and how difficult it is to establish that the enforcement of EEO legislation has had much influence. The credibility of such analyses is limited, however, because they ignore the social and political context in which the struggle for EEO has taken place, and the social and political consequences as well. On the other side are many broader, less technical analyses that conclude that the battle is having radical social, political, and economic consequences. Their portrayal of American society as being radically transformed by wild-eyed bureaucrats and irresponsible judges imposing quotas everywhere is, to say the least, exaggerated; but these analyses are useful because they show how important it is to be concerned about the broad social and political trends that are both cause and consequence of EEO legislation.

EEO legislation *has* made a difference. Nonwhite women have clearly benefited from the passage and implementation of EEO legislation; no matter how their incomes are measured, EEO legislation has helped them gain on white men. The picture is a little less clear for white women and nonwhite men, but I would argue that they have benefited as well. The earnings of white women in the labor force have not increased much relative to those of white men, but I think it is misleading to focus on earnings in the short run, even though most analysts do; group share is a more appropriate focus of concern. It is misleading to focus on earnings because so many more white women than men, proportionately, have entered the labor force in recent years; when so many women lack experience, their incomes will be low for a while and will drag down the average for all women in the labor force, making it appear incorrectly that the relative economic status of women is not improving. In fact, however, the money earned by the new entrants increases their economic well-being and the share of the national income going to women. An analysis focusing on the income of *all* women, not just those in the labor force—focusing on their group share, that is—shows that the relative income of white women has been increasing and that EEO legislation is responsible for much of the increase.

Nonwhite men have, at worst, not been harmed by EEO legislation. That is no small matter, because the gains made by women, particularly in group share, could easily have come at the expense of nonwhite men. Instead, EEO legislation seems to have had no net effect on the group share of nonwhite men and a positive effect on their earnings and total incomes.

Ultimately, decreases in prejudice were necessary if women and nonwhites were to increase their relative incomes, but they were not sufficient; it is the transformation of changes in attitudes into legislative prohibitions against discrimination that has been responsible for many of the gains made by women and nonwhites. As chapter 6 showed, changing attitudes have had no direct effect on the incomes of nonwhite men and women. Instead, the decreases in prejudice, *when encouraged and taken advantage of by the civil rights movement,* led to improved educational opportunities and the passage and enforcement of EEO legislation. These in turn led to increases in the relative incomes of nonwhite men and women. The situation was somewhat different for white women, because they gained directly from changing attitudes and had not suffered from lack of education. Yet much of their gain, too, has depended upon EEO legislation. Thus, changes in attitudes made economic change possible; political action made it a reality.

Democratic Politics and the Struggle for Equality

What does the fight for EEO tell us about the extent to which democratic politics can be used to redistribute rights, opportunities, and income in a society? I think it can tell us a great deal, when placed in the context of political theory and studies of other issues. The questions dealt with above are not simply questions about mechanics, motivated by a desire to take society apart, to see how it works. The questions are human ones because they deal with the opportunities and obstacles people face as they try to achieve their aspirations, particularly those aspirations that bring them into opposition to other people.

Any attempt to analyze democratic politics must confront two fundamentally opposed views about its potential utility as a means of redistributing rights, opportunities, and income. On one side is the pluralist view, according to which power is dispersed, the main actors in political conflict are ever-shifting coalitions of interest groups, government agencies and officials sometimes act on their own to influence political outcomes, and almost all groups may influence the resolution of issues that concern them. In the pluralist view of the American political process, Robert Dahl, its best-known proponent, has written, "there is a high probability that an active and legitimate group in the population can make itself heard effectively at some crucial stage in the process of decision" (1956, 145). Opposed to this view is one in which power is concentrated in the hands of a relatively small elite, the main actors are the elite and the institutions they run on the one side and the masses on the other, the government merely acts to sustain elite power, and most people can rarely influence the resolution of issues that affect their lives. This latter view, often called the "elitist" or "stratification" view, has many variants—Marxist, neo-Marxist, class dialectic, and so on (Whitt 1982; Polsby 1983). I think it is fair to say, however, that they all agree on some essential claims about American democracy—that the relatively poor and unorganized groups in the society are effectively prevented from influencing major political decisions and that, essentially, democratic politics is a sham, manipulated by elites so as to maintain their power and privilege.

Pluralists, therefore, maintain that democratic politics can regularly be used to redistribute rights, opportunities, and income; elitists claim that it rarely or never can be. Who offers the more accurate appraisal of the struggle for EEO? To answer this question, we must discover whose interests were at stake in the struggle, who had sufficient power to determine the outcome (thus far), and whose interests have been served.

Those whose interests were most obviously at stake were those being discriminated against on one side and those doing the discriminating on the other. Not all those involved in discrimination, either as victims or as perpetrators, were actively involved in the battle for EEO, however. Among the victims, by far the most highly organized and active protestors were blacks and Jews; among the discriminators, the most active in defense of the status quo were white southerners, most conspicuously through their representatives in Congress. It was fairly clear what each of these groups had to gain or lose in the fight for EEO. Blacks and Jews were seeking to improve their economic opportunities as well as to gain the civil rights accorded to others. White southerners were seeking to preserve a way of life organized to a considerable degree around the subjugation of blacks.

Other groups may have had something to gain or lose, but their interests are less obvious. According to some economists (e.g., Becker 1971), capitalists would gain from an end to discrimination because discrimination prevents the most efficient use of labor; others have claimed, however, that capitalists gain from dividing the working class on the basis of racial antagonism (see the review in Wilson 1980, chap. 1), and many capitalists and managers certainly resent the intrusion into their affairs involved in enforcement of EEO laws. White men may, in the long run, gain from living in a society in which the end of discrimination leads to an increase in economic efficiency and hence higher per capita income; but in the short run some will clearly suffer economically if forced to compete fairly with groups previously excluded from most good jobs (Lieberson 1980). Thus it is difficult to show that the material interests of most groups in the society would drive them unambiguously to support one side or the other in the fight for EEO. And, in fact, with a few exceptions, groups other than those most directly involved in discrimination acted as if their interests were either divided or not much affected by the fight—that is, they did not openly or actively participate in the congressional struggle.

When the struggle over economic opportunities was confined to dis-

criminators and their victims, there was little doubt about the outcome;
the economically more powerful group, which controlled access to jobs,
would win. Discrimination might decline somewhat as the result of
changing attitudes, and possibly other forces, but only very slowly, as
the result of decisions made by the more powerful at their discretion.

Seemingly faced with discrimination continuing indefinitely into the
future, those who were discriminated against responded in a way well
described by E. E. Schattschneider in his classic *The Semisovereign
People* (1960)—they tried to take the conflict over EEO out of the private arena, where they seemed doomed to lose, and bring it into the
public arena, where they hoped the balance of power would be more to
their advantage. That is, they tried to get the government, a group potentially more powerful than their direct adversaries, to adopt and imple-
ment legislation that would force discriminators to change their
behavior. Such a tactic could work only if the government could be
influenced to act on behalf of relatively poor and disadvantaged groups,
and if the government was in fact more powerful than their adversaries.

As we know, the government *was* moved to act on behalf of the
relatively poor and disadvantaged. The power to get the government to
do so rested, however, not with the poor and disadvantaged alone, but
with the group that Schattschneider emphasized often determines the
outcome of political conflict—the "audience" (1960, 2) or, in this
case, the public as a whole. The driving force behind congressional
action turns out to have been public opinion.

This finding is quite compatible with the pluralist view, but not with
the elitist view. Yet there was another kind of power involved in the
adoption of Title 7, a kind of power that does not fit neatly into either
view. There was a limit on the power of the public in the fight for EEO
legislation. Public opinion demanded that Congress do something to
prohibit employment discrimination, but not that it do anything in particular; that is, with regard to this issue, like most others, the public made
general demands but was neither willing nor able to be very specific
about how they should be satisfied. In determining what, specifically,
Congress would do about EEO, great power must be attributed to the
authors of the classic EEO bill, who, through the "power of the first
draft," effectively set the terms of future congressional action. They
appear to have done so, not very surprisingly, by writing a statute em-
bodying language and approaches familiar from other statutes. The EEO
law, therefore, is quite conservative in some ways—respectful of prop-

erty and of business, oriented toward conciliation, employing elaborate procedures, focusing on individual cases. Was this an instance in which elites made use of the historical biases of American political institutions—a bias that even prominent pluralists agree is "against change" (Dahl and Lindblom 1976, xliii)—to nullify the apparent power of the masses? Was it an instance in which the public's attitudes, delicately poised between a willingness to favor equality of opportunity and a distaste for moves guaranteeing equality of results (Lipset and Schneider 1978), were accurately reflected in the statute? Or was it both? There is really no way to tell.

There is still, of course, the question of results. Whose interests have been served by the adoption of EEO legislation? Again, there are obvious beneficiaries—the blacks and women whose incomes are higher now than they would have been without the law. In the short term there has been a price to be paid for these gains. Certainly the many major corporations, government agencies, and unions that have lost EEO suits or have agreed in consent decrees to change their employment practices and compensate people they have discriminated against must believe they have lost something. People who have not gotten jobs they would have gotten in the past because the competition may involve more and different kinds of people have lost something as well. In the long term, it may be argued, society as a whole will gain from EEO; in the short term, however, many corporations and individuals no doubt see themselves as paying a real price for it. From their point of view, the disadvantaged have gained and the better-off have lost—an outcome more compatible with the pluralist than the elitist view.

Thus the American public can get the federal government to redistribute rights, opportunities, and income, at least with regard to EEO. But was the struggle for EEO typical, or was it a fluke, an exception to a general rule of elite dominance and public impotence? A growing body of evidence indicates that the case of EEO was not a fluke, that the government is frequently, if not always, responsive to the public on major issues. The government's responsiveness to public opinion on EEO, for example, is not at all unusual. The three issues the public has been most consistently concerned about for the past fifty years have been the economy, war, and civil rights. On economic issues, Congress does respond to the public. At the end of his comprehensive study of political control of the economy, Edward Tufte concluded that "under conditions of partisan political competition . . . to a significant degree, the economic priorities of the party elected to run the government are carried out. This democratic control of economic outcomes is impressive" (1978, 142–43). At the time he wrote the book he felt obliged to qualify his conclusion by adding that such democratic control was impressive "particularly when compared to the extent of such control for other issues" (1978, 143). But the qualification is unnecessary, at least with regard to the two other issues the public has cared most about. As I have shown previously, public opinion had a powerful influence on congressional action on the Vietnam War (Burstein and Freudenburg 1978; Burstein 1979c), and this book and previous articles have demonstrated its influence on EEO and other civil rights legislation (Burstein 1979a). There are, of course, some issues on which Congress ignores public opinion (see, e.g., Weissberg 1976), but recent studies show that the number of issues on which Congress responds to public opinion is very substantial indeed (Page and Shapiro 1983).

Similarly, other, more specific conclusions following from the study of EEO are consistent with the findings of other researchers, though the number of even roughly comparable studies is small. It may be a general phenomenon, for example, that the success of a social movement depends upon changes in the social and political context over which it has little or no control. Comparing a farm workers' movement that succeeded with one that failed, Jenkins and Perrow conclude (1977, 266) that "The critical factor separating the National Farm Labor Union failure from the United Farm Worker success was the societal response to insurgent demands." (The former received little public support, the latter a great deal.) "The dramatic turnabout in the political environment originated in economic trends and political realignments that took place quite independent of any 'push' from insurgents."

The same argument can be made about the influence of lobbying and leadership on congressional action. Some have argued that lobbyists and political leaders can rarely get legislators to act in opposition to the desires of their constituents (e.g., Kingdon 1981; Jackson 1974). The analysis of EEO buttresses these claims, showing how the effect of lobbying the leadership (as well as social protest) seems to depend upon public opinion.

On balance, therefore, there is much evidence consistent with the pluralist view—the government does respond to the public and may even be brought to act on behalf of the poor and disadvantaged. There is, however, a ready reply to this claim: even after the civil rights movements, the thirty years of work by the proponents in Congress, the adoption of legislation, and the expenditure of hundreds of millions of dollars on its enforcement, it will still be a very long time before the incomes of blacks and women approach those of white men. American democratic institutions may respond to the poor and disadvantaged, but not much, and only very grudgingly. Major change is almost impossible to bring about; those who hold power have actually been forced to concede very little.

At this point, I think, a weakness of both the pluralist and the elitist positions becomes apparent. Neither specifies with any precision just how responsive a system has to be, how much influence various groups have to have, or how rapid change must be for a political system to be described as pluralist or elitist. Pluralists and elitists often seem to be looking at the same glass and getting into bitter arguments over whether it is half full or half empty. Thus, for example, the pluralist Robert Dahl devotes much of his book *Pluralist Democracy in the United States* (1967) to describing civil war, revolution, ethnic, religious, and regional differences, the civil rights movement, and conflict of all kinds. He shows how difficult it is for those who want political change to succeed, but his conclusion is sanguine (1967, 428): "Success [for a group trying to get a policy adopted], if it ever arrives, often takes years; many defeats may occur during the intervening generations. An idea born out of its time may struggle desperately to survive. . . . Considered in this perspective, the citizen interested in political action may feel himself to be a victim of forces over which he can exert no control. . . . This, I think, is too one-sidedly pessimistic a view of man's fate . . . in important ways changes in policy depend on the actions of individuals. . . . The day of victory may be long in coming. . . . But unless individuals were to act . . . then the changes we all witness in our own times would, surely, never occur."

Taking the elitist perspective, in contrast (though he might not like the label), William Gamson, in a study that shows social protest often succeeds, concludes (1975, 142–43), "The pluralist image, then, is a half-truth. . . . Some of these unruly and scrappy challengers do eventually become members [of the polity]. . . . Entry is not prohibited for those with the gumption, the persistence, and the skill to pursue it long enough. But this is, at best, cold comfort. Beyond the unsuccessful challengers studied here there may lie others unable to generate enough effort to mount even a visible protest. If it costs so much to succeed, how can we be confident that there are not countless would-be challengers who are deterred by the mere prospect?''

Both Dahl and Gamson see the struggle for political success as long and often difficult, with no guarantee of success. Yet one of them concludes that the pluralist view is correct, while the other sees it as a half-truth. Who is right? There is simply no way to decide; the choice becomes, in the absence of explicit standards, a matter of personal predilection, or of mood, as much as anything else. And recent attempts to develop subtler or more sophisticated models of the distribution of power in America founder upon the same difficulty. J. Allen Whitt's statement that in the "class dialectic" model outcomes "usually favor dominant class interests, but may also reflect the power of opposing classes'' (1982, 32) hardly provides a useful guide to reaching conclusions about the distribution of power, because of its failure to specify what is meant by "usually" or "may also reflect."

I think that by now it is impossible to ignore the fact that the government is frequently responsive to the public. It is also impossible to ignore the fact that the response is often limited. Trying to force these facts into a mold, using them to decide whether the American political system is "really" pluralist or "really" elitist does not seem a fruitful endeavor, because both views are so vague. We need to know more about politics and to be more specific in our models before we can conclude that the American political system is "really" one thing or another.

The Limits of Political Action

This analysis has tried to show more fully and precisely than previous studies just how closely linked different aspects of politics are—how the effect of public opinion is related to social protest activity, and so forth. Yet it has also shown in three ways just how loosely politics is structured. The first aspect of this structural "looseness" is the gap between the general intention behind a policy and its specific formulation. As Hugh Heclo concluded in his study of social policy in Britain and Sweden: "Interests are self-serving but they have not been self-defining in the policy process" (1972, 300). Groups, that is, act in their own interest, but how those interests are translated into public policy is very much an open question. The opinions of the average individual, even one who is concerned about an issue, are usually so vague that they may translate into public policy in any number of ways. There are, for example, many possible ways of dealing with employment discrimination; American history provides some examples, and so does the experience of many European countries (Ratner 1980). What a law says may make great deal of difference to those it is supposed to affect, but laws may be written in a variety of ways without being in conflict with the desires of those demanding passage.

The second example of structural looseness stems from the way unforeseen problems and circumstances may weaken the connection between the expectations of the law's supporters and the eventual consequences of their actions. For example, few supporters of Title 7 understood how deeply and pervasively racist and sexist practices were incorporated in routine corporate practices, and so they did not foresee the extent to which personnel practices would be called into question once the law was passed; nor did they consider the ways sex discrimination differed from race discrimination and what the implications of a prohibition of sex discrimination might be. Many of the consequences of EEO legislation—on personnel practices, female labor force participation, educational institutions, sex roles, and the like—were not anticipated by those involved in the legislative debates and not even imagined by the average citizen who favored government action against discrimination. EEO is surely not the only issue that can be characterized this way. It is in essence unreasonable to assume that those responsible for the adoption of a policy can fully anticipate its likely consequences (cf. Skocpol 1980, 200).

The third example of looseness in the political process involves a great historical irony in the struggle for EEO, which demonstrates the difficulties involved in predicting long-term social trends. The irony is this: one of the groups most responsible for the adoption of EEO legislation has not utilized it, while another group that had no articulated interest in the legislation has proved to be its major beneficiary.

The movement for EEO was instigated largely by Jews and blacks, who were the most obvious victims of employment discrimination in American society. The campaign for EEO legislation took a very long time, however, and by the time it was adopted Jews had little need for it; anti-Semitism in the labor market had declined dramatically, and Jews had learned to avoid those sectors of the economy where it was still a problem (Jencks 1983a; Chiswick 1983). The number of EEO cases involving anti-Semitism has therefore been small.

The number of cases involving sex discrimination has, in contrast, been large and is increasing rapidly. Women, who were not for the most part involved in the struggle for EEO legislation on their own behalf, have proved to be its main beneficiaries, and their increasingly well-organized fight for equality may have ramifications far beyond those imagined by anyone involved in the congressional debate. Thus the situation of the Jews shows, to some extent, that groups organized to affect government action may accomplish much of what they want by other means, while groups insufficiently organized to influence government may gain government assistance nevertheless. In the battle against discrimination, the efforts of one group have helped another, sometimes accidentally.

Implications for the Study of Politics and Labor Markets

Simple Questions, Few Answers

The questions about EEO and democratic politics with which this book began were simple and straightforward. They proved very difficult to answer, however, partly because recent trends in the social sciences have revived that proverbial danger of academic life, knowing more and more about less and less, while reducing our ability to answer simple but important questions. Here are three examples of what I mean. First, most political scientists and many ordinary citizens agree that one of the most fundamental issues in democratic politics is the extent to which the government is responsive to public opinion. Until recently we have known very little about this, however, because many political scientists reacted to an apparent paucity of public opinion data on many issues by beginning to study the relation between public policy and variables presumably *related to* public opinion, for which data *were* available. For example, if people's opinions about economic policy were unknown, a researcher might relate data about their incomes to policy outcomes, having assumed that poor people prefer different policies than rich people. As the years went by, however, the researchers in effect forgot that they had begun with a concern about public opinion; the substitute variables came to be treated as important in their own right. The fundamental issue that motivated the research in the first place was forgotten, and virtually no progress was made in learning how public opinion affected public policy (Burstein 1981).

Second, social scientists have become less interested in finding out why particular policies were adopted than in showing that particular variables are important. As Heclo has written, "there is sometimes an unfortunate tendency for each discipline, or specialty within a discipline, to develop a proprietary interest in a variable, taking it as a matter of honor to prove than its variable is most important or at the very least is not cast into the outer darkness of statistical insignificance" (1972, 285). Thus there are people devoted to showing that social movements are important, that lobbying is important, that changes in the party balance are important. Much of this type of specialized research has proved useful, because it has led to important theoretical and methodological advances in our ability to analyze certain phenomena such as social movements (e.g., Gamson 1975); in fact much of the analysis in this book was based upon such advances. Unfortunately this emphasis on variables all too often means that no one is committed to showing how all the relevant variables fit together in the complex process that determines public policy. Such an approach is encouraged by the reward structure of academic disciplines and subdisciplines, but is an obstacle to describing the entire political process and to testing competing theories of politics. Everybody knows from common sense that policy is influenced by many things; this is one of those instances in which common sense is right, but one would never know that from reading many contemporary studies.

Third, social scientists tend to divide themselves into those who study the causes of legislative change and those who study the consequences. In the real world, people who want a law passed usually are not interested merely in seeing a new entry in the United States Code; they want the law to have some real impact. Those involved in the enforcement of legislation know that enforcement is affected by politics, just as passage was. The law itself is neither an end nor a beginning, but rather an intermediate stage in the political process. Yet it is seldom studied that way. The only book I know of that treats the political process formally as one that begins with pressures on the political system, continues through the legislative process, and moves on to subsequent changes in outcomes is Berk, Brackman, and Lesser's (1977) book on the California penal code, though Tufte's book on the economy (1978) and Wilensky's on welfare policy (1975) move in this direction as well. Part of the reason for this division between those who study causes and those who study consequences is the boundaries between academic disciplines; sociologists are most interested in certain causes of political

change, political scientists in others, and economists in the consequences. The result is that many of those interested in the causes of
political outcomes define as their outcome an intermediate stage of the
political process, such as the passage of legislation, and fail to see that
legislation may be given its real meaning only after passage, while those
examining the consequences of legislation may be mystified by what
they see because they fail to consider how the consequences are influenced by political and social change.

Getting Better Answers

While writing this book, I had to deal with a host of theoretical and
methodological problems, as every researcher does. Many of them were
peculiar to this project. But two types of problems were of more general
concern; in large part the product of the tendencies in the social sciences
just described, they were serious impediments to the study of politics
and income distribution. Describing the problems and determining how
they were dealt with, and with what consequences, may help improve
our capacity to study other issues and therefore our understanding of
politics and labor markets in general.

The first type of problem involved deciding what a study of EEO
should explain. In considering this, I found I had to rethink the analysis
of legislation, inequality, and social movements.

What is one explaining in a study of legislative change? Any politician, lawyer, or average citizen will agree that what a law says matters.
That is, it matters whether or not a law prohibits a particular activity,
applies to a particular group of people and so on. Most causal studies of
public policy, however, ignore the content of legislation (rare exceptions
include Berk, Brackman, and Lesser 1977 and Steinberg 1982), possibly because it is difficult to analyze quantitatively. But what sense
would this analysis make if it ignored the fact that discrimination against
women is prohibited?

Thus I decided to analyze not just why the law passed, but also why
it says what it does. Doing so led the way to some significant conclusions about the struggle for EEO—about the importance of ideas in the
legislative process, the focus of most legislators on doing something in
conjunction with their lack of concern with exactly what to do, the lack
of connection between the analysis of particular parts of a bill and its
eventual consequences, and the like. What laws say is important and
should not be so routinely ignored in future studies.

Rethinking the analysis of inequality was necessary and useful as well. EEO legislation was intended to reduce inequality, but there are many ways to conceptualize and measure inequality. Others have already pointed out, for example, that because EEO legislation is intended to affect how people earn income, not how they spend it, analyses should focus on income inequality between black and white individuals (who may earn income), not between black and white households (through which income is spent; see Jencks 1983a). Chapter 6 suggested, however, that focusing on individual incomes in routine ways when considering EEO may be misleading. EEO legislation is intended to affect not just how income is earned by workers, but also how it is distributed by institutions; in addition, because the enforcement of EEO legislation is affected by conflict between social groups and by the resources available to them, the future of EEO will depend on how income is distributed to entire groups, not just to individuals in the labor market. Thus, in the analysis of EEO, inequality of income among social groups should be considered, and in fact chapter 6 showed that examining group share rather than relative earnings had a significant effect on one's conclusions. If the distribution of income is treated as a purely economic matter, white women appear to be only slightly better off than they used to be, and EEO legislation may seem of little help. If income distribution is treated as partly a political matter, however, white women appear significantly better off, and EEO legislation may be shown to have had a positive effect.

The final concern was how to assess the impact of a social movement—in this case the movement for equal employment opportunity. An examination of previous work, especially quantitative work with claims to theoretical and methodological rigor, showed that studies of social movements failed to deal with legislation or its consequences (e.g., Gamson 1975; Jenkins and Perrow 1977), those dealing with civil rights or related issues provided little data on either the causes or the consequences of legislative change, and those dealing with the consequences of legislation ignored the social and political context in which enforcement was to take place. There were virtually no studies of how demands for government action led to legislation, following through to determine the consequences of the continuing demands *and* the legislation. Dealing with this problem meant drawing on past work on social movements, public opinion, legislative change, implementation, and so forth, and synthesizing it so that the factors considered by specialists in each area could be considered simultaneously.

Doing this was not just an intellectual exercise; it had substantial influence on the results of the study. The desire to follow the consequences of the demand for EEO through the political process as far as possible led to conclusions quite different from those of most previous studies, both about the causes of political change and about the nature of the consequences. The study of EEO showed that politics is a continuing process, not one in which outcomes are decided by dramatic events or one that ends at a particular moment, as when a law is signed by the president. The effectiveness of EEO legislation itself was not determined at the moment it was signed into law. Instead, enforcement has depended heavily upon the initiative of private individuals and concerned groups trying to raise money and maintain the organization necessary to pressure administrative agencies, courts, and employers into seeing that the law is obeyed. As people come to realize that politics continues after legislation is adopted (e.g., Sabatier 1975; Hayes 1981; Galanter 1974), it will become unacceptable to separate the determinants of policy from the study of its consequences.

The second type of problem I confronted in doing this study was *how to explain* the legislative and economic outcomes of the struggle for EEO. When attempting to do so, I found that I had to go beyond past work in dealing with public opinion, the complexities of social and political processes, and the time span involved in political change.

Public opinion, as already discussed, is of crucial theoretical importance in the study of democratic politics. Yet it has generally been ignored in empirical studies of democratic politics, and choosing to analyze it even though the available data were far from perfect was a major decision. Only since this book was begun has other systematic work been initiated on the effect of changes in public opinion on public policy (Page and Shapiro 1983).

When trying to draw on theory to help explain the processes leading to the passage and implementation of EEO legislation, I found myself facing major disjunctions between theory and research in the study of politics and stratification. Those who study both subjects know that the processes they are concerned about involve many variables. In addition, a growing body of work in politics (e.g., Godwin and Shepard 1976; Carmines 1974; Fiorina 1975; Kuklinski 1979; Kingdon 1981) and some work in stratification (Featherman and Hauser 1978, chap. 6) hypothesize that important aspects of politics and stratification involve interactions between relevant variables—for example, that elections, demonstrations, and lobbying may cause Congress to pay attention to public opinion without necessarily having a direct effect of their own, or that one consequence of EEO legislation would be to increase the strength of the relationship between education and income for blacks and women. Almost all empirical research, however, ignores these hypotheses and continues to consider the variables separately, often expressing confusion when the variables do not have the independent effects expected (see Burstein 1981 for a review). This book has shown that taking theory seriously and applying it to statistical analysis can affect one's conclusions in significant ways—showing, for example, that political leaders increased congressional response to public opinion while favorable public opinion heightened the power of leaders. Theory also made the lack of relationship between the party balance and congressional action not only understandable, but expected. Future quantitative work on politics should see fewer linear additive models and more with interaction effects.

The final issue in explaining the outcomes of the struggle for EEO concerned the time span involved in the genesis of major political change. Most analyses of civil rights legislation, and in fact of most legislation that seems to respond to especially urgent demands or needs, take an essentially episodic view of politics. That is, although it is acknowledged that long-term social changes may have preceded legislative action, the primary focus is on the dramatic events just before passage. This approach makes passage of such legislation appear to be an aberration, not part of normal social or political processes (cf. Gamson 1975), and narrows the search for causes, leading to a focus on the dramatic (e.g., demonstrations) and the neglect of more slowly developing manifestations of social change. In fact, as this analysis has shown, the fundamental determinants of legislative action are likely to be long-term social and political trends and organizational efforts; in addition, the exact form taken by the legislative action is likely to be strongly influenced by ideas current at the time the legislative debate began. History cannot be ignored.

This book is based upon a number of theoretical and methodological innovations, many developed by others but never applied together as they have been here. My conclusions would have been very different, and far less credible, without them.

Summing Up

As the United States began to rise out of the Great Depression of the 1930s it was, as it always has been, a land of both opportunity and obstacles. Americans had more freedom and equality than people almost anywhere else, but vast numbers found their ability to earn a living and hope of being rewarded for their efforts hindered by discrimination based on race, religion, national origin, or sex.

The movement for EEO sought to end such discrimination, and to a considerable extent its aim has been achieved. Anti-Semitism in the labor market is no longer a major issue; the relative incomes of blacks, women, and other groups have increased; the principle of equal opportunity is much more widely accepted than it was; and those who feel they have been discriminated against may get the aid of federal courts and administrative agencies in their attempts to gain fair treatment.

The struggle has been a long and difficult one, however, and is far from over. Studying it teaches us a great deal about politics and society in America. Those who wanted EEO legislation got it because American society actually worked as it was "supposed to," according to some of our more optimistic social analysts (e.g., Myrdal 1962; Lipset 1979)—that is, people acted on their egalitarian values and the government responded. Yet those who sought EEO legislation, and continue to fight for EEO, had an uphill battle, because they were acting in opposition to other important tendencies in American society—hostility toward members of allegedly "inferior" groups, rationalization of the status quo, the dominance of politics by elites not necessarily sympathetic to the plight of the oppressed, and the inclination to respond to social protest with repression rather than receptiveness to the demands being expressed. Congress and the public responded to pleas for fairness, but not readily; it took the proponents of EEO legislation over thirty years of great effort, vast expense, confrontation with danger, and even loss of life to achieve the passage of today's EEO law.

From the perspective of history, the passage of EEO legislation was just one especially important episode in a never-ending struggle. Changing attitudes and the adoption of legislation have helped those they were supposed to help, but they have not done so automatically. Continuing enforcement of the EEO law, and further changes in behavior by employers and union, depend upon continuous pressure by those discriminated against and their allies. There are always forces in every society that seek to achieve wealth and power at the expense of others; as Lipset has written, "The forces making for. . . inequality will seek, often successfully, to strengthen themselves" (1979, 343). The gains women, blacks, and members of other groups have made so far will help them in their future struggle; the fight for equal treatment becomes a little easier as those involved become a little more equal. But it will be a very long time before Americans can feel sure that individual merit and luck determine how they do economically, without discrimination's playing a considerable role as well.

Democratic politics can be used to change the distribution of income. Its effect is modest and slow and comes as the result of very great effort. But that does not mean it is inconsequential. As Polanyi has written, "The rate of change is often of no less importance than the direction of the change itself; but while the latter frequently does not depend upon our volition, it is the rate at which we allow change to take place which well may depend upon us" (1944, 36–37). Democratic politics has not ended discrimination or produced equality; but it has increased the opportunities available to millions of people and helped ensure that they would be treated fairly.

Appendix: Data from Congressional Hearings and the *New York Times*

Congressional Hearings

Data on witnesses testifying before congressional hearings on EEO were based on the coding of the hearings listed below. The data were presented in table 5.3 by Congress; to standardize the presentation, they were listed for the first year of each Congress regardless of when the hearing actually took place.

House Labor Committee, 78th Congress, 2d session, 1–16 June, 1944, on bills H.R. 3986, 4004, 4005.

House Labor Committee, 78th Congress, 2d session (78-2), 16 November 1944, on bills H.R. 3986, 4004, 4005.

Senate Education and Labor Committee, 78-2, 30 August–8 September 1944, on bill S. 2048.

Senate Education and Labor Committee, 79-1, 12–14 May 1945, on S. 101, 459.

House Rules Committee, 79-1, 8 March–26 April 1945, on H.R. 2232.

Senate Labor and Public Welfare Committee, 80-1, 11 June–18 July 1947, on S. 984.

House Education and Labor Committee, 81-1, 10–26 May 1949, on H.R. 4453.

Senate Labor and Public Welfare Committee, 83-2, 23 February–3 March 1954, on S. 692.

House Judiciary Committee, 84-1, 13–27 July 1955, on H.R. 389.

House Judiciary Committee, 86-1, 4 March–1 May 1959, on H.R. 300.

House Education and Labor Committee, 87-1, 23–24, 26–27 October, 3–5 November 1961, special subcommittee hearings.

House Education and Labor Committee, 87-2, 15–24 January 1962, special subcommittee hearings.

Senate Labor and Public Welfare Committee, 88-1, 24 July–20 August 1963, on S. 773, 1210, 1211, 1937.

Data from the *New York Times*

Many of the data used in this book were drawn fom stories in the *New York Times*—the data on demonstrations described in figure 4.1, on riots in figure 4.2, on anti-rights demonstrations, injuries and property damage, killings, and official violence in figure 4.3, and on delegations in table 5.3. This part of the appendix provides a brief rationale for the data collection, a summary of the coding manual that guided the data collection itself, and some data on the reliability of the data collection procedures.

Rationale

Many variables believed to influence political outcomes have traditionally been studied only qualitatively, and hypotheses about their effect have therefore been difficult to test. As discussed above in chapters 1, 4, and 8, for example, many people have believed that congressional action on civil rights (as well as other issues, such as the Vietnam War) was affected by demonstrations but have been unable to determine whether their belief was correct because they did not have data to relate to congressional action, except for a few of the largest demonstrations. In recent years, however, a small but growing group of social scientists has concluded that valid time-series data on many of the more visible aspects of politics could be collected by drawing on an obvious but hitherto untapped data source—major newspapers, particularly, in the American context, the *New York Times*. When this study and immediately preceding ones (Burstein and Freudenburg 1978) were begun, the use of the newspaper stories as a source of data for quantitative research on politics, particularly social protest, was in its infancy. By now, however, such data have been used in a number of major studies. The properties of the data are known, their reliability and validity have been assessed fairly systematically, and we know which kinds of events are reliably reported by the *Times* and which are not (at least with regard to the kinds of events potentially relevant to this study). Similar types of data are also being collected for different countries and historical periods. Though problems remain, and such data must still be used and interpreted cautiously, it is widely agreed that the data derived from stories in the *New York Times* convey a generally accurate picture of the events and time trends analyzed in this book and are far better than any other actual or potentially available data. Relevant works describing the development of methods of content analysis of *New York Times* stories and other, similar data sources include those by Tilly (1969, 1978), Snyder and Kelly (1977), Jenkins and Perrow (1977), Sugimoto (1978), Danzger (1975), and McAdam (1982). Relevant works on content analysis as a general method of inquiry include Scott (1955), Markoff, Shapiro, and Weitman (1974), Holsti (1969), and Krippendorff (1980).

Data used in this project were taken from stories in the *New York Times*, almost entirely as summarized in the annual *New York Times Index*, published between 1940 and 1978. Coders recorded specific aspects of stories—whether there had been a civil rights demonstration on a particular day, on whose behalf it had been held, whether it concerned EEO—according to a very detailed set of instructions that is partly reproduced below. The data were then compiled by year and put into form in which they have been described in the preceding chapters. It should be noted that data for this book were sought in the *New York Times Index* under a wider range of subject headings than apparently used in any previous research on American politics; the headings were civil rights and/or civil liberties; freedom and human rights; minorities; Negroes; women; labor, under subheadings discrimination and women; education, under subheadings racial integration, equal educational opportunities, Negro education, and student activities; and cross-references where appropriate.

The Coding Manual

What follows is the set of instructions given to coders gathering data from the *New York Times;* the general introduction and some technical details, examples, and exhortations to coders have been omitted.

Data Selection Procedures

Coding data from the *New York Times Index* involves two types of decisions. Since most of the events reported are irrelevant to the task at hand, the coders will first decide whether the event belongs in the sample. Once an event is included, the coder must decide how to code it.

General rules: Rely primarily on the abstracts; the selection criteria and detailed coding directions are designed so that actions can be coded using only information in the abstracts. Try to avoid looking up the original articles on microfilm. This simply takes too much time. The major exception is for counting events.

Location in the index: Select events only from abstracts under the following topics [listed above].

Location of the event and of target groups: code only events that occurred in one of the fifty United States or the District of Columbia. Do not code actions in overseas possessions (including Puerto Rico). Qualifying actions must be in regard to or by American minority groups or women.

Counting Events

General rules: One count per action per day. Count actions, not reports. For most actions counting is straightforward; a single action occurred on a single day. Large-scale or long-term actions may last more than one day. Boycotts, strikes, and riots are especially likely to be of this type. Count one for each day the long-term event is reported on in the *Index*. For a single story that apparently refers to multiple actions: (*a*) If the story clearly indicates that several actions occurred (e.g., a rally, followed by a march, followed by a riot), code each action separately: (*b*) If the story refers to multiple actions of the same type, count each action separately if the number is specified: (*c*) If the number of actions is not specified exactly, refer to the original article: (*d*) If the abstract indicates that actions occurred in several named locations, count one action per location. Use the rule that there cannot be more than one demonstration of a particular type per city per day.

Target Group

For each mode of action, the event must be in regard (pro or con) to a minority or minorities covered by EEO legislation. The determination of target group varies slightly by mode of action. For delegations, demonstrations, strikes, and boycotts, ask what the aim of the action is in regard to what target groups. For unofficial violence, ask against what minority group or its associates the violence was perpetrated. For official violence, determine target group by the aim of the main event in which a peaceful demonstrator was participating, where appropriate. For riots and racial disorders, the target group is not coded, but the perpetrators of the event must be one of these groups. Target group is coded as one of five mutually exclusive categories:

Negroes: references to "blacks," "negroes," "colored." "Negroes" is the heading under which most of this material will be found in the *Index*. References to "racial" issues are coded here *if* there are contextual cues that the reference is specifically to blacks.

Women: There should not be much of a problem with this code. Do not include gay rights references unless they are part of a more general feminist protest.

Jews: Any references to the civil rights of Jews or to anti-Semitism. Be sure the reference is to Jews in this country, especially for the World War II period. References to "religious" bias go here if contextual cues indicate the reference is to Jews.

General: Code here events in regard to any combination of Negroes, women, Jews, either among those three or along with some other specified minority or minorities; and code here any general references to "civil rights" of minorities and references to both racial and religious prejudice as well as references scoring "discrimination" (pro or anti) without specific reference to a group.

Other: Code here any specific reference to another minority of race, religion, or national origin not included in Jews, women, and Negroes—for example, references to any *one* of Hispanic, Oriental, Islamic, Puerto Rican, Chicano, American Indian, and the like.

Aim, Pro/Anti

To be included in the sample, a delegation, demonstration, strike, or boycott must make some claim or contention regarding the civil rights of one of the groups covered by EEO legislation. (These aspects are not coded for official and unofficial violence or for riots.) For each event code two aspects of the contentions and claims: the *aim* (the particular rights involved in the claim) and the direction pro/anti (whether the claim supports or opposes the rights of the target group).

Aim: Aim is coded as either employment related or other. If employment, the aim of the action specifically refers to employment rights of the target group, either alone or in combination with other aims. References to economic rights should also be included here. If the aim is general, not specified, or specified as other than employment rights, code as "other."

Guidelines: *The claim must be contentious.* Do not include aims relating to black history and culture, women's history, and so forth, unless a contentious position regarding rights to these things is also explicitly involved. The contentious nature of an event can be interpreted fairly liberally; include allegations of "bias," "discrimination," "prejudice," "bigotry," and the like.

Clarification and examples of what is an employment aim: Include problems regarding Negroes, women, Jews, or other minorities in national defense or the armed services; include only references to the work or jobs that minorities and women carry out. Include references to discrimination in labor unions as employment. Discrimination in professional sports, especially in reference to blacks, is included as employment.

Coding the Equal Rights Amendment: Some protests over the ERA will not be coded since they are disagreements among groups of women over whether the ERA will or will not help women. Analogous disputes occur among other minorities and generally should be excluded. Note that aims generally regarding the ERA will be coded as "other" even though the ERA will affect employment. If the event specifically refers to employment aspects of the ERA, however, do code it under employment.

Do not include disputes about abortion rights unless they are part of a larger feminist claim. This exclusion was an admittedly arbitrary decision to avoid dealing with the complex issues of rights that are involved with abortion.

Coding of events involving political parties or candidates: Generally exclude rallies, speeches, and the like by political candidates. However, include demonstrations at political functions in certain situations; do not exclude all political party activity. Rallies and conventions by some specifically minority rights parties should be included as intrinsically contentious in nature; for example, Freedom Democratic party, Black Panther party, National Women's party.

Pro/anti: For this variable code whether the action and its contention are pro-rights of the target groups or anti-rights of the target group. This is generally rather easy to determine.

Modes of Action

There are six types of action to code: delegations, demonstrations, strikes and boycotts, official violence, unofficial violence, and riots and racial disorders. The first three types have certain features in common. They are all gatherings or popular collective actions with stated political positions or contentions regarding the civil rights of women, blacks, or other minorities of race, religion, or national origin. Popular action means action that does not include routine congressional activities, court activities, or routine government business. Collective action means group action, not action by lone individuals, though individuals acting on behalf of or as representatives of protest groups are included (as in delegations). Generally group activities will include at least five people.

We mean to include only activities whose political aim is quite clear. Most reports will indicate the political intent. Sometimes the coder will get the political intent from previous stories announcing the event. The political intent may be generally stated as "civil rights." We do not include events that involve dissension among groups within minorities or among minorities. Do not include nonpolitical events by minorities, even if they may have some latent political effect. Official and unofficial violence and riots do not have stated political aims, though we hypothesize that they have both political motivations and impact.

Delegations

Delegations are meetings between protest groups or other interested groups or their representatives and policymaking federal or state government officials in which feelings, grievances, or plans of action on civil rights issues are conveyed, discussed, or presented.

"Meetings": the key theme here is the legitimating function of "face-to-face" meetings between protesting representatives and policymakers. Hence do not include telegrams, letters, or other one-way communications. Include actions described as "delegations," since we can assume these were face to face. Also include events described as "lobbying." Also include other oral interpersonal communications between protest movement leaders and government officials. Do not include announcements of lobbying campaigns. Include meetings between protest movement leaders and government officials, whether instigated by officials or by protest leaders.

"Protest or other interested groups or their representatives": May be as few as one lobbyist or representative; must represent or oppose the interests of minorities or women as listed under target group; and must be recognized as a leader in some way. Generally exclude people holding political office as protest representatives.

"Policymaking federal or state government officials": Include members of Congress, federal or state officials, and their staff; do not include delegations to city officials. Officials must be policymaking or at least have some official potential for influencing policy. Hence, in addition to the preceding, include delegations to executive branch minority group commissions. Do not include minority presentations to political parties or political conventions; continue to exclude all purely political campaign activities. Do not include testimony at congressional hearings, since this material is being coded directly from other documents.

"Feelings, grievances, or plans of action on civil rights issues are conveyed, discussed, or presented": The meeting must involve some presentation of the delegation's views on a civil rights issue pertaining to some minority group or women.

Demonstrations

Here we define a demonstration as a public display by a group of five or more individuals expressing a political position or contention of support for or opposition to the civil rights of women, blacks, or other minorities of race, religion, or national origin.

"Public display": Demonstrations vary widely in the form of display they involve. In this project the following types will be the most common: Marches and rallies are usually named as such in the *Index*. Also include parades if appropriate aim is indicated. Likewise, include mass meetings with appropriate stated aims. Sit-ins and pickets are usually named as such in the *Index*. Lie-ins, pray-ins, and similar variations usually occurring at the alleged or symbolic site of injustice are also included here. Unspecified demonstrations for civil rights are often reported by the *Index* simply as "demonstrations." Include these here. Also include the occasional unusual modes of protest that are clearly demonstrations as defined above. Note that demonstrations, delegations, and strikes and boycotts are intended to be mutually exclusive categories.

Do not include small-scale heckling.

The display must involve some form of active protest. Written expressions of group feeling are specifically excluded, as are newspaper advertisements, letter-writing campaigns, and the like. Some group must actually get together and do something to qualify the event for this category. Verbal protests alone do not qualify.

"Expression of political contention or aim regarding civil rights": Follow the rules for determining "aim" and "pro/anti" in assessing and coding the contentious nature of demonstrations. No demonstration is to be coded unless some appropriate aim is explicitly stated or can be inferred.

Do not include routine holiday celebrations and related marches and rallies such as Columbus Day, even if they happen to touch on civil rights issues.

Role of violence: Most demonstrations at least begin peacefully. Do not be concerned to code all violence in demonstrations. If a demonstration evolves into what qualifies as a riot, it will also be coded as such. If there is official or unofficial violence perpetrated against peaceful demonstrations, that will be coded under one of those categories.

Strikes and Boycotts

Webster's Dictionary defines a strike as "a temporary stoppage of normal operations and activities designed as a protest against an action or condition." To boycott is "to combine against (a person, employer, a group of persons, or a nation) in a policy of nonintercourse for economic or political reasons; withhold wholly or partly social or business intercourse from as an expression of disapproval or means of coercion."

Strikes and boycotts are coded together because of the similarities in these modes of action. Both are based on refusals to participate in previously established forms of interaction. Both also tend to be "economic" actions. That is, very often economic goods are involved, with workers refusing to work, citizens refusing to purchase, and such. Note that this is not always the case, however, as in school boycotts. Both types of event are also probably equally underreported by the papers since they often last for long periods and thus may become unnewsworthy.

Strikes and boycotts must be collective actions by five or more individuals. A single institution may boycott, however, and be included, as when a school drops out of segregated sports—five or more individuals are involved as part of the institution.

Code only reports of actual events. Do not include citations like "Detroit boycott fails." We want events where some action actually took place, not just calls for action.

Strikes and boycotts must have a relevant civil rights aim regarding a relevant minority.

See the "counting" section for basic rules on counting strikes and boycotts. Because of the relatively poor reporting, we use a rather inclusive method overall for counting days of a boycott or strike, although our rules for initially including the event are strict. We code up to one boycott per day per city, with any reference to the boycott qualifying a day for inclusion. The references to the boycotts include actions (such as carpooling during a bus boycott), rallies, demonstrations, and other protests regarding the boycott, and also verbal references to the boycott in sermons, speeches, letters, and other events. References to legal actions coming out of the boycott will also qualify a particular day for inclusion as a boycott day.

Rallies, marches, delegations, and other categories of protest are coded as events separate from the boycott even if they are in regard to the boycott.

Unofficial Violence

Unofficial violence is defined as unofficial violence against women or minority group members or their associates who are identified in some way with civil rights causes.

"Unofficial" means not perpetrated by public officials; we also include here some actions perpetrated by unknown persons (see below).

Victims of such violence must be members of one of the minority groups we are interested in or be associated with such a group (as in white supporters of the black civil rights movement). If property damage is involved, the property must belong to a minority or be somehow (perhaps symbolically) associated with a minority.

The victims of violence must be associated with some cause in support of a minority's civil rights.

The association with a civil rights cause is an important dimension; we do not want to include "ordinary" criminal behavior. Code only violence that occurs because of the victims' actual or symbolic representation of minority rights. The distinction is problematic because violence against blacks has been part of the structure of discrimination against blacks, especially in the South. We want to measure not such dicrimination per se but political action regarding discrimination. Some events are so blatant that we include them even if a civil rights cause is not implicated. Anything described as a lynching should be included, even if the lynched persons are not clearly civil rights activists. About other murders we are stricter, requiring that there be some clearly relevant motivation. One mechanical inclusion criterion here is that any event listed under "civil rights" or a "civil rights" subheading under a group heading like "women" or "Negroes" will qualify providing it also meets the other requirements of this category.

Code only references to specific, actual incidents of violence. Code three types of violence: property damage, personal injury, and death. Counting is somewhat different for this mode of action: count deaths by head, injuries only by incident, and damage by place (that is, if a church and a home are burned, count as two). For any one incident, code only the most serious violence, that is, code deaths if any; if no deaths, code injuries; if no injuries, code damage.

Death, personal injury, and property damage are generally self-explanatory. Note the following clarifications: Be sure to include here incidents of white violence against peaceful demonstrators. Include throwing rocks at people as injury, even if no injuries are actually reported. Include cross burnings here when they happen at a victim's home or at another place symbolically associated with victim groups; code as property damage. Other cross burnings by groups may qualify as demonstrations, such as the Klan's burning a cross at a rally. Include burnings or desecration of black churches or Jewish synagogues.

Official Violence

Official violence is defined as violence by public officials against peaceful protestors; for example, the use of dogs and nightsticks against peaceful marchers. The idea is to measure instances of excessive police brutality to persons and undue damage to their property or persons given the protest activity such individuals are involved in.

Public officials include any local, state, or federal law enforcement officials, but also any other government officials. Do not include ordinary, legitimate police responses to violent protestors or rioters. Include any use of tear gas and shooting of unarmed demonstrators.

Because of the ambiguous nature of reports and charges, and because of the difficulty of always determining what is "excessive," we are fairly strict in our coding:

Do not include charges against police except if something as severe as death or substantial injury is reported; that is, charges of police brutality must include some additional evidence to qualify the event for inclusion.

Nonviolent harassment or vaguely alleged harassment is not included. Accusations of brutality were common during black protests—be sure there is some evidence of the kind of property and personal damage we are looking for. This probably underestimates the extent of police brutality but is the best we can do with this data set. Do not include harassment arrests of civil rights protestors, for example, discretionary arrests for minor infringements of the law.

Code only actions against civil rights protestors or demonstrators. Brutality against minorities arrested for non–civil rights activities, though very common, is not included here.

Riots and Racial Disorders

Because of what Tilly calls the "extraordinary, devastating, and ill-bounded" nature of collective violence (1969, 17), riots are difficult to deal with methodologically. Following Tilly's model, we developed a detailed procedure for deciding whether to include events as riots/racial disorders. It is based on the idea that we are interested in riots not as events in themselves but as they may influence the legislative process. As such, four aspects of events are important: their collective nature and magnitude; their violence; their racial character; and their threat to ordinary processes and agents of social control. The original intent was to code only large-scale riots that fit all four of these criteria. Because of the lack of detail in the *Index* reports, we relaxed our restrictions so as to include smaller-scale racial disorders. Each event must still be violent, racial, and minimally collective.

Any event described in the *Index* as a riot with a racial or ethnic basis is to be included, even if other cues are inadequate. The racial character of a disorder can be determined by whether the riot or disorder is called "racial" or described by some similar adjective, involves racial minorities as rioters, or is listed under the heading "Negroes."

Many article summaries use the nouns "violence," "disorder," or "disturbance," with few or no further cues describing the event. Arbitrarily, adjectives or forms of these nouns that imply multiple incidents will qualify the event for inclusion if the implication is also that more than one incident occurred on the same day in the same city. Such references are still subject to the one count/city/day rule and are coded as one disorder. Very brief incidents should be excluded if there are no other cues.

Other cues: Number of participants, if explicitly mentioned, should be at least fifty minority persons, excluding police and other officials, or there should be at least five resulting arrests, or the number of police sent to respond should be described as large.

Reliability of the Coding Procedures

One criterion of the quality of measurement is reliability, which is essentially repeatability, or the likelihood that two measurements of the same phenomenon will produce the same result. In content analysis, reliability has, as a practical matter, meant the extent to which two or more individuals, coding the same material, agree on their codes.

Assessing the reliability of the coding of *New York Times* data used here had two aspects, because the coding of the data itself involved two tasks: selecting events for inclusion in the data set, and assigning those events to the various coding categories. Although in practice coders performed these tasks virtually simultaneously, it is both theoretically and methodologically important to assess the success of each aspect of the procedure separately.

Assessing the reliability of the process by which already-selected events were assigned to coding categories was the less problematic of the two aspects. Each annual volume of the *New York Times Index* was coded by at least two people. The average reliability across all pairs of individuals, using Scott's measure (1955), was .87. This seems comparable to the reliabilities attained in other studies using similar types of data, though in fact reporting of reliability coefficients and related information tends to be sketchy (see, e.g., McAdam 1982, 237).

More problematic is assessing the reliability of the process in which coders decide what to code. Although the search for codable data is part of all content-analysis procedures, there appears to have been no systematic discussion of procedures for estimating the reliability with which coders complete the search for data. I have not been able to find any such discussion in the recent literature on the use of print media in the study of conflict and civil rights, either.

The problems involved in trying to gauge what may be called "inclusion reliability" are substantial, particularly when one is trying to get data on a particular type of content (about "events") that was not part of the formal structure of the source material (the *New York Times Index* is structured around years, subject headings, and articles, not events). We may get some sense of how reliable the inclusion process was by considering what proportion of all events coded by *any* coder were coded by *all* coders; that is, For what proportion of events any coder believed were relevant did all the coders agree? The problem with this approach is that it greatly underestimates the reliability of the coding process. Coders read far more material than they coded, because most of the events they read about were irrelevant for the purposes of the study (for example, all the articles about blacks not dealing with civil rights). Yet without having a complete record of all events the coders read about (which would have involved multiplying their task manyfold and was therefore completely impractical), there is no way to tell how often they agreed to exclude an article from consideration.

As a practical matter, the problems associated with inclusion in this study may be evaluated as being of various degrees of seriousness, depending upon one's implicit standards and point of view.

Because this problem is not discussed in comparable studies, there is no standard for comparison, no way of deciding how satisfactory the inclusion process was, either absolutely or in comparison with other studies. It was certainly true that during the development of the coding scheme a great deal of time was devoted to developing clear criteria for inclusion; the amount of effort that had to be devoted to this was far greater than most works on coding would lead one to believe, and I am sure the results of this study were no worse than the results of others widely known in the literature on social protest (e.g., McAdam 1982; Jenkins and Perrow 1977).

More specifically relevant to this data, one analysis of nearly seven hundred events coded by two people indicated that the coders initially disagreed on inclusion a quarter of the time—that is, a quarter of all the events were included by one but not the other. A quarter seems like a lot. If we remember, however, that most articles they read were the subject of agreement *not* to code, the problem seems less serious. If we assume, for example, that 10 percent of all stories read were coded by one or the other, then the rate of disagreement between them is less than 3 percent, since they both agreed to exclude 90 percent of all potentially relevant material and disagreed on only a quarter of the rest.

When a detailed analysis of the disagreements was conducted, the coders and a third party agreed in 80 percent of the disputed cases that the event in question should have been coded. Thus the major consequence of unreliability in inclusion decisions seems to be in underestimating the amount of political activity occurring. We have no reason to believe that the reliability varied significantly over time or that the conclusions of this study have been affected. Nevertheless, it is clear that more research is needed on inclusion reliability and its effect on the findings of studies based upon content analysis.

Notes

Chapter 1

1. See U.S. Congress, House Committee on Education and Labor 1963, particularly the testimony of Raymond Hilliard.

2. See the testimony by Mitchell and Powell, U.S. Congress, House Special Subcommittee of the Committee on Education and Labor 1949, 65, 293; see also Schwartz 1967, 5–6; Von Eschen, Kirk, and Pinard 1969; Wilson and Varner 1973. The women's movement is similar to the civil rights movement in the great importance attributed to achieving equal employment opportunity; see, for example, Robinson 1979, 427; Florer 1973, chap. 3.

3. See, e.g., Lipset 1979; White 1982; Sowell 1981; Jencks 1983a,b.

4. This does not mean, of course, that "public opinion" as measured in any particular survey will be translated directly into public policy. Over two hundred years of theoretical debate and empirical analysis have shown that majority rule is a complex and problematic process. However subtle the arguments become, though, there remain many people who conclude that in a democracy, policy is ultimately determined by majority preferences; see, e.g., Kingdon 1977; Mayhew 1974; Dahl 1956; Page and Shapiro 1983.

5. See the discussion in Steinberg 1982, 212–13, and also Lipset 1979, xxiii–xxxi; Lindblom 1977, 353; Tufte 1978; Hibbs 1977.

6. For variations on this theme, see Piven and Cloward 1971; Sowell 1981; Isaac and Kelly 1981; Lazear 1979; and the reviews in Button 1978, chaps. 1 and 5, and Steinberg 1982, 213–16.

7. See Lipset 1979 for an excellent discussion of the ongoing importance of this struggle.

8. Studies that attribute importance to some or all of these factors include Berman 1966; Franklin 1967; Dye 1971; Sundquist 1968; Wirmark 1974; Lytle 1966; Fleming 1965; Garrow 1978; Lichtman 1969; Schlei 1976; Lawson 1976; Morgan 1970.

9. On public opinion, see Page 1978; on social movements, see Gamson 1975; Tilly 1978; McAdam 1982; Jenkins and Perrow 1977; Snyder and Kelly 1979; on congressional action, see Walker 1977; Steinberg 1982; Berk, Brackman, and Lesser 1977; cf. Tufte 1978.

10. For example, Gamson's seminal work on social movements in American history says next to nothing about their influence on any legislature; McAdam's account of blacks' involvement in social movements refers to Congress only in passing; and

Jenkins and Perrow's account of the farm workers' movement frequently mentions federal action but says nothing concrete on what brought it about.

11. Political scientists mention social movement organizations when they cannot avoid it (when discussing civil rights, for example), but neither the rise of such organizations nor their influence on policy is included in their formal theories in any serious way; see, e.g., Dahl 1967; Dye 1975; and the discussion in Gamson 1975; but see also Tarrow 1983.

12. Typical examples of sociologists' work on discrimination that mention that law may be important but then fail to consider it include Farley 1977; Featherman and Hauser 1976, 464; Snyder and Hudis 1976, 215, 231. The shortcomings of economists' work are discussed in chapter 6.

13. White 1982; Hill 1977.

14. On the background of organized action against employment discrimination, see, for example, Blumrosen 1971; Chafe 1977, chap. 2; Kesselman 1948; Ruchames 1953.

15. The logic of this argument is presented in Steinberg 1982 and Silberman and Durden 1976.

16. On the drive for the executive order and the order itself, see Hill 1977, chap. 4; Morgan 1970; Norgren and Hill 1964, chap. 7; Sovern 1966, chap. 2.

Chapter 2

1. For sophisticated analyses of public opinion and the place of the Supreme Court in the political process, see Cox 1976, chap. 5; Horowitz 1977; McCloskey 1960, chap. 7. Of course, strong and widespread public support for civil rights legislation might have led to some congressional activity, and really intense concern could have led to a movement for a constitutional amendment to overturn the Court's rulings; I do not want to attribute absolute power to the Court. But there was no such intense public concern, and there is little doubt that the Court's rulings discouraged those who hoped to return civil rights to the public agenda.

2. Data on Supreme Court cases is from Mead Data Central 1976 and Berger 1967. Cases included are those dealing with discrimination against individuals or groups on the basis of race, religion, national origin, or sex. Of the 122 cases discovered, only 10 did not deal with racial discrimination. "Victory" was accorded the side alleging discrimination if it won all or nearly all the substantive legal points raised in the case.

3. The phrases are found, sometimes with very minor variations in wording (substituting "religion" for "creed," for instance), in the first EEO bill to be the subject of congressional hearings, the first state EEO law, the first EEO bill to be passed by either house or Congress, and Title 7, as well as many other bills and laws; see U.S. Congress, House Committee on Labor 1944; *Laws of New York* 1945; U.S. Congress, *Congressional Record,* 1950, 2162–65; and 42 U.S.C. 2000e et seq.

4. When EEO bills were first debated in Congress, the 1866 law was considered unenforceable because of a series of Supreme Court decisions; it was resurrected by the Supreme Court as a remedy for private discrimination in 1968 (*Jones v. Mayer,* 392 U.S. 409). There were some state and local laws against discrimination in certain

aspects of employment before the 1940s; these too read very differently from contemporary laws (see Bonfield 1967).

5. The works drawn on most heavily were Berk, Brackman, and Lesser 1977 and Steinberg 1982, particularly the former. See also the roughly comparable categorization in the *Legislative History* of the 1972 bills (U.S. Congress, Senate Committee on Labor and Public Welfare 1972, 2040 ff).

6. The complete text of most bills, particularly those introduced before the early 1970s, is for all practical purposes inaccessible. Summaries of the bills prepared by the Legislative Reference Service of the Library of Congress were therefore coded instead (U.S. Library of Congress 1942–74). The summaries convey the essence of the bills and, given the simplicity of the coding scheme, provide all the information necessary for the analysis. To test the validity of the summaries, bills for which texts were readily available—those published as part of congressional hearings—were compared with the summaries. Though many details were left out of the summaries, their accuracy for purposes of the coding scheme used here was close to perfect. Many of the summaries were coded independently by two people; their rate of agreement was over 95 percent.

7. When a member of Congress sponsored more than one bill, each was counted so long as they differed in content. If a member sponsored more than one bill with the same content (as determined by the coding scheme), duplicates were eliminated from the analysis.

8. Washington, D.C., now prohibits employment discrimination on the basis of thirteen different attributes: race, color, religion, national origin, sex, age, marital status, personal appearance, sexual orientation, family responsibilities, physical handicap, matriculation, and political affiliation; see Bureau of National Affairs 1977, 453:1609.

9. On the similarities among proposals, see Bonfield 1967; Maslow and Robison 1953; Norgren and Hill 1964, chap. 5; Sovern 1966.

10. See Kesselman 1948; Ruchames 1953. Many other groups played a role in EEO politics; these three were simply the most prominent in the early stages.

11. See, for example, the comments by Senator Aiken, U.S. Congress, Senate Committee on Education and Labor 1944, 96–99, 118; also see U.S. Congress, Senate Committee on Education and Labor 1946.

12. Not including minor perfecting amendments, the 1964 leadership substitute, cloture, passage, or conference committee reports.

13. See U.S. Congress, House Committee on Education and Labor 1963; Congressional Quarterly 1964, 352. Legislation against age discrimination in employment passed in 1967 but had a history essentially separate from EEO legislation dealing with race and other characteristics.

14. All bills have had some exemptions—employers and unions below a certain size (often fifty employees or members in the early years), religious organizations, some social and fraternal groups, and so forth. These cannot be dealt with in detail here, but in general the exemptions, like the basic coverage, have remained fairly constant over the years, with the tendency being to close loopholes over time.

15. Extending coverage to the federal government is not quite the same as the

other extensions, because the president already had prohibited discrimination by executive order. Making the prohibition statutory is a way of reducing executive discretion and imposing congressional ideas about enforcement.

16. H.R. 3986 of 1944, the first bill on which hearings were held, declared it unlawful to "refuse to hire," to "discharge," or to discriminate in "compensation or in other terms or conditions of employment" and to discriminate against persons because they oppose practices forbidden by the bill. The 1945 New York State law declares it an unlawful employment practice to "refuse to hire or employ or to bar or to discharge from employment . . . or to discriminate against . . . in compensation or in terms, conditions, or privileges of employment." It also forbids discriminating against people because they oppose any practices forbidden under the law.

17. Blumrosen argues that liberals were wrong in their belief that administrative enforcement would be more effective than judicial enforcement (1971, chap. 1). He claims that they were enamored of the National Labor Relations Board (NLRB) type of approach for ideological reasons and refused to take into account the substantial experience (by 1964) of state EEO agencies, which were generally both of the NLRB type and failures at reducing employment discrimination. In addition, both the liberals and the Justice Department may have underestimated the potential power given the attorney general because of their focus on individuals' complaints of discrimination rather than on systematic discrimination.

18. Statistical studies of legislatures do not generally deal with issues on which there is little legislation and few roll call votes; instead, they focus on changes in laws already on the books, roll call voting, expenditures, and the actions of individual legislators; for reviews, see Burstein and Freudenburg 1978 and Berk, Brackman, and Lesser 1977.

19. See, for example, Ferejohn 1974, 15, on environmental protection legislation, Bailey 1950, 55–56, 153–55, on economic legislation, and Franklin and Tappin 1977 and Leece and Berrington 1977 on the British Parliament. The most systematic quantitive treatment of levels of sponsorship over time is Walker's (1977), but he uses it as an indicator of the activity of individual members of Congress rather than as a way of characterizing activity on an issue.

20. The number of sponsors in table 2.1 is lower than the number in the figures because some members of Congress sponsored more than one bill per congress; above, sponsorships were counted; here, members of Congress. The 1950 bill may have passed as part of major push for liberal legislation initiated by Democrats encouraged by the 1948 election of President Truman and their large gains in the House and Senate, especially the House. But support for the initiatives proved shallow; most of the proposals (for example, EEO) were not adopted until much later, and some (repeal of provisions of the Taft-Hartley Act, for example) never have been adopted.

21. The major exception to the general rule was the Senate in the early 1950s, when sponsorship increased rapidly and then declined. This upsurge may have been the result of Senator Humphrey's period of active involvement on the Labor and Public Welfare Committee, which dealt with EEO bills, but it does represent an anomaly in the overall picture.

22. The law has been amended three times since 1972. The amendments involved changing the form of the EEOC's annual report, placing administrative law judges rather than hearing examiners in charge of certain parts of the administrative process,

and eliminating a loophole in the definition of sex discrimination; none of the changes was the subject of much debate, and none altered the structure of Title 7 in any substantial way (see Jones 1979, 5–21).

23. Modern civil rights legislation in general may be seen as having its roots in the New Deal; it was part of the New Deal "package" of policies, but it was also the part that was most divisive and took longest to enact into law (Brady 1982).

Chapter 3

1. See Lytle 1966; Berman 1966; Schlei 1976; Fleming 1965. What many writers do is to explain the passage of civil rights legislation by pointing to forces other than public opinion. They should be seen as implicitly hypothesizing that public preferences had little influence on Congress; because they are rarely explicit, however, we can only infer that this is what they really mean.

2. For a thorough discussion of the problems involved in measuring aspects of public opinion and relating them to political outcomes, see Weissberg 1976 and Page and Shapiro 1983; see also Cell 1974; Stigler 1972; Page 1978.

3. The search was conducted in the holdings of the Roper Public Opinion Research Center, the national election studies of the University of Michigan Center for Political Studies, the General Social Survey of the National Opinion Research Center, comprehensive studies of public opinion, and other sources. See Hastings and Southwick 1974; Center for Political Studies 1964, 1968, 1970, 1972; Gallup 1972; *Gallup Opinion Index* 1964–78; Davis 1973, 1975, 1976, 1977, 1978; Schwartz 1967; Simon 1974.

4. Note that the analysis here focuses on what has been called "collective representation"—representation of the public as a whole by Congress—rather than "dyadic representation"—representation of individual constituencies by their own representatives—because my concern is with the link between legislation, a collective outcome, and the preferences of the public as a whole (see Weissberg 1978). The evidence presented will not tell us what motivates individual members of Congress, but it will enable us to discover whether Congress as a whole acts as if its members are motivated by their desire to satisfy constituents (cf. Tufte 1978). Members of Congress themselves, as well as other involved public figures such as President Johnson, usually attributed their own actions and those of others to moral imperatives and the pressure of public opinion; see Johnson's speech upon signing the Civil Rights Act of 1964 (reported in the *New York Times*, 3 July 1964, 9); Talmadge 1955; and the report of the congressional debate in the *Congressional Record* (1964, 110, part 2:1391–2840).

5. Again, the basic questions are reported in table 3.1; there have been minor and inconsequential changes in the wording in different polls.

6. The figures are influenced somewhat by the fact that the questions were asked of members of each group as part of the sample (with the sometime exception of blacks). For the two groups that constitute a large proportion of the population—Catholics and women—favorable responses from group members can have a significant effect on the results. Catholics are much more willing to vote for a Catholic than other people are, but women have been no more likely to vote for a woman than men have.

7. The trend on the "Catholic president" question may be less uniform than the others because only this question became relevant to an actual candidate, John F. Kennedy in 1960.

8. The 1945 data point, indicating that just 14 percent of the public approved women's working, was seen as an aberration induced by fears of a postwar depression; when the depression did not materialize, the percentage approving immediately increased to 39 percent, so the 1945 data point was eliminated from the analysis. The question on equal pay was likewise excluded from the statistical analysis, because the shortness of the period during which the question was asked, combined with the lack of a clear trend (R^2 with time = .58) made it impossible to have any confidence in estimates for recent years.

9. The focus is on the total number of sponsors, rather than sponsors in the House and Senate separately, because focusing on the total smooths out the effect of idiosyncratic personal or parliamentary factors. The statistical results are generally the same no matter what measure of sponsorship is used.

10. The two attitude measures are so highly correlated that including both in the same equation produces results that cannot be sensibly interpreted; R^2 for that equation is .76, the same as for the equation on women alone. Lagging the attitude variables by a year—estimating the effect of attitudes averaged over the election year and the first year of a congress (1940–41, 1942–43, etc.) rather than the two years of a congress—led to lower estimates of R^2, so the effect of attitudes on sponsorship is taken to be (relatively) immediate rather than delayed. One objection that may be raised is that the correlation between sponsorship and public opinion is high simply because sponsorship, like public opinion, increases fairly steadily over time—a similarly high correlation could be found between sponsorship and any variable that increases the same way, such as the consumer price index or the population of China. Common sense and political theory tell us, however, that a correlation between public opinion and legislative action has a sensible explanation, while the other correlations do not.

11. The enforcement provisions were amended in committee and by the Senate leadership and never put to a separate vote. The addition of the sex discrimination provision was voted on separately in the House, but not in a roll call vote, so there is no record of who voted for it and who against; it was not voted on separately in the Senate. And the proposal to extend coverage to governments was not made until later.

12. Because several of the percentages in each column are very similar or identical and are within the range of sampling error in the public opinion column, there is no point in formally calculating rank-order coefficients.

13. See the statements by Senator Dominick of Colorado, summarized in Congressional Quarterly 1972, 248–49.

14. Patterns in House voting on administrative enforcement in 1966 and in Senate voting on administrative enforcement and the coverage of governments in 1970 were the same as the 1971–72 patterns.

15. The proportion that favored leaving EEO up to the states in the questions asked in 1952 and 1953 was almost the same as the proportion answering that the federal government should go "none of the way" in 1948 and 1949; because the "leave it up to the states" response was the weakest available, it may be seen as the equivalent of proposing to do nothing.

16. The adoptions of each kind of law are so highly correlated that including both at once in an equation leads to estimates that are uninterpretable.

Chapter 4

1. A demonstration was defined as a peaceful public display by a group of five or more people expressing support for the civil rights of women, blacks, or other minorities as defined by race, religion, or national origin. Rallies, sit-ins, picketing, boycotts (a major civil rights tactic), strikes related to civil rights, and similar events were included.

The basic event coded was the demonstration-city-day, one demonstration in one city on one day. A demonstration lasting longer than one day was counted for each day it continued. Limitations on the information and resources available for coding made it impossible to take into account the number of participants, but the number of participants in a given year is known to be highly correlated with the number of demonstrations, and little is lost by examining the number of demonstrations rather than the number of participants.

Each demonstration was categorized according to whether it concerned EEO or some other issue, and on whose behalf it had been held (blacks, women, etc.).

2. Events were defined as riots when they were explicitly described as such in the *New York Times* or when the event was described as violent and clearly involved fairly large numbers of minority group members acting in opposition to the police or other agents of social control (more than fifty minority group members, for example, or large numbers of police or arrests mentioned). As with demonstrations, the basic event was the riot-city-day, with one event per city per day being counted. Some of the problems of formally defining and tabulating riots are discussed by Tilly 1969.

3. Because the emphasis is on the apparently illegitimate use of force against peaceful protestors, other types of police/citizen encounters were not counted, including police responses to riots or other violent behavior, harassment, arrests of civil rights protestors, and brutality against minorities arrested for nonmovement activities.

4. With only sixteen congresses to work with and a relatively large number of independent variables, many of which are highly correlated with each other, there are severe limitations on multivariate analysis—if the estimates are to mean anything, only a small number of variables can be included in an equation at one time, and care must be taken not to include variables whose collinearity causes problems in the estimates. The simplest way to get a sense of how public opinion and other variables affect congressional action is to estimate the coefficients for a series of equations, each including one variable in addition to pro-EEO attitudes. This procedure will not provide estimates of the effect of each variable controlling for all the others, but it will tell us if they may all be seen as somehow affecting Congress.

The Durbin-Watson d statistic showed that serial correlation was a potential problem in the ordinary least squares (OLS) equations for general demonstrations and *New York Times* coverage, possibly leading to exaggerated estimates of t- and F-statistics and of R^2. A variant of generalized least squares (GLS) estimation was used to overcome this problem; the procedure used is described in Wonnacott and Wonnacott 1970, 331–32; the program is Peck's 1981. The results were in fact more conservative than those using OLS. The conclusions for analyses that run only through 1964 were identical to those presented in the table and therefore are not shown separately.

5. This is a "best" equation, with variables not related to salience at the .05 level trimmed (see Leamer 1978) and with multicollinearity problems avoided by eliminating superfluous variables. Note that here, in contrast to analyses of congressional action, where the two-year congress was the unit of analysis, the unit of analysis in this equation is the single year. In GLS equations with pro-EEO attitudes as the dependent variable, no measure of pro- or anti-rights activity or media coverage had a statistically significant (at the .05 level) effect on pro-EEO attitudes.

Chapter 5

1. This is not to say that elected representatives will never vote on the basis of idealism, doing what they feel is morally right rather than what is popular. But we have every reason to think that this happens most often on issues the public cares little about and infrequently on issues of public concern (Kingdon 1977). As Dahl has written, "In a rough sense, the essence of all competitive politics is bribery of the electorate by politicians" (1956, 68).

The magnitude of the challenge presented to the Democrats and Republicans by civil rights is exemplified by the threats they faced from other parties and candidates who felt that neither major party was dealing satisfactorily with civil rights and other issues—the states' rights (Dixiecrat) and Progressive parties in 1948, George Wallace in 1968.

2. According to the 1960 national election survey conducted by the Survey Research Center of the University of Michigan, when the public was asked which party was more likely to see to it that blacks got fair treatment in jobs and housing, 46 percent said there would be no difference and the proportion choosing the Democrats (19 percent) was almost identical to the proportion choosing the Republicans; the rest had no opinion (Campbell et al. 1970, question 22B). The situation changed later; by 1968, a clear plurality of those asked felt the Democrats would be more likely to help blacks (Political Behavior Program 1973, question 23A).

3. The statistical relation between sponsorship and percentage Democratic remains virtually zero when calculated for each house of Congress separately and when "percentage Democratic" is calculated in different ways (such as the average percentage Democratic for the House and Senate). Multivariate analyses, including the party balance in questions with public opinion and other variables, produce the same result.

4. The definition of lobbying in federal law involves spending money to influence legislation. A typical broad definition is in Meek and Wade 1976, 420. Lobbying is often defined as an activity of interest groups; see McCarthy and Zald 1977, 1218; Sabatier 1975; Gamson 1975, 139–41; Wilson 1973, chaps. 15–16.

5. It is apparently quite common for congressional hearings to be one-sided (see Hayes 1981, 26), but it seems surprising here because both sides felt so strongly about the issue.

6. One may be dubious about the extent to which either the ministers or the labor leaders who testified represented the wishes of the average member of their organizations. They did represent relatively liberal organizations, however, so their public statements were probably not too unrepresentative.

7. The correlations presented in table 5.4 are consistent with multivariate regression equations taking lobbying and pro-EEO attitudes into account simultaneously. For testimony and private amicus briefs, the equations are as follows (t-statistics in parentheses under coefficients; those significant at .05 are *; ** means significant at .01):

Sponsors = -591.4** + 1.59** (pro-EEO attitudes) + .11 (pro-EEO witnesses)
        (-3.6)   (6.0)   (.53)
                    Adjusted R^2 = .69   Durbin-Watson d = .7
  Sponsors = -60.8** + 1.61** (pro-EEO attitudes) + .60 (private briefs)
        (-3.8)   (6.1)   (.86)
                    Adjusted R^2 = .70   Durbin-Watson d = 1.0

8. The relevant equations are:

Sponsors = -53.7** + 1.50** (pro-EEO attitudes) + 1.23 (EEO delegations)
        (-3.3)   (5.0)   (.5)
                  Adjusted R^2 = .69   Durbin-Watson d = .7
Sponsors = -64.8** + 1.81** (pro-EEO attitudes) $-.80$ (general delegations)
    (-4.3)   (6.5)   (-1.7)
                  Adjusted R^2 = .74   Durbin-Watson d = 1.2
  Sponsors = -63.1** + 1.75** (pro-EEO attitudes) $-.96$ (government briefs)
      (-3.9) ·   (5.9)   (-1.1)
                  Adjusted R^2 = .71   Durbin-Watson d = .9

9. The data reported here and in the rest of this section are based on this group of formal leaders. Considering each house separately does not affect the results; neither does considering each party separately. Considering a smaller group (e.g., leaving out committee chairs) weakens the relationships somewhat. Republicans controlled the House and Senate in 1947–48 and 1953–54; Democrats did so at all other times. Senate committees numbered thirty-three through 1946, fifteen to seventeen thereafter; House committees numbered forty-seven to forty-eight through 1946, nineteen to twenty-one thereafter.

10. Especially persistent leader sponsors in the 1940s and early 1950s were Democratic representatives Celler (New York; Judiciary Committee) and Norton (New Jersey; Labor Committee); Democratic senators Murray (Montana; Education and Labor committees) and Neely (West Virginia; District of Columbia Committee) and Republican senators Aiken (Vermont; Expenditures in Executive Departments, and Agriculture and Forestry committees), Saltonstall (Massachusetts; Republican whip and Armed Services Committee), Langer (North Dakota; Civil Service and Judiciary committees), and Tobey (New Hampshire; Commerce Committee). It is worth noting that many of the senators were from states with relatively small minority populations and so were probably not acting as a result of urgent demands by constituents; their support for EEO would not have resulted in much opposition, either.

11. The correlation between sponsorship by leaders and total sponsorship is technically spurious to some degree because the leaders' sponsorships are part of the total. Their sponsorships were included because they do count, after all, as part of the total amount of support for EEO legislation.

12. The data on presidential stands were taken from the *Congressional Quarterly* and elsewhere and refer to whether the president favored enforceable EEO legislation, opposed it, or took no position (Congressional Quarterly 1964, 677; 1972, 14-H; Berman 1970; Morgan 1970). Two dummy variables were then constructed, the first scored 1 if the president supported EEO legislation and 0 otherwise, the second scored 1 if the president opposed legislation and 0 otherwise. The "correlation" of .42 is actually the multiple R of these two variables on sponsorships.

13. The equation in table 5.5 is a "best" equation, the one best combining high explained variance, low multicollinearity, high Durbin-Watson d, and small number of relevant variables in an equation consistent with theory (see Leamer 1978).

14. See Kingdon 1977. Members of Congress may even favor a bill when doing so will symbolize support for a cause important to some constituents, but only as long as passage is just a remote possibility (Hayes 1981). If passage becomes more likely and other constituents realize it would damage their material interests, opposition from constituents may increase, and some former supporters may become opponents. The recent history of the Equal Rights Amendment provides examples of this.

Chapter 6

1. The earliest econometric studies seemed to show that EEO legislation had a significant positive effect on the relative income of nonwhites, particularly nonwhite men (Freeman 1973; Masters 1975); some legal scholars were dubious about these conclusions (Bell 1977), though others thought EEO laws would have a significant effect after a long delay (Hill 1977). Recent econometric studies tend to converge on the conclusion that EEO laws have not had a significant effect (Butler and Heckman 1977; Lazear 1979).

2. There are, by this time, a number of economic theories of discrimination; see the reviews by Marshall 1974 and Blau and Jusenius 1976. Nearly all empirical work on the effect of EEO legislation is modeled on the classic studies by Masters 1975, chap. 6, Freeman 1973, and Landes 1968, however; they in turn base their studies on the theoretical work of Becker 1971 (first edition 1957). One contemporary dispute concerns the relative virtues of cross-sectional as opposed to time-series studies of the effect of EEO legislation. The major advantage of the time-series approach is that broad patterns of social change and the passage of legislation are more easily taken into account than in the cross-sectional approach (see Sawhill 1979, 355).

3. See also Addison and Siebert 1979, 230. The only empirical attempt to measure taste for discrimination (before Burstein 1979a) in a study of EEO legislation is Bergmann and Lyle's (1971) study of occupational differences across metropolitan areas and industries. Using the 1968 Wallace vote as a proxy for white taste for discrimination, they found that this variable explained black/white differences better than either education or the existence of a state fair employment practices law. But they did not use actual attitude data or follow up on the idea. See Beller 1982, 173, for a typical recent instance of referring to the importance of attitudes (or "climate") while leaving them out of the analysis.

4. Here the black/white comparison differs somewhat from the female/male comparison, because men and women, unlike blacks and whites, usually live together and share income. Nonparticipation in the labor force by many women living in such

circumstances is truly voluntary. Nevertheless, it has become clearer in recent years that female nonparticipation in the labor force must be treated as problematic rather than being taken for granted. It is also plain that contributions of time and money to women's political organizations have increased as well. The situations of women and blacks are far from identical, but there are enough similarities to warrant viewing women, as well as other groups, as potentially self-conscious political actors.

5. A thorough justification for the use of such a group share measure is provided by Villemez and Rowe 1975 in their comparison of blacks and whites; they focused only on men with income, however. Fossett and South 1983 claim that this measure (called the "distributional fairness index" in their paper and in Villemez and Rowe) has one flaw, despite its many virtues as a measure of inequality: it varies with the relative size of different groups, a factor they consider irrelevant to the conceptualization of intergroup inequality. Here, however, as I have just argued, relative group size is *not* irrelevant.

6. The estimates for nonwhite men and women are ordinary least squares (OLS) estimates. "Adj. R^2" is R^2 adjusted for degrees of freedom. D-W d is the Durbin-Watson d statistic. The statistic showed that serial correlation was a potential problem in the OLS equations for white women, possibly leading to exaggerated estimates of t- and F-statistics and of R^2. A variant of generalized least squares estimation (GLS) was used to overcome this problem; the procedure used is described in Wonnacott and Wonnacott 1970, 331–32; the program used is Peck's (1981). The results were in fact more conservative than those for OLS. Although some of the independent variables were fairly strongly correlated with each other, the use of recently developed regression diagnostics indicated that collinearity did not significantly affect the possibility of estimating coefficients (Belsley, Kuh, and Welsch 1980, chap. 3).

7. This hypothesis is consistent with the finding of statistically significant serial correlation in the equations for white women, noted earlier.

Chapter 7

1. The specific projections should not be taken too literally; too many unforeseen things can happen during the next thirty or forty years for simple projections to be very accurate. Yet the projections are quite reasonable in light of the experience of other racial and ethnic groups and cannot be dismissed lightly.

2. See the views expressed in, for example, White 1982, Sawyer 1981b, and Glazer 1978 and summarized in Benokraitis and Feagin 1978, chap. 6. "Reverse discrimination" has never been satisfactorily defined but is commonly taken to mean treating women or nonwhites better than comparable white men (see Jones 1982). In the *Weber* case (*Steelworkers v. Weber*, 443 U.S. 193 [1981]), Weber's employer and union had voluntarily adopted an affirmative action plan that involved preferring black applicants for a craft training program over whites to some extent.

3. The effect of family background on adult achievement has tended to be less for women and blacks than for white men, largely because discrimination prevented parents from helping their children very much; nevertheless the effect of family background is substantial (Jencks et al. 1979; Featherman and Hauser 1978; Rosenfeld 1978; Marini 1978).

4. If discrimination did disappear completely, it would obviously cease to have

any effect on relative incomes; but this is not likely to happen soon (see Jencks et al. 1979, 210; Burstein 1985).

5. In fact, many of the best-known court cases involving claims of reverse discrimination are concerned with opportunities for training and education rather than for jobs—for example, *DeFunis v. Odegaard* (law school admission; 416 U.S. 312 [1975]); *University of California Regents v. Bakke* (medical school admission; 438 U.S. 265 [1980]); and *Steelworkers v. Weber* (craft training program; 443 U.S. 193 [1981]).

6. The fight over access to education seems to be turning to some degree into a fight over some basic attributes of educational institutions—how merit is defined, what sorts of entrance criteria are appropriate, and so forth. This is shocking to some people, but the rules and norms guiding the operation of today's institutions of higher education were themselves the product of previous conflicts between social groups and are not as self-evident as many believe; see Gorelick 1981.

7. Wilson 1980, Thurow 1980, and others make this point forcefully and argue that some groups that have suffered from discrimination, particularly poorly educated blacks, are likely to be helped only by major economic reforms. This amounts to saying that the solution to their problem will be as much political as economic.

8. The Note deals solely with issues involving seniority, but the approaches discussed are easily generalized to other employment issues.

9. Probably still the best single treatment of all the complex ethical and practical issues involved in enforcing EEO legislation is the article by Fiss 1971.

10. This last approach is similar to the "Feagin plan," devised by the sociologist Joe Feagin, in which some of the effects of past discrimination would be overcome by having a competition in which *all* jobs, including those now occupied, would be thrown open to all applicants on the basis of merit. Needless to say, Professor Feagin does not really expect his plan to be adopted.

11. In *Affirmative Discrimination,* Nathan Glazer expresses surprise that the "apparently inexorable" movement toward distributing jobs on the basis of race and ethnic group may slow (1978, ix–x). How a movement supported mainly by the economically deprived and politically unorganized and opposed by major economic interests and the dominant social group (white men) could move forward inexorably is not clear. Many social scientists have trouble believing that the plans even of elites are "inexorably" implemented; the idea that disadvantaged groups could have such power is rather novel.

References

Aaron, Henry. 1978. *Politics and the professors*. Washington, D.C.: Brookings Institution.

Abramson, Joan. 1977. Measuring success; or, Whatever happened to affirmative action? *Civil Rights Digest* 9:14–27.

———. 1979. *Old boys—new women: The politics of sex discrimination*. New York: Praeger.

Abramson, Paul, John Aldrich, and David Rohde. 1983. *Change and continuity in the 1980 elections*. Rev. ed. Washington, D.C.: CQ Press.

Addison, John T., and W. Stanley Siebert. 1979. *The market for labor*. Santa Monica, Calif.: Goodyear.

Angle, J., and D. A. Wissmann. 1981. Gender, college major, and earnings. *Sociology of Education* 54:25–33.

Backstrom, Charles. 1977. Congress and the public: How representative is the one of the other? *American Politics Quarterly* 5:411–35.

Bailey, Steven. 1950. *Congress makes a law: The story behind the Employment Act of 1946*. New York: Columbia University Press.

Bardolph, Richard. 1970. *The civil rights record*. New York: Crowell.

Barrett, Nancy S. 1979. Women in the job market. In *The subtle revolution: Women at work*, ed. Ralph E. Smith, 31–62. Washington, D.C.: Urban Institute.

Bartholet, Elizabeth. 1982. Applications of Title VII to jobs in high places. *Harvard Law Review* 95:947–1027.

Beck, E. M. 1980. Discrimination and white economic loss. *Social Forces* 59:148–68.

Becker, Gary. 1971. *The economics of discrimination*. 2d ed. Chicago: University of Chicago Press.

———. 1981. *A treatise on the family*. Cambridge: Harvard University Press.

Bell, Derrick, Jr. 1977. Forward: Equal employment law and the continuing need for self-help. *Loyola University of Chicago Law Journal* 8:681–86.

Bell, Duran. 1974. The economic basis of employee discrimination. In *Patterns of racial discrimination*, ed. G. von Furstenberg, A. Horowitz, and B. Harrison, 121–35. Lexington, Mass.: Heath.

Beller, Andrea. 1979. The impact of equal employment opportunity laws on the male-female earnings differential. In *Women in the labor market,* ed. Cynthia Lloyd, Emily Andrews, and Curtis Gilroy, 304–30.New York: Columbia University Press.

————. 1982. The impact of equal opportunity policy on sex differentials in earnings and occupations. *American Economic Review* (papers and proceedings) 72:171–75.

Belsley, David, Edwin Kuh, and Roy Welsch. 1980. *Regression diagnostics.* New York: Wiley.

Belton, Robert. 1978. A comparative review of public and private enforcement of the Civil Rights Act of 1964. *Vanderbilt Law Review* 31:905–61.

————. 1981. Discrimination and affirmative action. *North Carolina Law Review* 59:531–98.

Benokraitis, Nijole, and Joe Feagin. 1978. *Affirmative action and equal opportunity.* Boulder, Colo.: Westview Press.

Berger, Morroe. 1967. *Equality by statute.* Rev. ed. New York: Doubleday.

Bergmann, Barbara, and Jerolyn Lyle. 1971. The occupational standing of Negroes by areas and industries. *Journal of Human Resources* 6:411–33.

Berk, Richard, Harold Brackman, and Selma Lesser. 1977. *A measure of justice.* New York: Academic Press.

Berman, Daniel. 1966. *A bill becomes a law: Congress enacts civil rights legislation.* New York: Macmillan.

Berman, William. 1970. *The politics of civil rights in the Truman administration.* Columbus: Ohio State University Press.

Blau, Francine D. 1984. Discrimination against women: Theory and evidence. In *Labor economics: Modern views,* ed. William Darity, Jr., 53–90. Boston: Kluwer-Nijhoff.

Blau, Francine, and Carol Jusenius. 1976. Economists' approaches to sex segregation in the labor market. *Signs* 1:181–99.

Blumrosen, Alfred. 1971. *Black employment and the law.* New Brunswick, N.J.: Rutgers University Press.

Bonacich, Edna, and John Modell. 1980. *The economic basis of ethnic solidarity.* Berkeley: University of California Press.

Bonfield, Arthur. 1967. The origin and development of American fair employment legislation. *Iowa Law Review* 52:1043–92.

Brady, David. 1982. Congressional party realignment and the transformation of public policy in three realignment eras. *American Journal of Political Science* 26:333–60.

Braybrook, Arthur, and Charles Lindblom. 1963. *A strategy of decision.* New York: Free Press.

Bureau of National Affairs. 1969–78. *Fair employment practice cases.* Vols. 1–15. Washington, D.C.: Bureau of National Affairs.

_____. 1977. *Fair employment practices.* Vol. 6, part 2. Washington, D.C.: Bureau of National Affairs.

Burstein, Paul. 1979a. Equal employment opportunity legislation and the incomes of women and nonwhites. *American Sociological Review* 44:367–91.

_____. 1979b. Public opinion, demonstrations, and the passage of antidiscrimination legislation. *Public Opinion Quarterly* 43:157–72.

_____. 1979c. Senate voting on the Vietnam War, 1964–1973. *Journal of Political and Military Sociology* 7:271–82.

_____. 1980. Attitudinal, demographic and electoral components of legislative change: Senate voting on civil rights. *Sociology and Social Research* 64:221–35.

_____. 1981. The sociology of democratic politics and government. In *Annual review of sociology,* ed. Alex Inkeles, 7:291–319. Palo Alto, Calif.: Annual Reviews.

_____. 1985. On equal opportunity and affirmative action. In *Research in race and ethnic relations,* ed. Cora B. Marrett and Cheryl Leggon, vol. 4. Greenwich, Conn.: JAI Press.

Burstein, Paul, and William Freudenburg. 1978. Changing public policy: The impact of public opinion, war costs, and anti-war demonstrations on Senate voting on Vietnam War motions, 1964–1973. *American Journal of Sociology* 84:99–122.

Butler, Richard, and James Heckman. 1977. The government's impact on the labor market status of black Americans. In *Equal rights and industrial relations,* ed. Leonard Hausman, Orley Ashenfelter, Bayard Rustin, Richard Schubert, and Donald Slaiman, 235–81. Madison, Wis.: Industrial Relations Research Association.

Button, James. 1978. *Black violence: Political impact of the 1960s riots.* Princeton: Princeton University Press.

Campbell, Angus, Philip Converse, Warren Miller, and Donald Stokes. 1970. *1960 election study.* Ann Arbor, Mich.: Inter-University Consortium for Political and Social Research.

Carmines, Edward. 1974. The mediating influence of state legislatures on the linkage between interparty competition and welfare policies. *American Political Science Review* 68:1118–24.

Cell, Donald. 1974. Policy influence without policy choice. *Journal of Political Economy* 82:1017–26.

Center for Political Studies. 1964, 1968, 1970, 1972. *American national election study.* Ann Arbor, Mich.: Inter-University Consortium for Political Research.

Chafe, William H. 1977. *Women and equality.* New York: Oxford University Press.

Chiswick, Barry R. 1983. The earnings and human capital of American Jews. *Journal of Human Resources* 18:313–36.

Commerce Clearing House. 1949–78. *Congressional index*. New York: Commerce Clearing House.

Congressional Quarterly. 1945–72. *Congressional quarterly almanac*. Washington, D.C.: Congressional Quarterly.

Congressional Quarterly Service. 1968. *Legislators and the lobbyists*. Washington, D.C.: Congressional Quarterly Service.

Cox, Archibald. 1976. *The role of the Supreme Court in American Government*. New York: Oxford University Press.

Dahl, Robert. 1956. *A preface to democratic theory*. Chicago: University of Chicago Press.

———. 1967. *Pluralist democracy in the United States*. Chicago: Rand McNally.

Dahl, Robert, and Charles E. Lindblom. 1976. *Politics, economics, and welfare*. Chicago: University of Chicago Press.

Danzger, M. Herbert. 1975. Validating conflict data. *American Sociological Review* 40:570–84.

Davis, James A. 1978. *General social surveys, 1972–1978: Cumulative codebook*. Chicago: National Opinion Research Center.

Domhoff, G. William. 1967. *Who rules America?* Englewood Cliffs, N.J.: Prentice-Hall.

Dorn, Edwin. 1979. *Rules and racial equality*. New Haven: Yale University Press.

Downs, Anthony. 1957. *An economic theory of democracy*. New York: Harper and Row.

———. 1972. Up and down with ecology—the issue-attention cycle. *Public Interest* 28:38–50.

Duncan, O. D. 1974. Comment. *Journal of Political Economy* 82:S109–10.

Dye, Thomas. 1971. *The politics of equality*. Indianapolis: Bobbs-Merrill.

———. 1975. *Understanding public policy*. 2d ed. Englewood Cliffs, N.J.: Prentice-Hall.

Employment discrimination law. 1982. *Boston College Law Review* 24:213–99.

Erikson, Robert. 1971. The relationship between party control and civil rights legislation in the American states. *Western Political Quarterly* 24:178–82.

Farley, Reynolds. 1977. Trends in racial inequalities: Have the gains of the 1960s disappeared in the 1970s? *American Sociological Review* 42:189–208.

Feagin, Joe. 1972. Civil rights voting by southern congressmen. *Journal of Politics* 34:484–99.

Featherman, David, and Robert Hauser. 1976. Sexual inequalities and socioeconomic achievement in the U.S., 1962–1973. *American Sociological Review* 41:462–83.

————. 1978. *Opportunity and change.* New York: Academic Press.

Ferejohn, John. 1974. *Pork barrel politics.* Stanford, Calif.: Stanford University Press.

Fernandez, John. 1981. *Racism and sexism in corporate life.* Lexington, Mass.: Lexington Books.

Ferree, Myra Marx. 1974. A woman for president? Changing responses, 1958–1972. *Public Opinion Quarterly* 38:390–99.

Fiorina, Morris. 1974. *Representatives, roll calls, and constituencies.* Lexington, Mass.: Lexington Books.

————. 1975. Constituency influence. *Political Methodology* 2:249–66.

Firms are disrupted by wave of pregnancy at manager level. 1981. *Wall Street Journal,* 20 July, 1, 14.

Fiss, Owen. 1971. A theory of fair employment laws. *University of Chicago Law Review* 38:235–314.

Fleming, Harold. 1965. The federal executive and civil rights: 1961–65. *Daedalus* 94:921–48.

Florer, John. 1973. NOW: The formative years. Ph.D. dissertation, Syracuse University.

Fossett, Mark, and Scott South. 1983. The measurement of intergroup income inequality. *Social Forces* 61:855–71.

Franklin, John Hope. 1967. *From slavery to freedom.* 3d ed. New York: Knopf.

Franklin, M. N., and M. Tappin. 1977. Early day motions as unobtrusive measures of backbench opinion in Britain. *British Journal of Political Science* 7:49–69.

Freeman, Jo. 1975. *The politics of women's liberation.* New York: Longman.

Freeman, Richard. 1973. Changes in the labor market for black Americans, 1948–1972. *Brookings Papers on Economic Activity* 1:67–120.

Galanter, Marc. 1974. Why the "haves" come out ahead. *Law and Society Review* 9:95–160.

Gallup, George. 1972. *Gallup poll: Public opinion, 1935–1971.* 3 vols. New York: Random House.

Gallup Opinion Index. 1964–76. Princeton, N.J.

Gamson, William. 1975. *The strategy of social protest.* Homewood, Ill.: Dorsey.

Garrow, David. 1978. *Protest at Selma: Martin Luther King, Jr., and the Voting Rights Act of 1965.* New Haven: Yale University Press.

Ginsberg, Benjamin. 1976. Elections and public policy. *American Political Science Review* 70:41–49.

Glazer, Nathan. 1978. *Affirmative discrimination.* New York: Basic Books.

Godwin, R. Kenneth, and W. Bruce Shepard. 1976. Political process and public expenditures. *American Political Science Review* 70:1127–35.

Gorelick, Sherry. 1981. *City College and the Jewish poor.* New Brunswick, N.J.: Rutgers University Press.

Gould, Stephen Jay. 1981. *The mismeasure of man.* New York: Norton.

Griffin, Larry J., and Karl L. Alexander. 1978. Schooling and socioeconomic attainments. *American Journal of Sociology* 84:319–47.

Gunther, Gerald. 1975. *Cases and materials on constitutional law.* 9th ed. Mineola, N.Y.: Foundation Press.

Hastings, Philip, and Jessie Southwick. 1974. *Survey data for trend analysis.* Williamstown, Mass.: Roper Public Opinion Research Center.

Haworth, Joan G., James Gwartney, and Charles Haworth. 1975. Earnings, productivity, and changes in employment during the 1960's. *American Economic Review* 65:158–68.

Hayes, Michael. 1981. *Lobbyists and legislators.* New Brunswick, N.J.: Rutgers University Press.

Heclo, Hugh. 1972. *Modern social politics in Britain and Sweden.* New Haven: Yale University Press.

Herbers, John. 1982. Reagan's changes on rights are starting to have impact. *New York Times* (national edition), 24 January, 1.

Hibbs, Douglas, Jr. 1977. Political parties and macroeconomic policy. *American Political Science Review* 71:1467–87.

Hill, Herbert. 1977. *Black labor and the American legal system.* Vol. 1. *Race, work, and the law.* Washington, D.C.: Bureau of National Affairs.

Holsti, Ole. 1969. *Content analysis for the social sciences and humanities.* Reading, Mass.: Addison-Wesley.

Hopkins, Anne. 1980. Perceptions of employment discrimination in the public sector. *Public Administration Review* 40:131–37.

Horowitz, Donald L. 1977. *The courts and social policy.* Washington, D.C.: Brookings Institution.

Isaac, Larry, and William R. Kelly. 1981. Racial insurgency, the state, and welfare expansion. *American Journal of Sociology* 86:1348–86.

It's the thought that matters. 1981. *Fortune,* 1 June, 26–28.

Jackson, John E. 1974. *Constituencies and leaders in Congress.* Cambridge: Harvard University Press.

Javits, Jacob K. 1964. Additional views. In *The Equal Employment Opportunity Act,* 37 ff., Senate Report 867, 88th Congr., 2d sess., report on S. 1937. Washington, D.C.

Jencks, Christopher. 1983a. Discrimination and Thomas Sowell. *New York Review of Books* 30:33–38.

———. 1983b. Special treatment for blacks? *New York Review of Books* 30:12–19.

Jencks, Christopher, Susan Bartlett, Mary Corcoran, James Crouse, David Eaglesfield, Gregory Jackson, Kent McClelland, Peter Mueser, Michael Olneck, Joseph Schwartz, Sherry Ward, and Jill Williams. 1979. *Who gets ahead?* New York: Basic Books.

Jenkins, J. Craig, and Charles Perrow. 1977. Insurgency of the powerless: Farm worker movements. *American Sociological Review* 42:249–67.

Johnson, Lyndon B. 1971. *The vantage point.* New York: Holt, Rinehart and Winston.

Jones, James E., Jr. 1979. *Reference supplement: Discrimination in employment.* Washington, D.C.: Bureau of National Affairs.

———. 1982. "Reverse discrimination" in employment. *Howard Law Journal* 25:217–45.

Katznelson, Ira, and Mark Kesselman. 1975. *The politics of power.* New York: Harcourt, Brace, Jovanovich.

Kerckhoff, Alan C., and Robert A. Jackson. 1982. Types of education and the occupational attainments of young men. *Social Forces* 61:24–45.

Kesselman, Louis. 1948. *The social politics of FEPC.* Chapel Hill: University of North Carolina Press.

Kingdon, John. 1977. Models of legislative voting. *Journal of Politics* 39:563–95.

———. 1981. *Congressmen's voting decisions.* 2d ed. New York: Harper and Row.

Krippendorff, Klaus. 1980. *Content analysis.* Beverly Hills, Calif.: Sage Publications.

Krislov, Samuel. 1963. The amicus curiae brief: From friendship to advocacy. *Yale Law Journal* 72:694–721.

Kuklinski, James H. 1979. Representative-constituency linkages. *Legislative Studies Quarterly* 4:121–40.

Landes, William. 1968. The economics of fair employment laws. *Journal of Political Economy* 76:507–52.

Laws of New York. 1945. Albany, N.Y.

Lawson, Steven F. 1976. *Black ballots: Voting rights in the South, 1944–69.* New York: Columbia University Press.

Lazear, Edward. 1979. The narrowing of black-white wage differences is illusory. *American Economic Review* 69:553–64.

Leamer, Edward. 1978. *Specification searches.* New York: Wiley.

Leece, J., and H. Berrington. 1977. Measurements of backbench attitudes by Guttman scaling of early day motions. *British Journal of Political Science* 7:529–41.

Levine, Erwin L. 1972. *The ghost of John C. Calhoun and American politics.* Saratoga Springs, N.Y.: Skidmore College.

Levine, Marvin, and Anthony Montcalmo. 1971. The Equal Employment Opportunity Commission: Progress, problems, prospects. *Labor Law Journal* 22:771–79.

Levitan, Sar, William Johnston, and Robert Taggart. 1975. *Still a dream: The changing status of blacks since 1960.* Cambridge: Harvard University Press.

Lichtman, Allan. 1969. The federal assault against voting discrimination in the Deep South, 1957–1967. *Journal of Negro History* 54:346–67.

Lieberson, Stanley. 1980. *A piece of the pie.* Berkeley: University of California Press.

Lindblom, Charles E. 1977. *Politics and markets.* New York: Basic Books.

Lipset, Seymour Martin. 1979. *The first new nation.* New York: Norton.

———. 1981. *Political man.* Expanded ed. Baltimore: Johns Hopkins University Press.

Lipset, S. M., and Stein Rokkan. 1967. Cleavage structures, party systems, and voter alignments. In *Party systems and voter alignments,* ed. S. M. Lipsett and Stein Rokkan, 1–64. New York: Free Press.

Lipset, S. M., and William Schneider. 1978. The Bakke case: How would it be decided at the bar of public opinion? *Public Opinion* (March/April), 38–44.

Lipsky, Michael. 1968. Protest as a political resource. *American Political Science Review* 62:1144–58.

Lloyd, Cynthia, Emily Andrews, and Curtis Gilroy, eds. 1979. *Women in the labor market.* New York: Columbia University Press.

Lockard, Duane. 1968. *Toward equal opportunity.* New York: Macmillan.

Looking Backward. 1980. *Wall Street Journal,* 2 December, 34.

Lueptow, L. B. 1981. Sex-typing and change in the occupational choice of high school seniors: 1964–1975. *Sociology of Education* 54:16–24.

Lytle, Clifford. 1966. The history of the civil rights bill of 1964. *Journal of Negro History* 51:275–96.

McAdam, Doug. 1982. *Political process and the development of black insurgency, 1930–1970.* Chicago: University of Chicago Press.

McCarthy, John D., and Mayer Zald. 1977. Resource mobilization and social movements. *American Journal of Sociology* 82:1212–41.

McCloskey, Robert. 1960. *The American Supreme Court.* Chicago: University of Chicago Press.

Marini, Margaret Mooney. 1978. Sex differences in the determination of adolescent aspirations: A review of research. *Sex Roles* 4:723–53.

Markoff, John, Gilbert Shapiro, and Sasha Weitman. 1974. Toward the integration of content analysis and general methodology. In *Sociological methodology 1975,* ed. David Heise, 1–58. San Francisco: Jossey-Bass.

Marshall, Ray. 1974. The economics of racial discrimination: A survey. *Journal of Economic Literature* 12:849–71.

Marshall, T. H. 1964. *Class, citizenship, and social development.* Garden City, N.Y.: Doubleday.

Maslow, Will. 1946. FEPC—a case history in parliamentary maneuver. *University of Chicago Law Review* 13:407–44.

Maslow, Will, and Joseph Robison. 1953. Civil rights legislation and the fight for equality, 1862–1952. *University of Chicago Law Review* 20:363–413.

Mason, Karen Oppenheim, John Czajka, and Sara Arber. 1976. Change in U.S. women's sex role attitudes, 1964–74. *American Sociological Review* 41:573–96.

Masters, Stanley. 1975. *Black-white income differentials.* New York: Academic Press.

Mayhew, David. 1974. *Congress: The electoral connection.* New Haven: Yale University Press.

Mead Data Central. 1976. *Lexis.* New York: Mead Data Central.

Meek, Roy, and Larry Wade. 1976. *Democracy in America.* North Scituate, Mass.: Duxbury Press.

Miller, Joanne, and Howard H. Garrison. 1982. Sex roles: The division of labor at home and in the workplace. In *Annual review of sociology,* ed. Ralph H. Turner and James F. Short, Jr., 8:237–62. Palo Alto, Calif.: Annual Reviews.

Miller, Warren. 1979. *American national election study, 1978.* Ann Arbor, Mich.: Inter-University Consortium for Political and Social Research.

Miller, Warren, and Donald Stokes. 1966. Constituency influence in Congress. In *Elections and the political order,* ed. Angus Campbell, Philip Converse, Warren Miller, and Donald Stokes, 351–72. New York: Wiley.

Mills, C. Wright. 1956. *The power elite.* New York: Oxford University Press.

Miroff, Bruce. 1981. Presidential leverage over social movements: The Johnson White House and civil rights. *Journal of Politics* 43:2–23.

Monroe, Alan. 1978. Public opinion and public policy, 1960–1974. Paper presented at the annual meeting of the American Political Science Association, New York.

Morgan, Ruth. 1970. *The president and civil rights.* New York: St. Martin's Press.

Morris, Aldon. 1981. Black southern sit-in movement. *American Sociological Review* 46:744–67.

Myrdal, Gunnar. 1962. *An American dilemma.* New York: Harper and Row. Originally published 1944.

New bias on hiring rules. 1981. *Business Week,* 25 May, 123–27.

Norgren, Paul, and Samuel Hill. 1964. *Toward fair employment.* New York: Columbia University Press.

Norton, Eleanor Holmes. 1981. An assessment from an enforcement perspective. In *Consultations on the affirmative action statement of the U.S. Commission on Civil Rights,* 75–81. Washington, D.C.: U.S. Commission on Civil Rights.

Oberschall, Anthony. 1973. *Social conflict and social movements.* Englewood Cliffs, N.J.: Prentice-Hall.

———. 1979. Protracted conflict. In *The dynamics of social movements,* ed.

Mayer N. Zald and John D. McCarthy, 45–70. Cambridge, Mass.: Winthrop.

O'Connor, Karen, and Lee Epstein. 1981–82. Amicus curiae participation in U.S. Supreme Court litigation. *Law and Society Review* 16:311–20.

Oppenheimer, Valerie. 1970. *The female labor force in the United States.* Population Monograph Series, no. 5. Berkeley and Los Angeles: University of California Press.

Orfield, Gary. 1975. *Congressional power: Congress and social change.* New York: Harcourt Brace Jovanovich.

Page, Benjamin. 1978. *Choices and echoes in presidential elections.* Chicago: University of Chicago Press.

Page, Benjamin, and Robert Y. Shapiro. 1983. Effects of public opinion on policy. *American Political Science Review* 77:175–90.

Parsons, Talcott. 1959. "Voting" and the equilibrium of the American political system. In *American voting behavior,* ed. Eugene Burdick and Arthur Brodbeck, 80–120. Glencoe, Ill.: Free Press.

Peck, Jon K. 1981. *PEC user's manual.* Version 8.1. New Haven: Yale University.

Peres, Richard. 1978. *Dealing with employment discrimination.* New York: McGraw-Hill.

Pilisuk, Marc, and Thomas Hayden. 1965. Is there a military industrial complex which prevents peace? *Journal of Social Issues* 21:67–117.

Piven, Frances Fox, and Richard Cloward. 1971. *Regulating the poor.* New York: Pantheon.

Polanyi, Karl. 1944. *The great transformation.* Boston: Beacon.

Pole, J. R. 1978. *The pursuit of equality in American history.* Berkeley: University of California Press.

Political Behavior Program. 1973. *1968 election study.* Ann Arbor, Mich.: Inter-University Consortium for Political and Social Research.

Polsby, Nelson W. 1983. *Community power and political theory.* 2d ed. New Haven: Yale University Press.

———. 1984. *Political innovation in America.* New Haven: Yale University Press.

Ratner, Ronnie. 1979. *Labor market inequality and equal opportunity policy for women.* Albany: State University of New York, Center for Women in Government.

———, ed. 1980. *Equal employment policy for women.* Philadelphia: Temple University Press.

Reed, Leonard. 1981. What's wrong with affirmative action. *Washington Monthly* 12:24–31.

Robinson, Donald A. 1979. Two movements in pursuit of equal employment opportunity. *Signs* 4:413–33.

Rosenfeld, Rachel. 1978. Women's intergenerational occupational mobility. *American Sociological Review* 43:36–46.

Ruchames, Louis. 1953. *Race, jobs, and politics: The story of FEPC.* New York: Columbia University Press.

Sabatier, Paul. 1975. Social movements and regulatory agencies. *Policy Sciences* 6:301–42.

Sawhill, Isabel. 1979. Comment. In *Women in the labor market,* ed. Cynthia Lloyd, Emily Andrews, and Curtis Gilroy, 352–55. New York: Columbia University Press.

Sawyer, Kathy. 1981a. Job bias regulators enforce the law down to the decimal point. *Washington Post,* 5 May, A2.

————. 1981b. Senate panel starts hearings on constitutionality of affirmative action. *Washington Post,* 5 May, A2.

Schattschneider, E. E. 1960. *The semisovereign people.* New York: Holt, Rinehart and Winston.

Schlei, Norbert. 1976. Foreword. In *Employment discrimination law,* ed. Barbars Schlei and Paul Grossman, vii–xiii. Washington, D.C.: Bureau of National Affairs.

Schwartz, Mildred. 1967. *Trends in white attitudes toward Negroes.* Chicago: National Opinion Research Center.

Scott, Andrew, and Margaret Hunt. 1966. *Congress and lobbies: Image and reality.* Chapel Hill: University of North Carolina Press.

Scott, William A. 1955. Reliability of content analysis. *Public Opinion Quarterly* 19:321–25.

Shay, Frank. 1938. *Judge Lynch: His first hundred years.* New York: Biblo and Tannen.

Shuman, Howard. 1957. Senate rules and the civil rights bill. *American Political Science Review* 51:955–75.

Silberman, Jonathan I., and Garey Durden. 1976. Determining legislative preferences on the minimum wage. *Journal of Political Economy* 84:317–29.

Simon, Herbert. 1957. *Models of man.* New York: Wiley.

Simon, Rita James. 1974. *Public opinion in America: 1936–1970.* Chicago: Rand McNally.

Skocpol, Theda. 1980. Political response to capitalist crisis. *Politics and Society* 10:155–201.

Smith, A. Wade. 1981. Racial tolerance as a function of group position. *American Sociological Review* 46:558–73.

Smith, Richard. 1979. Lobbying influence in Congress. Paper presented at the annual meeting of the American Political Science Association, Washington, D.C.

Smith, Tom W. 1980. America's most important problem—a trend analysis, 1946–1976. *Public Opinion Quarterly* 44:164–80.

Snyder, David, and Paula Hudis. 1976. Occupational income and the effects of minority competition and segregation. *American Sociological Review* 41:209–34.

Snyder, David, and William Kelly. 1977. Conflict intensity, media sensitivity, and the validity of newspaper data. *American Sociological Review* 42:105–23.

———. 1979. Strategies for investigating violence and social change. In *The dynamics of social movements*, ed. Mayer N. Zald and John D. McCarthy, 212–37. Cambridge, Mass.: Winthrop.

Sovern, Michael. 1966. *Legal restraints on racial discrimination in employment*. New York: Twentieth Century Fund.

Sowell, Thomas. 1981. *Markets and minorities*. New York: Basic Books.

Steel, Lewis M. 1983. Why attorneys won't take civil rights cases. *Nation* 236:362–64.

Steinberg, Ronnie. 1982. *Wages and hours*. New Brunswick, N.J.: Rutgers University Press.

Stember, Charles H., et al. 1966. *Jews in the mind of America*. New York: Basic Books.

Stern, Robert, Walter Gove, and Omer Galle. 1976. Equality for blacks and women: An essay on relative progress. *Social Science Quarterly* 56:664–72.

Stigler, George. 1972. Economic competition and political competition. *Public Choice* 13:91–106.

Stinchcombe, Arthur. 1978. *Theoretical methods in social history*. New York: Academic Press.

Stolzenberg, Ross. 1980. The measurement and decomposition of causal effects in nonlinear and nonadditive models. In *Sociological methodology 1980*, ed. Karl Schuessler, 459–88. San Francisco: Jossey-Bass.

Sugimoto, Yoshio. 1978. Measurement of popular disturbance. *Social Science Research* 7:284–97.

Sullivan, John, and Robert O'Connor. 1972. Electoral choice and popular control of public policy. *American Political Science Review* 66:1256–68.

Sundquist, James. 1968. *Politics and policy: The Eisenhower, Kennedy, and Johnson years*. Washington, D.C.: Brookings Institution.

Talmadge, Herman. 1955. *You and segregation*. Birmingham, Ala.: Vulcan Press.

Tarrow, Sidney. 1983. *Struggling to reform: Social movements and policy change during cycles of protest*. Occasional Paper no. 15, Western Societies Program. Ithaca, N.Y.: Center for International Studies, Cornell University.

Taylor, D. Garth, Paul Sheatsley, and Andrew Greeley. 1978. Attitudes toward racial intergration. *Scientific American* 238:42–49.

Thernstrom, Stephan. 1973. *The other Bostonians.* Cambridge: Harvard University Press.

Thornton, Arland, and Deborah S. Freedman. 1979. Changes in the sex role attitudes of women, 1962–1977. *American Sociological Review* 44:832–42.

Thurow, Lester. 1975. *Generating inequality.* New York: Basic Books.

————. 1980. *The zero-sum society.* New York: Basic Books.

Tilly, Charles. 1969. Methods for the study of collective violence. In*Problems in research on community violence,* ed. Ralph Conant and MollyApple Levin, 15–43. New York: Praeger.

————. 1978. *From mobilization to revolution.* Reading, Mass.: Addison-Wesley.

Title VII, seniority discrimination, and the incumbent Negro. 1967. *Harvard Law Review* 80:1260–83.

Tufte, Edward. 1978. *Political control of the economy.* Princeton: Princeton University Press.

U.S. Bureau of the Census. 1958. *Current population reports.* Series P-20. Washington, D.C.: Government Printing Office.

————. 1960–77. *Current population reports.* Series P-60. Washington, D.C.: Government Printing Office.

U.S. Commission on Civil Rights. 1977. *The federal civil rights enforcement effort, 1977.* Washington, D.C.: Government Printing Office.

U.S. Congress. 1940–74. *Congressional directory.* Washington, D.C.: Government Printing Office.

————. 1941–72. *Congressional record.* Washington, D.C.: Government Printing Office.

U.S. Congress, House Committee on Education and Labor. 1963. *Hearings on Equal Employment Opportunity, H.R. 405 and similar bills.* Washington, D.C.: Government Printing Office.

U.S. Congress, House Committee on Labor. 1944. *Hearings on H.R. 3986 . . . to Prohibit Discrimination in Employment.* Washington, D.C.: Government Printing Office.

U.S. Congress, House Committee on the Judiciary. 1963. *Hearings on H.R. 7152.* Washington, D.C.: Government Printing Office.

U.S. Congress, House Special Subcommittee of the Committee on Education and Labor. 1949. *Hearings on H.R. 4453 and companion bills.* Washington, D.C.: Government Printing Office.

U.S. Congress, Senate Committee on Appropriations. 1970. *Hearings on state, justice . . . appropriations.* 91st Congr., 2d sess. Washington, D.C.: Government Printing Office.

U.S. Congress, Senate Committee on Education and Labor. 1944. *Hearings on*

S. 2048, Fair Employment Practices Act. Washington, D.C.: Government Printing Office.

————. 1946. *Hearings on S. 1178, Equal Pay for Equal Work.* Washington, D.C.: Government Printing Office.

U.S. Congress, Senate Committee on Labor and Public Welfare. 1972. *Legislative history of the Equal Employment Opportunity Act of 1972.* Washington, D.C.: Government Printing Office.

U.S. Department of Labor. 1974. *Manpower report of the president.* Washington, D.C.: Government Printing Office.

————. 1977, 1980. *Handbook of labor statistics.* Washington, D.C.: Government Printing Office.

————. 1978. *Employment and training report of the president.* Washington, D.C.: Government Printing Office.

U.S. Equal Employment Opportunity Commission. 1966–78. *Annual report.* Washington, D.C.: Government Printing Office.

U.S. Library of Congress, Legislative Reference Service. 1942–74. *Digest of public general bills and resolutions.* Washington, D.C.: Government Printing Office.

U.S. Office of Management and Budget. 1971–80. *Budget of the U.S. government, special analyses.* Washington, D.C.: Government Printing Office.

————. 1982. *Budget of the U.S. government, 1983.* Special analysis J: Civil rights activities. Washington, D.C.: Government Printing Office.

U.S. Women's Bureau. 1970. *Laws on sex discrimination in employment.* Washington, D.C.: Government Printing Office.

Vanek, Joann. 1981. Household work, wage work, and sexual equality. In *Women and household labor,* ed. Sarah F. Berk, 275–91. Beverly Hills, Calif.: Sage Publications.

Villemez, Wayne J. 1977. Male economic gain from female subordination. *Social Forces* 56:626–36.

Villemez, Wayne J., and Alan Rowe. 1975. Black economic gains in the sixties: A methodological critique and reassessment. *Social Forces* 54:181–93.

Von Eschen, Donald, Jerome Kirk, and Maurice Pinard. 1969. The disintegration of the Negro non-violent movement. *Journal of Peace Research,* 215–34.

Waite, Linda. 1978. Protecting female labor force participation from sex-role attitudes. Paper presented at the annual meeting of the American Sociological Association, San Francisco.

Walker, Jack L. 1977. Setting the agenda in the U.S. Senate: A theory of problem selection. *British Journal of Political Science* 7:423–46.

Wallace, Phyllis. 1976. *Equal employment and the AT&T case.* Cambridge: MIT Press.

Weissberg, Robert. 1976. *Public opinion and American democracy.* Englewood Cliffs, N.J.: Prentice-Hall.

_____. 1978. Collective vs. dyadic representation. *American Political Science Review* 72:535–47.

Welch, Finis. 1973. Education and racial discrimination. In *Discrimination in labor markets,* ed. Orley Ashenfelter and Albert Rees, 43–81. Princeton: Princeton University Press.

White, Theodore H. 1982. Summing Up. *New York Times Magazine,* 25 April, 32 ff.

Whitt, J. Allen. 1982. *Urban elites and mass transportation.* Princeton: Princeton University Press.

Wilensky, Harold. 1967. *Organizational intelligence.* New York: Basic Books.

_____. 1975. *The welfare state and equality.* Berkeley: University of California Press.

Wilson, James Q. 1973. *Political organizations.* New York: Basic Books.

Wilson, Warner, and William Varner. 1973. The rank order of discrimination. *Phylon* 34 (March):30–42.

Wilson, William J. 1980. *The declining significance of race.* 2d ed. Chicago: University of Chicago Press.

Wirmark, Bo. 1974. Nonviolent methods and the American civil rights movement, 1955–1965. *Journal of Peace Research* 11:115–32.

Wonnacott, Ronald, and Thomas Wonnacott. 1970. *Econometrics.* New York: Wiley.

Woodward, C. Vann. 1966. *The strange career of Jim Crow.* New York: Oxford University Press.

Index